THE FUTURE OF CENTRAL AMERICA

This book is

CONTRIBUTORS

Adolfo Aguilar Zinser

Isaac Cohen

Richard R. Fagen

Piero Gleijeses

Xabier Gorostiaga

William M. LeoGrande

Luis Maira

Mario Ojeda

Olga Pellicer

Gert Rosenthal

Clint E. Smith

Pedro Vuskovic

Sponsored by the
Project on United States–
Mexico Relations

The Future of Central America

POLICY CHOICES FOR THE U.S. AND MEXICO

Edited by Richard R. Fagen
and Olga Pellicer

STANFORD UNIVERSITY PRESS, STANFORD, CALIFORNIA

Stanford University Press, Stanford, California
© 1983 by the Board of Trustees of the
Leland Stanford Junior University
Printed in the United States of America
Cloth ISBN 0-8047-1177-1
Paper ISBN 0-8047-1190-9
Original edition 1983
Last figure below indicates year of this printing:
93 92 91 90 89 88 87 86 85 84

Preface

FROM its inception, the Project on United States–Mexico Relations planned to encourage work on foreign policy. At the outset, three issues were selected for consideration: energy, North-South negotiations, and Central America. At a preliminary meeting in October 1981, held in Washington, D.C., we discussed all three issues. It soon became clear, however, that the Central American question was what most interested and divided participants. We thus decided to concentrate on Central America at the next meeting of the group, which was to be held the following June in Guanajuato, Mexico. With that in mind, we invited scholars and practitioners not only from Mexico and the United States, which is the normal practice of the Project, but also from Central America. The essays presented in the following pages were all prepared for that meeting, discussed in lengthy and sometimes heated sessions, and then revised for publication.

Because we felt that rapid publication was important for topics of such urgency, we set very short deadlines for revisions as well as a tight translating and editing schedule. Meeting these deadlines and schedule would not have been possible without the full cooperation of all participants, Stanford University Press, and our three excellent translators, Barbara Mauger, Donald Share, and Paula V. Smith.

We are also very much indebted to our hosts in Washington and Guanajuato. During our preliminary meetings at the School of Advanced International Studies of Johns Hopkins University, the Honorable Lucius D. Battle, Chairman of the Foreign Policy Institute, and Professor Riorden Roett, Director of the Latin

American Studies Program, graciously provided facilities and substantive contributions. In Mexico, we enjoyed the hospitality and the magnificent facilities of the Guanajuato branch of the Center for Studies of the Third World.

Finally, we are grateful to the more than three dozen people who participated in one or both meetings, but whose names do not appear in this book—with the exception of a few who are mentioned in the closing essay. They contributed significantly to making the debates in Washington and Guanajuato honest, to-the-point, and, we hope, useful to all concerned. The problems in Central America are so profound, and the human costs so high, that the least safe and comfortable scholars and practitioners can do is tell the truth as they see it and participate to the best of their abilities in the search for peace and justice in the region.

Richard R. Fagen
Olga Pellicer

Contents

Contributors

ADOLFO AGUILAR ZINSER is a Senior Researcher at the Center for Studies of the Third World, in Mexico City.

ISAAC COHEN is a Senior Analyst for the Economic Commission for Latin America, in Mexico City.

RICHARD R. FAGEN is Gildred Professor of Latin American Studies at Stanford University.

PIERO GLEIJESES is Adjunct Professor of American Foreign Policy and Latin American Studies at the School of Advanced International Studies of Johns Hopkins University.

XABIER GOROSTIAGA is Director of the Institute for Economic and Social Research, in Managua, Nicaragua.

WILLIAM M. LEOGRANDE is Assistant Professor of Political Science at American University.

LUIS MAIRA is Director of the Institute for the Study of the United States at the Centro de Investigación y Docencia Económica, in Mexico City.

MARIO OJEDA is Professor of International Studies at El Colegio de México, in Mexico City.

OLGA PELLICER is Director of the Department of International Politics at the Centro de Investigación y Docencia Económica, in Mexico City.

GERT ROSENTHAL is Director of the Mexico City Office of the Economic Commission for Latin America.

CLINT E. SMITH is the U.S. Deputy Coordinator of the Project on United States–Mexico Relations, at Stanford University.

PEDRO VUSKOVIC is a Senior Researcher in the Department of International Economics at the Centro de Investigación y Docencia Económica, in Mexico City.

Foreword

THIS VOLUME is the second in a series on United States–Mexico relations sponsored by the Project on United States–Mexico Relations and published by Stanford University Press. The first volume, *U.S.-Mexico Relations: Economic and Social Aspects*, edited by Clark W. Reynolds and Carlos Tello, appeared earlier this year. The third volume, *U.S.-Mexico Relations: Agriculture and Rural Development*, edited by Bruce F. Johnston, Cassio Luiselli F., Celso Cartas, and Clint E. Smith, is currently in press.

The Project on United States–Mexico Relations is fully binational in conception, support, and membership, though it by no means excludes participants from countries other than the United States and Mexico. The objective of the Project is three-fold: to explore jointly future development prospects of both countries in an historical perspective; to further the process of mutual understanding; and to provide a framework for formulating binational policies that respect the cultural, political, and economic autonomy of each country, and yet also recognize the reality of ever-increasing interdependence.

Each of the Project's working groups, including future ones on North American energy relations, United States–Mexico finance and trade, labor market development, and approaches to rationalizing interdependence, brings together representatives from the academic community and the private and public sectors. Participants are committed to a broad interdisciplinary approach, in which the United States and Mexico are both perceived to be continuously "developing" countries, with different histories, cultures, values, technologies, and economic circumstances, yet sharing a fundamental commitment to economic and technological progress and to human rights.

In such an approach, both countries are understood to be mutable, responding to internal and external forces within an international system that is itself, on a larger scale, grappling with similar issues. In terms of the practicality of such analysis for both the United States and Mexico, and the implications of such analysis for a better understanding of the process of organic interdependence, the fact that representatives from each country often disagree as much among themselves as with representatives from outside their homeland does not prevent all from sharing the common purpose of searching for means to make the process of interdependence more rational, humane, and just.

Clark W. Reynolds
Carlos Tello M.

THE FUTURE OF CENTRAL AMERICA

Introduction

Richard R. Fagen and Olga Pellicer

THE essays in this volume were first presented as papers and in discussions at a conference held in Guanajuato, Mexico, in June 1982. In a deeper sense they are the result of the profound crisis that is wracking Central America.

At Guanajuato, and at a preliminary meeting that took place in Washington in October 1981, we focused our attention on a somewhat limited set of questions: How, we asked ourselves, are the United States and Mexico—the two dominant (although still very unequal) powers in the region—involved in the Central American crisis? What are their policies toward Central America, and what are the implications of those policies for their relationship with each other? What kinds of policies would, in the long run, contribute to peace, stability, and well-being in the region?

We would be less than candid if we were to claim that we have addressed all of these questions in the detail they deserve. Nor, given the rhythms of academic publishing, could we hope to provide an up-to-date analysis of fast-breaking events in Mexico City, in Washington, or in the region. Rather, we have concentrated on highlighting aspects of Central American realities and U.S. and Mexican policies that seem likely to be both relatively lasting and undeniably important over the next few years. In broad outline, these are as follows:

The nature of the Central American crisis and the objective limitations on restructuring domestic (national) policies.

Perceptions of the crisis in the United States and the policy options under discussion.

Mexican policies toward Central America and their implications for relations with the United States.

The Guatemalan case: dilemmas for the United States and Mexico.

The Nicaraguan case: dilemmas of a revolutionary government in a context of crisis.

There are two essays on each of these themes, except for the Nicaraguan case, and a concluding essay in which Clint Smith summarizes some of the more policy-relevant discussions that took place both in Washington and in Guanajuato.

The most notable omission from the list is an analysis of El Salvador. Of course, the Salvadoran case enters into the essays on both Mexican and U.S. policies toward the region, but we decided not to commission a paper specifically on El Salvador precisely because the topic has received so much scholarly and journalistic attention over the past few years.[1] The reverse is true for Guatemala; emphasis is given to this case because relatively little attention has been paid to what we feel is the most poorly understood and potentially far-reaching of all the situations of insurgency in the area.

Furthermore, as the essays by Piero Gleijeses and Adolfo Aguilar Zinser make clear, the problems raised by the Guatemalan case for both the U.S. and the Mexican governments are of a different order than, for example, those raised by El Salvador. For U.S. policy makers, a centrist or reformist solution to the Guatemalan crisis will be almost impossible to engineer. For Mexican policy makers, coming to terms with a revolutionary situation on their southern border is quite different from dealing with a revolution-in-power in Nicaragua or a popular insurgency in El Salvador. The proper starting point is not, however, either the analysis of individual cases or particular bilateral issues. Rather, it is the Central American crisis as a whole that initially commands our attention.

---

[1] In English, see, for example, Robert Armstrong and Janet Shenk, *El Salvador: The Face of Revolution* (Boston, Mass., 1982); Cynthia Arnson, *El Salvador: A Revolution Confronts the United States* (Washington, D.C., 1982); Central Information Office, *El Salvador: Background to the Crisis* (Cambridge, Mass., 1982); Marvin E. Gettleman et al., eds., *El Salvador: Central America in the New Cold War* (New York, 1981); Arnon Hadar, *The United States and El Salvador* (Berkeley, Calif., 1981); Tommie Sue Montgomery, *Revolution in El Salvador: Origins and Evolution* (Boulder, Colo., 1982).

THE CENTRAL AMERICAN CRISIS

By 1982 it could truly be said that the reformist alternative was dead or dying in almost all countries in Central America. The hope of the 1960's and 1970's—always more widespread in the United States than in the region itself—that economic growth would bring political liberalization and widespread benefits to the masses was everywhere in ruins. In Nicaragua, a massive insurrectional movement had overthrown the Somoza dictatorship and introduced a new political and economic agenda. In El Salvador and Guatemala, prolonged guerrilla struggles had replaced reformist attempts to dislodge oligarchic and military power. In Honduras, the elected civilian government was increasingly hostage to an ever more active military. Even in Costa Rica, the reformist experiment par excellence of Central America, mounting political and economic problems threatened to destabilize the only liberal democracy on the Isthmus.

As Isaac Cohen and Gert Rosenthal point out in their essay, and as Luis Maira and Pedro Vuskovic also emphasize, the structural crisis that complicated and challenged reformism has deep historic roots. In societies in which oligarchic and later military rule would not yield to pressures for social and political reform, even the dramatic economic growth of the 1960's and 1970's did not result in either the overall lessening of inequality or the participation of marginalized groups in the new order. To the contrary, in several countries the gaps between rich and poor, between the powerful and the powerless, widened at the same time that aggregate income was growing rapidly and once-simple economies were modernizing and diversifying.

Furthermore, at least in Nicaragua, El Salvador, and Guatemala, and to a lesser extent in Honduras, the legitimacy of electoral politics was savaged by repeated fraud, military coups, and often the outright murder of the emerging leadership of center or center-left political groups and parties. The politics of reform, at first deeply wedded to electoral strategies, increasingly embraced oppositional activities of other sorts (strikes, mass protests), and finally was forced to choose between ineffectiveness and possibly physical elimination on the one hand or an alliance with the armed opposition on the other. By the 1980's, the choice for many ex-reformists had become relatively stark: death, exile, alliance with guerrilla movements, or a devil's pact with the military.

If the reformist's dream of electoral politics, social reform, economic growth, and substantial "spreading of benefits" was largely exhausted in Central America by 1982, the authoritarian dream (or nightmare) was not. Powerful elites in all Central American nations—and their allies abroad—still believed that the immediate crisis could be managed if sufficiently large dosages of repression were administered. That tens of thousands might die and hundreds of thousands be forced to flee their homes and even their countries seemed not to matter to the architects of the authoritarian response.

Reality, however, has not evolved as the authoritarians had hoped. On the one hand, neither modest nor massive dosages of repression have brought increased political stability to the area. To the contrary, the past few years have witnessed a sharp upswing in political instability as violence and counterviolence displace negotiation and dialogue in Central America. On the other hand, even in those isolated instances when repression has brought a momentary quiescence to one or another country, it has become clear that needed social changes do not easily spring from the ashes of conflict. At a minimum, reformism held out the hope that social change and progress would result from the public policies advocated in its name. Authoritarianism, at least in the militarized form that it assumes in Central America today, holds out no such hope. It is little more than a methodology, bloody and discredited, for attempting to stem changes that more and more residents of the region are coming both to understand and to actively seek.

As a methodology for inhibiting change, at least in the short run, repression is not without its successes. As Piero Gleijeses suggests in his essay on Guatemala, if success is measured simply in terms of "preventing the access to power" of progressive or left-leaning governments, then the Guatemalan military (with a little help from their friends in Washington in 1954) have so far been successful. In the face of an utterly ruthless and relatively well-trained and equipped military machine, the reformist alternative can be totally destroyed and the guerrilla alternative made long and costly indeed. The Nicaraguan case notwithstanding, the ultimate success of armed insurrections in El Salvador and Guatemala is by no means guaranteed.

That the revolutionary alternative faces a long and difficult march in Central America should surprise no one familiar with the history of similar movements in other parts of the world. The length and difficulty of the march is, furthermore, deeply conditioned by a host of local realities as well. The particular terrain on which the guerrilla struggle is being fought, and the special part played by ex-President José Napoleón Duarte in keeping the reformist illusion alive, distinguish the Salvadoran case from that of both Nicaragua and Guatemala. The Guatemalan struggle is complicated by the ethnic division so central to that society as well as by Guatemala's geographical contiguity to Mexico.

Another factor that makes the Central American case somewhat special is the hegemonic and clearly antirevolutionary role historically played by the United States in the area. As emphasized in the essays by Luis Maira and William LeoGrande, that role is deeply rooted in certain strategic and ideological conceptions central to the conduct of U.S. foreign policy. As such, it will not easily be diminished.

To complete the panorama, it is necessary to say something about Nicaragua. Xabier Gorostiaga's essay on the dilemmas of the Nicaraguan Revolution underlines the difficulties encountered as a revolutionary government-in-power tries to make good its promise to offer a developmental alternative obeying the "logic of the majority." Not only must the pledge to benefit the masses be translated into meaningful and successful public policies, but this must be done in an environment that is now less propitious and supportive than was the case when the government first came to power in mid-1979.

The structural crisis of the region, for example, continues to deepen. Inflation and indebtedness mount. Local wars threaten to become generalized and internationalized. And, as Vuskovic suggests in his essay, it is becoming increasingly difficult to imagine sustained development taking place in any one country unless its neighbors also enjoy peace and prosperity. Central American realities make solutions that transcend the limits of strictly national and nationalistic perspectives particularly urgent. Yet, to date, Nicaragua stands alone, surrounded by critics and enemies.

There is, however, another side to the coin—another direction in which the causality runs. The Nicaraguan Revolution has had special regional and international responsibilities thrust upon it, and a wide variety of particular meanings attached to it. Although this is a heavy burden to bear in such a hostile, difficult, and rapidly changing environment, the Revolution will continue to be closely watched to see if a "pluralist," mixed-economy transition to socialism is possible.

This scrutiny is so intense, and the evaluative criteria that are applied are so demanding, that even under the best of circumstances it would not be possible for the Sandinist Revolution to live up to all the expectations that others have for it. There is, however, no escaping the historic role in which the Nicaraguans have been cast. Revolutionary movements in El Salvador and Guatemala win and lose friends in response to events in Nicaragua. Enemies of progressive change exploit every error or problem (real or imagined) in Nicaragua in a ceaseless effort to discredit other radical movements. Bankers, priests, and politicians of various stripes watch the course of the Revolution in a continuing attempt to decide if the institutions they represent can live with a transformation as profound as the one now underway in Nicaragua.

Like Costa Rica's time of troubles, the insurgent movements in El Salvador and Guatemala, and the presence of foreign powers and actors, Nicaragua's revolution is a structural feature of the 1980's in Central America. As such, added importance is given to the question explicitly or implicitly asked by almost all of the essays: What crisis-resolving political and economic options are available for Central American countries? A more complete rendering of this question would add the phrase, "given the multiple lessons that can be drawn from the Nicaraguan Revolution."

UNITED STATES POLICY

The very existence of the Nicaraguan Revolution provides new opportunities for U.S. policymakers intent on impeding or destroying revolutionary movements in Central America. With the Sandinists in power, there is actually something less elusive than guerrilla movements against which to do battle. The Nicaraguan developmental effort, which even with the best of luck would be plagued by problems, has now become the object of massive attempts at delegitimation and destabilization.

The critique of U.S. policy contained in the essays as a whole, however, goes well beyond the Nicaraguan case. What is being questioned is the ability—or the lack thereof—of the United States (as a society, not just as a government) to come to terms with revolutionary change of any kind in the Caribbean Basin. The postwar record, episode after episode, is not encouraging: the CIA-engineered coup against the Arbenz government in Guatemala in 1954; the aggressions against the Cuban Revolution almost from its outset (including, of course, the Bay of Pigs invasion of 1961); the invasion of the Dominican Republic in 1965 when Washington feared that a "Castro-like regime" might be installed; the overt hostility under the Nixon and Ford administrations toward the reformist Manley government in Jamaica.

If we were to fill in the details, and add to this the most overt imperialist actions in Central America and the Caribbean for the hundred years before the Second World War, the record would be even blacker and the list much longer. In addition, with a few honorable exceptions, it would make little difference what party was in power, what the domestic economic situation of the United States was at the moment, or what voices or domestic criticisms were raised. The main policy thrust would be similar, for the sources of U.S. attempts to control events in the Caribbean Basin, to prevent the access to power of regimes that truly dispute U.S. hegemony, lie very deep in the history, structure, and political culture of the United States.

The historical longevity and profundity of imperialist practice in the Caribbean Basin raise two additional issues. The first is essentially an hypothesis: cold war and East-West tensions are perhaps less important for explaining U.S. actions than both defenders and critics of Reagan's policies in the region would have us believe. Ideologically, of course, cold war tensions are both useful and much used to explain and justify policy. But imperialist practices predate the Cold War and may (if history allows the hypothesis to be tested) outlive it as well. The United States will not easily surrender its empire, particularly since most official voices deny that it has one.

The second issue is less an hypothesis and more a well-substantiated observation: for a variety of reasons, the capacity of the United States to act imperially in the region has been diminished. This trend has been most dramatic during the post-Vietnam period. Even the Reagan administration has found its policy options sharply constrained by a combination of domestic and international factors (from the Catholic Church at home to allied governments abroad) that would have been unthinkable as little as fifteen years ago. There is, however, another side to the shrinking of imperialist options. The strength of revolutionary movements in Central America makes "cheap and easy" solutions impossible. To maintain control of the empire in a period of economic crisis and in the face of broadly based insurgencies requires a commitment of resources that the U.S. government is increasingly unable to muster. Thus, as the essay by Luis Maira suggests, there now exists a basic structural tension between a still vigorous imperialist ideology and a reduced capacity to control events in what was once an area of unquestioned United States supremacy.

MEXICAN POLICY

The United States is not the only external actor of importance in the drama that is unfolding in Central America. One of the other significant factors in the current situation is the role that certain Latin American countries, which until recently had little interest in Central America, are coming to play. Among these countries, the most deeply involved is Mexico.

After a certain indifference toward political problems to the south of its border, in 1979 Mexico emerged as the key advocate of international collaboration with the Nicaraguan Revolution. Similarly, Mexico strongly advocated a negotiated solution to the civil war in El Salvador, and promulgated plans designed to lessen tensions in the area. Finally, in conjunction with Venezuela, through the San José agreement, Mexico became party to an energy program that embodied the most important mechanism of economic aid at work in the region.

Another significant aspect of Mexican policy toward Central America has been its impact on international public opinion, particularly on liberals and the press in the United States. As underlined by Olga Pellicer in her essay, many U.S. newspapers have repeatedly editorialized in favor of the incorporation into U.S. policy of Mexican points of view. "Without Mexican involvement, there can be no Central American policy worthy of the name," said the *New York Times*.[2]

Nevertheless, as would be the case with any regional actor holding a position in open conflict with the dominant power, Mexico's capacity to influence events in Central America operates under significant constraints. The most important such constraint derives from the failure of the Reagan administration to recognize the validity of Mexican initiatives. There are two reasons for this. On the one hand, the United States does not want to share influence in a region that for many decades has been considered a private preserve of its own interests. On the other hand—and this is more specific to the particular vision of the Reagan administration itself—it is felt that Mexican officials have lost sight of what really matters in Central America. Bound up as they are in defense of the Sandinist Revolution—so the U.S. argument goes—Mexicans fail to recognize the danger of subversion emanating from Central America, threatening even the very heartland of Mexico.

This second set of arguments has acquired additional urgency since late 1981. With the end of the petroleum-induced boom, an unprecedented deterioration of the Mexican economy has set in. As emphasized in Mario Ojeda's essay, this has weakened—and will continue to weaken—Mexico's international negotiating power. More specifically, Mexican policy in Central America is under serious pressures.

What is implied is not an abandonment of the traditional principles of Mexican foreign policy, such as self-determination, non-intervention, and national sovereignty over natural resources. Nor is the nationalistic ideology of the Mexican government being called into question. Rather, a number of more specific changes may well ensue.

It is possible that the U.S. government will try to link Mexico's financial problems to its own regional foreign policy. Some sort of "tradeoff" might well be sought in which the restruc-

[2] *New York Times*, March 17, 1982, p. A-22.

turing of international credits for Mexico would be made conditional on a change in Mexican positions on security and economic development in Central America and the Caribbean Basin in a direction more congruent with U.S. positions.

It is also possible that Mexico's actions in Central America might be constrained by U.S. efforts to apply to the analysis of domestic politics in Mexico the same scheme used in the rest of the region. In this scheme, any expression of discontent in Mexico—and such expressions are almost inevitable, given the seriousness of social and economic problems—will be seen as creating fertile conditions for "subversion" coming from Cuba or Nicaragua. When this occurs, in the eyes of some U.S. policy makers, Mexico will truly have become part of Central America—and will have to be treated as such.

The opportunities for constraining Mexican policy in this fashion find their most fertile terrain in relation to Guatemala. It is with respect to Mexico's southern frontier that advocates of the "conservative vision" of Central America (in Luis Maira's words) are most likely to find arguments and motives for convincing their Mexican counterparts of the real subversive threat embodied in the revolutionary movements of the region. As Adolfo Aguilar Zinser points out, Guatemala is already viewed by many Mexican policymakers as a special case. And given the proximity of guerrilla struggles to the border with Mexico, the overlap of indigenous populations on both sides of the border, and the probable sharpening of the armed struggle in Guatemala, some Mexican policymakers would need little more justification for viewing Guatemala as even more special.

Despite these problems, the overall perspectives for Mexican policy toward Central America are not entirely negative. As Olga Pellicer notes in her essay, a number of circumstances, and in particular the defeat of the Christian Democrats in the Salvadoran elections of March 1982, have led to a change in the policies of the other major Latin American actor in the region, Venezuela. The Mexican-Venezuelan initiative of September 1982, advocating discussion between Honduras and Nicaragua, may be a bellwether of things to come. Although this initiative seems not to have had much effect, it may signal the beginnings of an alliance that could provide at least a partial counterweight to the policies of the United States in the region.

TOWARD A DIFFERENT U.S. POLICY

Despite what was said earlier about diminishing U.S. ability to maintain control of Central America, all contributors to this volume would agree that by a large margin the United States continues to be the main actor in the region. And, as William LeoGrande's essay on U.S. policy argues, in Nicaragua, El Salvador, Guatemala, and probably in Honduras as well, the Reagan administration has taken positions and advocated policies almost surely guaranteed to deepen both the regional and the national crises, widen the arena of conflict, and prolong the bloodshed. It is thus critical that alternative policies for the United States be developed, policies both bold enough to meet the challenges posed by Central America and sufficiently plausible eventually to attract substantial support in the United States and elsewhere.

Although this is not the forum in which to outline such an alternative in detail, the essays in this volume (and the discussions in Washington and Guanajuato) suggest at least the following guidelines for a new U.S. approach:

The approach must openly recognize the reasons for and the legitimacy of radical movements for social-economic-political change in the region.

The approach must be regional in scope, even if specific policies are tuned to the peculiarities of each national situation. It must seek to create the bases for unity and cooperation in the region, not the bases for setting one nation against another.

The approach must put negotiation at the center of a strategy for conflict resolution, both nationally and internationally, not military measures.

The approach must incorporate a basic rethinking of Cuba-U.S. relations, for there can be no long-run stability in the Caribbean Basin while the United States continues to treat Cuba as an outlaw nation and while Cuba reacts accordingly.

The approach must, to the fullest extent possible, involve and be coordinated with other major actors in the area (e.g., Mexico, Venezuela).

The approach must be based on a careful and circumscribed definition of vital U.S. interests in the region. Questions of national security must be realistically posed in ways appropriate to the closing years of the twentieth century.

The subtext implicit in these very general points is critical. The approach implies an announced willingness on the part of the United States to live with radical and even revolutionary regimes in Central America as long as they do not pose a direct security threat to the United States. Precisely because of this security issue, in Guanajuato it was felt that, in order to have even the faintest chance of being viable in the American political system, this new approach to Central America would have to embody a clear understanding that nonalignment on the part of such regimes would be a *sine qua non* of U.S. acceptance.

At first glance an approach of this sort seems utopian, especially in view of what was said earlier about the historical record of the United States in the Caribbean Basin. The hope must be, therefore, that a process of learning is a possibility. In the context of the current situation in both the United States and Central America, the discussions in Guanajuato and in Washington suggested at least two major points where learning seemed to be particularly necessary.

The first has to do with accepting the fact that the forms of political and economic organization which are so much a part of U.S. history and ideology are in substantial measure not viable in today's Central America. For example, traditional liberal political practices, as illustrated by the results of the March 1982 elections in El Salvador, simply do not respond to the problems of a society wracked by civil war. Nor are private enterprise and the free play of market forces going to resolve the economic problems faced by Nicaragua—nor for that matter by Costa Rica or Honduras either. This is not to say that alternative visions of political and economic order are immediately at hand, but it is to insist that the failed solutions of the past do not hold the key to the future.

The second arena of potential learning has to do with the new realities of power and politics in the Caribbean Basin. The Cuban Revolution with its special relationship to the Soviet Union, the Nicaraguan Revolution, the regional roles being played by Mexico and Venezuela, the powerful pressures for fundamental change that are generated by poverty and violence throughout Central America, are all part of these new realities. As much as many U.S. citizens might wish to turn back the clock to 1960—or even to 1920 in some cases—this will not happen. Thinking about the future must reflect the present, not mythical longings for a set of relations that has passed from the historical agenda.

In Guanajuato Mexican voices were particularly eloquent and persistent in the discussion about current realities and their relationship to the future. The repeated offers of the Mexican government to act as a channel of communication between revolutionary forces in Central America and the U.S. government were viewed as embodying real opportunities, opportunities both misunderstood and missed by the Reagan administration. What is at issue is not whether the United States has the right to develop and conduct its own foreign policy toward the region. Of course it does. What was being questioned, and what continues to be relevant, is the capacity of the United States to understand fully how profoundly the region to its south has changed, and how crucial it is to develop policies that take those changes into account. Mexico's experience and contacts are surely relevant to that challenge.

At a more procedural level, there is also reason for some optimism. Crises at times bring forth the political will necessary to break boldly with the past, and certainly crisis is endemic today in Central America. Furthermore, new administrations have historically found openings during their first year in office to attempt bold departures from past policies.[3]

Given the historic role of the United States in the region, and the close association of the U.S. government with conservative elites, this kind of initiative would send shock waves from the Canal to the Rio Grande. It would, as the saying goes, dramatically change the correlation of forces in Central America— even before any additional concrete steps were taken (such as ending military aid to repressive regimes). What would follow is impossible to predict in detail, but a very different political dynamic would certainly be set in motion in the region.

[3] Although on a smaller scale and of a different order than what is being suggested here, the Carter administration's decision to make the renegotiation of the Panama Canal treaties its first foreign policy initiative was further complicated by the need to secure formal congressional approval for the new treaties. This would not be an element of a new initiative on Central America.

Yet, over the longer run, change might not be as dramatic as some hope and others fear. One of the lessons of Nicaragua is how resistant to change, no matter how deeply desired by incumbent elites and their followers, are the basic contours of economic and social systems. Under almost any imaginable set of new economic relations, the small, agro-exporting economies of Central America would still be closely tied to the international capitalist system—borrowing, buying, and selling in that system, with both the advantages and disadvantages implied. And even if political arrangements came to differ widely from idealized U.S. visions of democracy, they would still be experienced by many Central Americans as a vast improvement on the realities under which they suffer today.

It is also important, however, to emphasize that there is no possible set of new political and economic arrangements that could solve the deep crisis of Central America in the short run. Decades of inequality, exploitation, and violence have left wounds that cut to the very quick of Central American societies, and those wounds will not fully heal in this decade. All we can ask is that U.S. policies cease being part of the problem of Central America and begin to be constructive elements in a much-to-be-hoped-for eventual solution.

The Dimensions of Economic Policy Space in Central America

Isaac Cohen and Gert Rosenthal

INTRODUCTION

Probably more has been written about Central America in the last three years than in the previous thirty. Most of these writings try to explain why the region has been so unstable and turbulent; many analyze the role of external actors—particularly the United States—in the dynamics of the region. The international community has also become increasingly aware of the region, and many ideas have been forwarded on how to reestablish stability and foster the well-being of the populations of its several countries. At times, emphasis is laid on the need for fostering more tolerant, open, and pluralistic societies, where such universal values as human dignity, material well-being, and representative democracy are observed. All of the governments of the region profess to support these values wholeheartedly, but the record of the past few years, with the honorable exception of Costa Rica, is not encouraging. For their part, official declarations of various external actors interested in the region —among others, the United States, Mexico, Canada, Venezuela, France, Germany, and Spain—stress the need to support the "moderate forces" within these societies, but their definitions of who represents such forces differ drastically, and at any rate the support for such moderation sometimes goes little beyond lip service.

In the context of increasing polarization that characterizes most of the countries of the region, however, the "middle ground" or "center" is hard to discern. In terms of economic policy, for example, there are rather stringent constraints on those measures designed to promote reforms, the limits being imposed by domestic conditions as well as by external actors.

The purpose here is to explore the limited dimensions of economic policy space in Central America. The ideas are still of a highly preliminary nature, and possibly more questions are raised than answered. The hypothesis is that gradual economic and social reforms, as part of the forces of change, have not fared well in most of the countries of the region, and that their viability has become even more questionable in recent years. In part, this is due to the ambivalent character of U.S. foreign policy in the region, which has pursued both reformist and security objectives—the latter having prevalence "in the crunch." As Stanley Hoffmann pointed out some years ago, "In Latin America the United States simultaneously makes efforts towards development and progress which cannot succeed unless they shake oligarchies and dislodge vested interests, and efforts to prevent subversion and insurgency which consist in rushing to the threatened gates and which therefore strengthen the *status quo*."[1] Central America offers striking examples in support of this statement.

SALIENT CHARACTERISTICS OF CENTRAL AMERICAN ECONOMIES AND SOCIETIES

A minimum understanding of how Central American economies and societies function is indispensable as a background to discussing the dimensions of policy space in the region.

The first and most basic characteristic of these countries is their extreme dependence on events that occur outside their very limited boundaries, both national and regional. The quest for a key export product—be it gold, cacao, indigo, coffee, bananas, sugar, or cotton—has been a constant in the region's history, ever since the Spanish conquest.[2] This fact has strongly affected the economic, social, and political structure of all five countries; at the same time, because the influence it exacts is not the same for each of them, it also helps to explain why important differences exist.

[1]Stanley Hoffmann, *Gulliver's Troubles, or the Setting of American Foreign Policy* (New York, 1968), p. 187.
[2]Murdo J. MacLeod, *Spanish Central America: A Socioeconomic History, 1520–1720* (Berkeley, Calif., 1973).

The export sector has always been the main "engine of growth" of these economies, as well as the main source of capital accumulation and employment opportunities. In modern times, although during the sixties and seventies a fairly dynamic import substitution process was initiated under the aegis of Central American economic integration, and the export sector itself became increasingly diversified, rates of growth still were and continue to be a function of the performance of exports. In fact, not surprisingly, the level of intraregional trade is also a function of the traditional export sector, since intraregional trade rises with rates of growth. Furthermore, contrary to the expectation of some analysts that import substitution would lessen the degree of "openness" of the Central American economies, the proportion of both exports and imports to gross domestic product (GDP) systematically increased as incomes rose. Thus, for the region as a whole, the exports as a proportion of GDP rose from less than 19 percent in 1950 to well over 30 percent in 1980, and that of imports from 16 percent to over 35 percent. (For some countries, such as Honduras, this proportion was over 40 percent.) It is no wonder, then, that all these countries are sensitive to changes in the international economy, a fact that has been magnified in recent years as this dependence began to affect not only trade, but also capital flows associated with increasing rates of external savings. Thus, in the early eighties, most of these countries are adversely affected not only by the recession in the developed countries—and particularly that of their main trading partner, the United States—but also by the very high levels of interest rates, which take an increasing share of export earnings in order to service the ever-higher levels of external debt.

The exploitation of one or several basic commodities, furthermore, has been a determinant in establishing the nature of the division of labor, owing to the labor-intensive character of the principal export crops. In the case of coffee, cotton, and sugar in particular, the demand for workers is seasonal, which explains the dualistic but interdependent nature of agriculture in the economies where these crops are prevalent. There the *campesino* basically produces foodstuffs for subsistence, sometimes with some excedents for the domestic, mostly urban market, and also constitutes the reserve pool of labor required seasonally by the exploitation of traditional exports. The complex interrelationships between the large number of small, subsistence-type agricultural units producing for domestic consumption and the relatively reduced number of medium to large units producing for external markets explain not only the characteristics of the economies, but also some of the most marked peculiarities of the social structures of the region.

The availability of labor, in effect, has played such a strategic role throughout the history of Central America's development, that some of the basic differences exhibited between countries can be explained, to a large extent, by the varying nature of labor relations. Thus, in the case of Costa Rica, the relative scarcity of labor and the late emergence of a key export product—coffee, in the mid-nineteenth century—partially explain the country's more egalitarian social structure. On the other hand, Guatemala and El Salvador, with relatively high population densities and the early introduction of key export crops, would represent the opposite extreme, with Honduras and Nicaragua occupying an intermediate position. Furthermore, in those countries where the main export crop during most of the twentieth century—bananas—required a permanent supply of labor, the dualistic nature of agriculture was somewhat less pronounced.

Finally, another characteristic of the emphasis on the exploitation of a few key export products has been the virtual absence of intrinsic or induced linkage effects of these productive activities. Neither the producers nor external agents have been able to invest the economic surplus derived from their exploitation in relatively more self-sustaining and less dependent activities. In effect, probably one of the most outstanding characteristics of Central American development is the fact that the exploitation of new export products only reiterated this phenomenon. The traditional producers did not diversify or integrate their activities, nor was the state able to extract an important portion of the surplus generated by the traditional producers and divert it to other productive activities. This does not mean that contemporary Central America has not witnessed the introduction of new activities, but only that these have been juxtaposed upon the traditional productive structures, which persist and constitute themselves into formidable obstacles or limits to modernization in the region.

These salient characteristics of the Central American economies also help to explain the extreme inequalities in income distribution that have been present, with varying degrees, in all
countries and are a function of both land tenure and the nature
of the above-mentioned labor markets. Not surprisingly, the income structure is most unequal in those countries that have relatively high population to land ratios, and rapid population
growth, coupled with large seasonal migrations of labor between
minifundia and *latifundia*, as in Guatemala and El Salvador.

The progressive juxtaposition, since the end of World War II,
of new layers of economic activity upon the basic, traditional
socioeconomic structure has contributed to diversified economies, but has not decisively transformed preexisting conditions.
This diversification, coupled with a relatively satisfactory level
of growth,[3] contributed to increasing urbanization and the
emergence of middle sectors basically in the services, the incipient industrialization process, and the growing bureaucracy.

The overwhelming importance of the few export products
has also decisively influenced the role of the state, oriented
basically toward securing the basic conditions for their exploitation. From this key orientation of public policy also derives
the almost symbiotic relationship that has tenaciously persisted,
until recent times, between the public sector and the dominant
entrepreneurial classes, despite the inroads of modernization
and the new activities that have been introduced. In more recent
times governments have sought legitimacy from the emerging
middle sectors, but those sectors, not having been fully integrated, have also been the source of the radical challenges to the
dominant group. Except in Costa Rica, the campesinos have remained largely unmobilized, passive witnesses and victims of
social systems characterized by their elitist nature.

Those systems, in effect, greatly hinder formal social organizations, with varying degrees of intensity from country to country. The dominant entrepreneurs are well organized through
chambers of agriculture, industry, and commerce, and through
multiple other mechanisms that effectively represent their interests, yet at the same time other groups of society lack any means

---

[3] For the region as a whole, real GDP grew at an annual average rate of 5.3% between
1950 and 1980. Nicaragua and Costa Rica had higher than average rates; Honduras
registered a lower than average rate.

at all of organized expression. Unions are weak in most of the countries, especially in the rural areas, with the exception of the laborers of the banana enclaves who receive certain government encouragement to counter foreign capital. Neither organized labor, nor—much less—the campesinos, are represented in any important decision-making board, such as those that govern the central banks and other official or semi-official agencies. In sum, social organization tends to reinforce inequitable patterns in income distribution that vary with the effectiveness of pressure groups.

Finally, the structuring of the Central American economies around one or a very few key export products has had a profound effect on patterns of authority. Not only the symbiotic relationship between the dominant economic groups and governments, but also the legacy of corruption in violation of colonial rules, and especially the repressive methods imposed to assure an adequate supply of labor—forced recruitment of labor in previous eras, vagrancy laws, and something akin to debt peonage in more recent times—have all contributed to the relatively rigid political systems in most of the countries (Costa Rica would again be the exception), with virtually no representation for the majority of the population. To this day, most of the Central American political systems are authoritarian; the dominant entrepreneurial classes are paternalistic; and political confrontations remain elitist, despite the inroads of modernization.

LIMITS TO THE DIMENSIONS OF ECONOMIC POLICY SPACE

Throughout their history as independent nations, and especially since the end of World War II, those actors within the Central American societies that have pursued change have persistently tried to alter some of the main characteristics already described; that is, their goals have included decreasing the dependency of their economies on international phenomena, altering the social structure and the relation between capital and labor, establishing more egalitarian societies, and increasing the level of participation of the majority of the population in their respective countries' affairs. They have had to tread a narrow and slippery path, especially in Guatemala, El Salvador, and, until 1979, Nicaragua, finding that the dimensions of economic policy space, on the one hand, and the degree of political participation, on the other, are severely limited. Some, in their frustration at their incapacity to make major headway in the achievement of their goals, have reached the conclusion that the solution is to overthrow the existing social, economic, and political order by means of revolution. Others, either unwilling or unable to embrace violent means, have persisted in attempting to build consensus through persuasion, in the context of the tolerant and pluralistic societies that they pursue.

That there have been important changes in all Central American economies and societies is undeniable. During the past three decades populations have tripled, real per capita income has doubled, and foreign trade has multiplied by sixteen; the countries are more urbanized, societies more differentiated, economies more diversified, and physical space better integrated. Modernization has encroached upon many activities. However, it is debatable how much of this change is part of a deliberate policy and how much is the result of "trickle-down effects," which even those actors in the societies that support the status quo are willing to tolerate. There is considerable evidence that the changes that policy makers and decision makers have been able to bring about have been peripheral in the sense that, with very few exceptions, they have not adversely affected the basic interests of the dominant groups of the societies. In other words, new social and economic layers have been juxtaposed to pre-existent ones, without seriously threatening the persistence of the prior economic structure. Some of the constraints have been of an economic nature, but most of them have been more closely related to political limits. Those limits to this type of "additive development" were almost invariably reached over the previous three decades when the preceding structure was seriously threatened.

It is impossible, of course, to separate the realm of economic policy from that of political interaction, since they mutually reinforce each other. However, it might be useful to select three areas of what is conventionally associated with a "reformist platform" of economic policy to explain just how narrow the dimensions of economic policy space have been in Central America, and how the limits have varied from country to country. Those areas are: (a) the levels of taxation; (b) the participation of the public sector in the economies; and (c) the structure of land ownership. At least through the late 1970's, on all three counts, change has been slow in coming or even nonexistent, except, significantly, in Costa Rica and, to a lesser degree, in Honduras.

A good indicator of the level of taxation is the relation between total taxes collected and gross domestic product. While some important changes took place within the tax structures of all countries—the relative importance of direct taxation increased, while the relative importance of import duties decreased—in most of the countries of the region the level of taxation remained constant or increased only slightly during the past three decades (Table 1). Indeed, were it not for the substantial increase in the level of taxation in Nicaragua after the successful revolution of 1979, the relation of fiscal receipts to GDP for the region as a whole would have increased by only about one percentage point between 1955 and 1980. Furthermore, this level is extremely low compared to the one prevalent in other developing countries, either in Latin America or in the rest of the world. This circumstance is no accident: the dominant groups of society have been as reluctant to share their proportion of economic surplus with the public sector as they have been to share it with the work force through higher wages. Even new taxes, when governments were successful in legislating them, were usually regressive. Thus, the ability of the public sector to take a more active reformist stance was severely limited by financial constraints, and such increased expenditures as were undertaken were usually funded through deficit spending financed internally and externally.

The immediate postwar period, imbued with democratic ideals, marked an end to most of the "depression dictatorships" in Central America, ushering in a brief period of liberal reforms. This meant an enhanced role for the public sector in promoting economic development, in addition to its previous role of maintaining order, with the establishment of a plethora of new institutions—central banks, social security institutes, development banks—and the adoption of a generally more reformist stance on the part of governments. However, by the 1950's the role of the public sector in development became an important public issue, with the dominant groups of society taking a

TABLE I

Proportion of Tax Receipts to GDP in Central America, Selected Years,
1950–1980

Country	1950	1955	1960	1965	1970	1975	1980
Central America	6.9%	9.5%	9.3%	9.4%	9.7%	11.1%	11.4%
Guatemala	8.7	8.5	7.8	7.6	7.8	9.5	8.6
El Salvador	8.3	10.8	10.9	9.9	10.3	12.0	11.4
Honduras	6.0	7.3	10.1	9.7	11.2	12.1	13.7
Nicaragua	4.8	10.8	9.4	10.2	9.4	10.6	18.5
Costa Rica	10.2	10.1	10.0	11.8	12.1	12.7	11.4

SOURCE: Calculations based on official statistics.

strongly anti-dirigiste position, which persists to this day. Although during the fifties and sixties the public sector gradually absorbed some public utilities formerly in private—usually foreign—hands, such as those involved in the generation and distribution of electricity, railroad transportation, and domestic and international communications, governments as a rule scrupulously avoided getting involved in directly productive activities or in providing services that the private sector was interested in. The important exception to this rule can be found in Costa Rica, where banks were nationalized in the late forties, and petroleum refining and distribution were absorbed by the government in the mid-seventies.

The proportion of public expenditures to total GDP, which illustrates the limits to governments' participation in their economies, has been quite moderate as compared to other developing countries and grew only modestly until 1975 (Tables 2 and 3). This constraint is not only a function of the financial restrictions imposed by the capacity to increase fiscal revenues, but also the result of a doctrinaire opposition on the part of influential groups in the societies to an enhanced role for the public sector. The rationale was that fuller participation would represent a suboptimal allocation of resources (the state is considered inherently inefficient in everything it does), and that a greater mobilization of resources on the part of the public sector would stunt private initiative. This opposition also has had something to do with the fact that an enhanced role for the public sector could challenge the position of the dominant groups of society

TABLE 2

*Proportion of Central Government Expenditures to GDP in Central America,
Selected Years, 1960–1980*

Country	1960	1965	1970	1975	1980
Central America	*11.2%*	*10.8%*	*11.2%*	*12.8%*	*17.8%*
Guatemala	9.3	8.1	8.3	7.8	10.1
El Salvador	12.2	10.9	10.3	13.4	17.6
Honduras	12.2	10.8	14.7	15.0	18.1
Nicaragua	11.1	11.2	11.8	14.1	29.5
Costa Rica	13.3	13.8	13.7	17.9	20.5

SOURCE: Calculated on the basis of official statistics.

TABLE 3

*Proportion of Public Sector Expenditures to GDP in Central America,
Selected Years, 1950–1980*

Country	1950	1955	1960	1965	1970	1975	1980
Central America	*11.1%*	*13.2%*	*13.3%*	*13.1%*	*13.6%*	*14.9%*	*19.9%*
Guatemala	10.4	12.3	11.4	10.1	10.4	10.0	13.0
El Salvador	12.6	13.5	14.5	14.0	13.5	17.0	21.8
Honduras	9.8	11.8	14.3	13.1	18.2	18.4	22.2
Nicaragua	15.7	16.2	15.2	13.6	13.6	16.1	34.5
Costa Rica	8.4	14.2	13.4	17.6	17.0	19.1	21.9

SOURCE: Calculated on the basis of official statistics.

through the emergence of a new, important autonomous actor whose inclinations might not be entirely predictable.

It is true that since 1975 levels of expenditure have grown, as a result of the public sectors' efforts to counteract declining rates of private investment in the face of spreading political turbulence in the region, although significantly this phenomenon was less pronounced in Guatemala and El Salvador. Furthermore, this increased expenditure was financed in growing proportion by increased borrowing.

Increasing the level of expenditures beyond the financial limits imposed by fiscal receipts through resorting to deficit financing again illustrates the additive aspects of Central America's development: rather than raise the levels of taxation to finance their own investment programs, the governments resorted to the less painful route of seeking external assistance. As Table 4 shows, external public debt grew rapidly, especially in the 1970's, although at a lower rate for the countries with the most conservative fiscal policies, Guatemala and El Salvador. By the end of the decade, over one-quarter of the export earnings of Honduras, Nicaragua, and Costa Rica were earmarked for the service of public debt. Between 1980 and 1982, however, all three countries had unilaterally to suspend interest payments on that debt and to initiate negotiations for its rescheduling.

Thus, it appears that at present even the limits to additive development have been reached as far as public expenditures are concerned. It is relevant, therefore, to ask how governments can continue to promote change and provide services to their respective populations when, in the majority of the countries, their participation in gross domestic product is so modest and such important obstacles stand in the way of its increase.

The third area of public policy in which little progress was achieved during this period, until the Nicaraguan Revolution took place in 1979 and the much-heralded reforms were adopted by the government of El Salvador since 1980, is land tenure. Such redistribution as took place, with the possible exception of Honduras, was usually not at the expense of existing agricultural units, but in "colonization" projects of public land. This is yet one more example of the additive nature of reform, in order to avoid affecting the preestablished order. In those countries for

TABLE 4

External Debt and Debt Service in Central America, 1960, 1970, and 1980

Country	1960		1970		1980	
	Total debt (*million dollars*)	Debt service	Total debt (*million dollars*)	Debt service	Total debt (*million dollars*)	Debt service
Central America	93	3.1	564	6.9	4,950	14.6
Guatemala	24	1.7	106	7.4	500	2.3
El Salvador	24	2.6	88	3.6	477	3.4
Honduras	14	2.6	90	2.8	900	20.9
Nicaragua	5	4.3	146	10.4	1,500	13.4[a]
Costa Rica	26	5.2	134	9.7	1,573	21.2

NOTE: Total debt here consists of disbursed public and publicly guaranteed debt. The figure for debt service is the ratio of service of public debt to exports of goods and services.

[a] Actual payments, excluding service in arrears.

TABLE 5

The Structure of Land Tenure in El Salvador, 1961 and 1971

(percentages of the total)

Size of agricultural unit	1961		1971	
	No. of units	Total area	No. of units	Total area
Less than 1 hectare	47.18%	3.88%	48.90%	4.84%
1 to 1.99 has.	21.38	4.33	21.81	5.58
2 to 4.99 has.	16.63	7.43	16.03	9.09
5 to 9.99 has.	6.17	6.25	5.76	7.61
10 to 19.99 has.	3.76	7.42	3.38	8.74
20 to 49.99 has.	2.96	13.19	2.58	14.84
50 to 99.99 has.	0.98	9.78	0.83	10.62
100 to 999.99 has.	0.89	31.97	0.69	30.16
1,000 or more has.	0.05	15.74	0.02	8.51

SOURCE: Official statistics.

which statistics are available, the structure of land ownership has remained highly concentrated (Tables 5 and 6). Although the largest estates appear to have been subdivided—often, no doubt, within the same families—the situation in the mid-seventies was virtually unchanged from the one observed in the fifties. In Guatemala, for example, the largest 2 percent of agricultural units registered in the 1950 census controlled 66.6 percent of the land; in the 1979 census the largest 2 percent still controlled 58.7 percent of the land. On the other end of the scale, the smallest agricultural units making up 88 percent of the total number of units registered in the first census controlled 14.3 percent of the land; in the 1979 census the same 88 percent controlled only 16.0 percent of the land, in spite of the government's so-called colonization programs that distributed 545,000 hectares among 145,000 families. Although the proponents of evolutionary change gave much lip-service to the need for land reform, such reforms would surely have surpassed the limits that political realities—i.e., the interests of the dominant groups of society—imposed. Thus, over the thirty-year postwar period, only marginal improvements were achieved in the structure of land ownership.

It is apparent, then, that the forces in favor of peaceful change in Central America have had to maneuver within very confined limits. It would be unfair to say that there have been no reforms—even the additive type of development has been translated into different situations today as compared, say, to thirty years ago. It would nevertheless be accurate to state that there have been almost overwhelming obstacles in the way of those pacific changes that seriously challenge the preexisting order, at least in the majority of the countries. This in itself was no doubt a contributing element to the fact that those changes which have occurred in Nicaragua since 1979 required a violent revolution, at the cost of some 50,000 lives, and it has also contributed strongly to the polarization in the other countries of the region.

None of the constraints to raising the level of taxation—and hence the public sector's share in the economy—or to improving the structure of land tenure are to any important degree related

TABLE 6

The Structure of Land Tenure in Guatemala, 1950, 1964, and 1979

(percentages of the total)

Size of agricultural unit	1950		1964		1979	
	No. of units	Total area	No. of units	Total area	No. of units	Total area
Less than 1 manzana[a]	21.3%	.77%	20.4%	.95%	41.1%	1.45%
1–2 manzanas	26.3	2.54	23.6	2.77	19.4	2.70
2–5 manzanas	28.6	5.70	30.9	7.85	20.8	6.32
5–10 manzanas	12.2	5.32	12.4	7.04	8.4	5.66
10–32 manzanas	7.7	8.35	8.9	12.95	6.6	11.74
32–64 manzanas	1.8	5.10	1.6	5.90	1.5	6.70
1–10 caballerías	1.861	21.86	1.883	26.53	2.015	30.27
10–20 caballerías	.163	9.52	.134	10.03	.141	12.41
20–50 caballerías	.103	13.32	.071	11.22	.063	11.76
50–100 caballerías	.030	8.81	.014	4.92	.012	5.24
100–200 caballerías	.009	5.28	.007	5.17	.002	2.03
200 or more caballerías	.006	13.43	.002	4.67	.001	3.72

SOURCE: Official statistics.

[a] 1 manzana = 0.7 has.; 1 caballería = 64 manzanas.

to economic policy. It is generally recognized that economic rents in all of the countries are high, and that an increased tax burden would hardly be a significant limiting factor to overall savings and investment. Nor have persuasive arguments been put forth to the effect that large landholdings are more efficient than smaller ones, and that land reform would thus be counterproductive in terms of agricultural output. (The few attempts at land reform, as in Guatemala in 1951, have been accompanied by an understandable reluctance on the part of large landholders to invest.) On the whole, the main constraints have been of a political nature, since the dominant groups of society have tenaciously opposed the reform measures, perceiving them as a threat to their own relative position within their respective countries and societies.

It would be an oversimplification, however, to state that pacific reforms have been impeded simply because they are opposed by the dominant groups of these societies. Rather, the explanation requires a brief examination of political interaction in the Central American political arena, and an analysis of the way that external actors interact with the domestic actors.

HOW ARE THE LIMITS SET?

It has been implicit in the previous pages—for it is almost a cliché to state it explicitly—that among the domestic actors who confront each other in the political arena there is a constant interaction between those who seek to preserve the status quo and those who seek change. The dimensions of economic policy space are defined by the changes over time in the lines of political interaction between the former and at least those who seek change by peaceful means. Shifting and sporadic alliances have permitted some of the marginal reforms that were undertaken over the years; some were even pushed through as a result of contradictions within the ranks of the dominant groups of society. The very narrowness of the dimensions of policy space in most Central American countries and the persistence of the preexistent order, in turn, helped to strengthen the ranks of those actors who believe that change can come about only by the violent overthrow of the preexistent order. As a result, those who seek to preserve the status quo, feeling their own hegemonic role increasingly threatened, also turned to violence, with the consequent polarization of most of the region's societies and the attendant weakening of those "caught in the middle." Indeed, the reformist platform became ever more tenuous as its supporters, being perceived on the one hand as the forerunners of a new order and on the other as the salvagers of the status quo, fell victim to the violence of the other actors.

But none of the above, and especially the narrow dimensions of policy space—the only aspect pertinent to this paper—can be understood without examining the role of U.S. foreign policy in Central America. Even granting the increasing importance of several new external actors in the Central American arena, such as Mexico, Venezuela, and Cuba among others, their role is still of minor significance compared to the overwhelming importance in the region of the United States. Its impact—politically, culturally, and economically—has been of decisive importance in the contemporary evolution of Central America, and there is little evidence that what is regarded as a relative decline in U.S. power at the global level has translated itself into a similar decline in Central America. Thus, one can quite properly limit the analysis of external influences on political interaction in the region to an examination of the role played in Central America by the foreign policy of the United States.

The objectives of that policy were set according to the worldwide responsibilities that the United States has assumed since 1945 as a superpower, and exhibited the characteristic tension and alternation between realism and idealism, and the ambivalence born in conflicting goals. Hence, by intervening actively, in effect as another actor, in the dynamics of political interaction in the countries of the region, the United States introduced a world dimension to confrontations that would probably have been characterized by their local, if not parochial, nature.

As a consequence of its powerful influence in Central America, the United States has virtually had the capacity to set the geopolitical limits by throwing its asymmetrical weight on the side of those domestic actors whose objectives have been most congruent with its own global interests at any particular time. That external support has intermittently, and sometimes simultaneously, sought to promote pacific change and to contain communism; and, as suggested earlier, when these goals came into conflict, prevalence was inevitably given to the latter.

Probably the best manifestation of this capacity to set the limits to political change in the region can be found in the overthrow of the Arbenz regime in Guatemala in 1954. Within the framework of the ideological anxieties of the Cold War, when the overriding objective of U.S. foreign policy was the containment of communism, the transformations undertaken in Central America by what is now considered a populist-nationalist government were immediately perceived as a threat to the security of the hemisphere. This led, by means of the active support of the U.S. intelligence establishment, to the victory in Guatemala of those actors interested in preserving the status quo. That is, the defense of the international status quo, which inspired U.S. foreign policy during the Cold War years, found its counterpart in the anticommunism supported with enthusiasm by the most conservative sectors of Central American societies. In other words, the global aspects of U.S. policy offered one of the domestic actors a rationale, albeit imported from outside, to fend off any challenge to its hegemonic role.

Different threats have not always been countered with the same swiftness and intolerance. During the sixties, with the Cuban Revolution perceived as a new challenge to the security of the hemisphere, and the arrival of a Democratic administration in the White House, a different response was adopted. These were the years of the Alliance for Progress, which sought to counter the "risk of contagion" emanating from the Cuban example by financing peaceful reforms and simultaneously increasing the local armies' degree of professionalization in the techniques of counterinsurgency.

This component of U.S. foreign policy found supporters within the region among the most conservative sectors, while the reformist component found support among a handful of technocrats placed in strategic positions within the governments of the region. In fact, the increased levels of external financing available from the Alliance for Progress allowed for the emergence of a relatively autonomous basis of support for these reforms, which were severely criticized by the conservatives as interventionist or "dirigiste" and as hindrances to the functioning of free enterprise. Thus, the reforms rapidly confronted limits in the sense that they were perceived as threats to the traditional social structures, with the result that colonization projects were preferred to agrarian reforms; higher levels of external financing took the place of tax reforms; and some degree of public indicative planning was supported at the same time that "open door" policies toward private foreign investment were maintained.

Then, in 1963, two events brought the limits to reformism to the forefront. Two *coups d'état*, one in Guatemala and then one in Honduras, with different origins and different consequences, challenged the U.S. emphasis on the peaceful and democratic reforms that characterized the Alliance for Progress. In Guatemala, the coup unleashed a campaign of selective terrorism, which claimed many lives, to defeat the first radical threat presented by the appearance of an organized guerrilla movement. In Honduras, the sudden change of government inaugurated almost two decades of military rule and reforms—among them a very moderate agrarian reform—which helps to explain the relatively small degree of polarization in that country. In both cases, security considerations—i.e., the requirements of counterinsurgency—took precedence over reforms, with some change imposed from above in Honduras without consideration for the democratic ideals implicit in the "reformist platform."

On occasion, the foreign policy of the United States has hesitatingly accompanied change in Central America. First, the overthrow of the "depression dictatorships" in the forties was to a large degree a result of U.S. support for the heterogenous coalitions that by the end of World War II challenged the dictators throughout the region, with the notable exception of Anastasio Somoza in Nicaragua. Second, after initially exploring various alternatives, the Carter administration, evidencing an unusual degree of tolerance for change, did not oppose the overthrow of the Somoza dynasty in Nicaragua in 1979 by a heterogenous coalition reminiscent of those that had overthrown the "depression dictators" after the war. Soon these changes also confronted limits because they seemed to be moving the countries where they were taking place beyond the almost exclusive sphere of influence of the United States. Such was the case of Guatemala in the early fifties, and it is increasingly apparent that such is the case with the Sandinist regime in Nicaragua at present.

Thus, the foreign policy of the United States in Central America has had a decisive influence on change in the region. Wavering between the support of peaceful reforms and counterinsurgency, and at times even supporting or not opposing revolutionary change, the United States has been able—so far, at least—to define limits to change. The well-known oscillations of its foreign policy, between realism and idealism, help to explain why an idealist support for change has rapidly become checked by a realism more concerned with containing communism, or how an emphasis on counterinsurgency ended up decisively limiting the impact of such reforms.

Another consequence of U.S. foreign policy on the limits of change, probably even more significant, has been its impact on globalizing the terms of political conflict in Central America. Political conflict in the region has now acquired a dimension that almost always excludes compromise, although one has always to recall the exception offered by Costa Rica. By imposing on political confrontations a zero-sum dimension, because of the fact that they have been rationalized in terms of the global confrontation between communism and anticommunism, the United States has contributed to the containment of change in Central America within very narrow limits. Even peaceful change, not to mention revolutionary transformation, has rapidly provoked the suspicion that it will have negative consequences for the security of the region, understood until now in terms of the Isthmus's belonging to the almost exclusive sphere of influence of the United States.

Finally, these consequences of U.S. foreign policy in Central America have introduced a considerable propensity to polarization of political change there, which has decisively diminished the potential of negotiated, gradual, and reformist alternatives. Those actors interested in preserving the status quo—in whose ranks the United States frequently but not always appears—as well as those interested in radically transforming these societies, tend to define moderate alternatives either as ominous radical threats or as measures to strengthen the status quo, depending on the extreme of the political spectrum on which each one stands. In the end, of course, as is generally the case, the political effectiveness of these definitions depends on the relative strength of those who make them.

IS A REFORMIST APPROACH STILL VIABLE?

The prospects for a moderate, reformist, or "middle-of-the-road" outcome to political interaction, at least in the majority of the Central American countries, may be dim; nevertheless, change by political as opposed to military means should not be ruled out as a viable alternative. It might be accomplished by any one of at least three different scenarios that respond, in varying degrees, to what might be called a reformist platform.

The first scenario, which has been prevalent in Costa Rica in effect for over thirty years, might conceivably be valid for other countries of the region, although highly improbable for those in which polarization has proceeded to the degree that the domestic actors committed to reformist change have been greatly weakened or even virtually eliminated. Such a scenario presupposes, among other requisites, the support of the most important external actor in favor of the domestic actors, regardless of security considerations. It is therefore difficult to imagine that the existing situation, either in Guatemala or in El Salvador, can lead to such an outcome, given the realities of U.S. global foreign policy at the present time and the relative strength of those domestic actors willing to resort to force to impose their objectives. At any rate, at the conceptual level, at least, the possibility still exists.

A more promising scenario would consist, in effect, in bringing all domestic actors pursuing change—peaceful or not—into the "mainstream" of pluralistic, nationalistic, popular, and non-aligned programs, much in the vein of the original platform announced by the Government of National Reconstruction of Nicaragua that to this day appears still to be a possible outcome for the Sandinist Revolution. Such a scenario would, however, entail the redefinition of the geopolitical limits currently applied by the United States—accepting internal change in Central America as long as it does not fall within the sphere of influence of the other superpowers; yet the revolutionary forces would have to settle for something that falls short of the millennium.

The third possible scenario, which may be the most plausible, finds its precedents in Honduras and Panama during the sixties and especially the seventies. It consists of a reformist platform being imposed from above (in the cases cited, by military governments). For those who have sought democratic evolutionary change this is the least attractive scenario, since it lacks some vital ingredients of what is commonly perceived as the reformist platform: by its very nature it is not democratic, and it is also not participatory. Rather, these evolutionary changes in the economic and social spheres can be accompanied by autocratic and even repressive measures, as recent events in some countries have shown.

It should be stressed that the reformist platform, as understood in this paper, does not necessarily conform to any preconceived model. Certainly it does not mean imitating the U.S. political and economic systems; it does not even mean having "five other Costa Ricas" in the region. On the contrary, it would rely heavily on the capacity of each country's domestic forces to innovate, in accordance with its own needs and the dictates of circumstances. The concept would include the pursuit of evolutionary change toward more egalitarian, less dependent societies in terms of economic and social policy, and toward pluralistic, participative, and nationalistic systems as political goals. Can stability return to this turbulent part of the world with the fulfillment of such a platform? Only time will tell.

Economic Factors in the Evolution
of Central American Societies

Pedro Vuskovic

THE primary purpose of these preliminary notes—and they should be seen as no more than that—is solely to provide a point of reference for a more systematic consideration of the topics covered. The impetus derives from the impression that the terms of the debate on Central America, the scene of the most severe social struggles in contemporary Latin America, often dangerously confuse the meaning of the various options that characterize the alternative outcomes. Therefore, even among those who recognize the need for progressive social transformations, it is common to encounter a sort of anguished examination of "reformism's" potential for meeting current demands and aspirations. The implicit or explicit argument behind this search is that only reformism can prevent a "radicalization" process that is identified, in turn, with "Sovietizing" tendencies. The political leadership of the antigovernmental forces is therefore subject to constant pressure to adopt a social-democratic stance or to disavow their alleged role as a threat to "continental security."

Meanwhile, the real options available do not only depend on the intensity of the external pressures exerted in an attempt to impose a given ideological slant. The more fundamental factors clearly are: (1) conditions within the region itself and within each member nation; (2) the essential features that have developed throughout the course of these nations' historical evolution; and (3) the profound nature of the problems that have emerged as a result of this process—in particular, those of primarily economic significance.

Whatever weight is attributed to economic factors in the Central American crisis, it is undeniable that they form a very important antecedent for understanding the political and social scenario recently characterizing the countries of the region. Similarly, the significance of economic determinants in shaping the prospects for the future evolution of both the Central American countries and the region as a whole is evident. Furthermore, these factors highlight some specific features that sharply differentiate Central American conditions from those in many other Latin American countries. This examination of these distinctive economic factors is aimed primarily at furthering a better understanding of the social processes taking place in the region.

In order to substantiate this argument, it should first be pointed out that the severe economic and social problems characterizing the Central American countries are neither accompanied by, nor the result of, grossly insufficient rates of economic growth and development. To the contrary, they have been preceded by a long phase of dynamic economic expansion.

Of the many pertinent indicators, the following are particularly significant and demonstrate the large changes that occurred between 1950 and 1980: (1) total population grew 2½ times while the urban portion increased from 16 to 43 percent; (2) gross domestic product (GDP) per capita almost doubled, and total GDP grew at an average rate of 4.9 percent per year; (3) the current value of exports rose from $257 million to $4,765 million (an average annual increase of 10.2 percent) while the import coefficient increased from 16 to 34 percent; (4) electricity generating capacity grew more than 15 times, and the highway system almost tripled.[1]

A second indicator is that, despite the expansion, the Central American economies are still characterized by underdeveloped, dependent capitalism. Over the course of their historical evolution, the consequences of this type of capitalism, such as the distortion of social characteristics and the deformation of economic structures, have been carried to their extremes.

Among other nationally specific economic and social traits that distinguish the various countries, the following features are

---

[1]Gert Rosenthal, "Principales rasgos de la evolución de las economías centroamericanas desde la posguerra," in CECADE/CIDE, *Centroamérica: Crisis y política internacional* (Mexico, 1982).

commonly evident: (1) very high rates of urbanization relative to average income levels; (2) a marked preponderance of "tertiary" activities in the composition of the national product; and (3) an external sector that has a disproportionately large weight in the national economic structures. The situation in Nicaragua is singularly revealing with respect to the first point. More than half of its population is urban, despite its relatively low degree of industrialization, thus demonstrating a clear imbalance between the economic structure and the rural/urban distribution of the population. This fact immediately raises the question of what provides the bases of economic maintenance for this sector of the population.

Similarly, it should be pointed out that despite these countries' relatively small demographic dimensions, the proportion of the economically active population employed in stable and productive jobs is very low. The imbalance is so great that the unutilized portion of the available labor force constitutes one of the region's most severe problems as well as one of its most important potential resources to aid future development.

In El Salvador, for example, there is a flagrant contrast between very high un- and under-employment levels among the adult, male population and a high level of participation in the labor force by minors, women, and old people. According to the 1975 national census, the proportion of minors working or looking for work was 12 percent for the 10–14 age bracket and 40 percent for those 15 to 19 years old; 36 percent of men and women over 65 were working; and 35 percent of women between the ages of 15 and 64 were economically "active." In contrast, the open unemployment rate in the San Salvador metropolitan area was 10.3 percent in August 1974 according to official figures, which do not include the large number of people seeking work for the first time. Underutilization of labor was estimated as being 45 percent in 1971. This rate is also strongly influenced by seasonal changes in the labor force.

In general, the disparity between low but not insignificant average income levels and huge inadequacies in the standard of living for large sectors of the population is evident in almost all the countries of the region. Those insufficiencies are so great that around 1970 the average educational level among the economically active population in Honduras was two-and-one-half years of study, compared to almost four in Colombia and more than seven in Argentina. The proportion of the economically active population without any education in Honduras was 42.5 percent, in contrast to a little more than 20 percent in Colombia and only 4 percent in Argentina. The fact that 33 percent of the Salvadoran population was illiterate in 1978 points toward the same conclusion.

Similarly, social inequality is more pronounced in this region than in many other Latin American societies. With the exception of Costa Rica, deficiencies in meeting the basic necessities of wide sectors of the population are also greater.

The existence of such sharp distortions and inadequacies even after a long period of relatively rapid economic growth clearly suggests a number of economically and politically significant conclusions. In the first place, it lends support to the argument that the origin of these problems lies not in the rate of growth but rather in some essential characteristics of the predominant pattern of development and its inherent limitations in the Central American context. Specifically, Central America's whole historical experience sets relatively rigid constraints on the possibilities of capitalist development in these countries. Thus, it substantiates the need for a "noncapitalist path" to development.

The mere comprehension of this fact at the present time could have an important impact. It could influence the definition of international behavior toward the Central American popular movements and toward government programs proposed or implemented after the successful resolution of these struggles. Such an understanding would suggest that any program of external economic cooperation basically tied to fostering the same old pattern of development is ultimately destined to fail. In other words, the efficacy of any form of international cooperation depends on recognizing the necessity of searching for solutions based on profound social transformations of an essentially noncapitalist nature.

Having recognized the significance of past experience and accepted a vision of an essentially noncapitalist path, one must then identify other basic economic factors that condition the evolution of the Central American countries to a significant degree.

The absolute dimensions of each nation and of the five together should not be ignored or their importance underemphasized. The national populations range from a little over 2 million (Costa Rica) to a little over 7 million (Guatemala), and the population of the five countries together barely exceeds 20 million people. With a joint territorial surface of about 440,000 square kilometers, the population density is much greater than the Latin American average. However, among the five nations there are marked differences; for example, the number of inhabitants per square kilometer varies from almost 18 in Nicaragua to a little more than 190 in El Salvador. The Latin American average is less than 16 people per square kilometer (1980 estimates).

In addition to questioning the specific pattern and system of development, one must consider the "economic viability" of these countries, given these absolute dimensions. Central America is not exceptional within Latin America in this respect but rather is an example of a much more extensive problem. It should be remembered that, of twenty-four countries in the region (including Barbados, Guyana, Jamaica, and Trinidad-Tobago), sixteen have national populations of less than 10 million.

There are three singular characteristics that powerfully affect the determination of future options for these nations' political and economic evolutions: (1) the conditioning factors resulting from the complete openness of their economic systems; (2) the economic and political constraints emerging from the limitations and consequences of capitalist development; and (3) the nature of the struggle that creates the possibility of transformation, along with the social and economic legacy of this struggle.

In the Nicaraguan case, the importance of this last consideration is obvious. No significant element of national life remained untouched by the conflict. In addition to the dramatic sacrifice of many combatant and civilian lives during this struggle, there was a striking deterioration in the level of economic activity, huge losses of crops and harvests, and the continual destruction of infrastructure, productive equipment, housing, industrial plant, schools, and hospitals. The triumphant insurgents therefore face the enormous task of material reconstruction and of regaining past levels of production and trade that were, at their best, relatively meager. Further complicating the new government's task is a heavy legacy of commitments and indebtedness, a strong demand for jobs by enormous numbers of unemployed workers, and a large number of vital needs that have not been met for the great mass of the population. In addition, Nicaragua's international reserves are exhausted, there has been a massive loss of private capital "opportunely" sent out of the country, and the public treasury has been plundered.

Today, the Salvadoran people's struggle is repeating the pattern. Its political leadership will have to cope with similar "legacies."

Thus, the picture is extraordinarily complex, with the interaction of both "structural" and "conjunctural" political and economic factors and the corresponding demands, pressures, and aspirations of all types.

Given this set of difficulties and obstacles, it becomes ever more evident that dependent capitalism, which cannot promote Central American development on its own terms, will be even less effective when confronted by the magnitude of these new challenges. It is on this concrete plane, not on the level of abstract ideological definitions, that the question of the viability or inviability of reformist proposals will be determined.

Proposals for revolutionary societal transformation, especially socialist ones, are supported by historical experience; they also undoubtedly open up new possibilities and potentials. Their mere proclamation, however, does not eliminate the need to provide new solutions to the continuing economic constraints. Revolutionaries too must choose among various basic, fixed options and then define the corresponding strategies.

The recent movement in Nicaragua and the current popular struggles in El Salvador and Guatemala have tended, as is logical, to take a relatively short-term view. They have focused on the more immediate tasks of reconstruction and reactivation that necessarily follow the revolutionary victory rather than devising grand schemes for the future. This is clearly a legitimate and unavoidable orientation. But the decisions derived from this focus belong by nature to a transitory phase. Even during this initial period, it is important that a longer-term perspective be taken when solutions are being devised for the most immediate problems of reconstruction.

Such a perspective should recognize the contradictory signals present in the current situation. On the one hand, there are enormous difficulties created by the low level of development of the productive forces. On the other hand, some of the obstacles are less difficult because of the relative simplicity of the existing social demands and the resultingly less complex productive structures. Therefore, in contrast to other countries in the Latin American region described as being in the middle stages of development, Central America has the disadvantages of extremely fragile economic structures, great difficulties in achieving self-sustaining growth, and extremely high levels of external dependence. It also has the comparative advantage, however, that social pressures exerted by the masses, in the form of demands and immediate aspirations, are focused primarily on basic necessities. It has not had to cope, for the most part, with the legacies of a more advanced productive structure, nor has it faced the pressures exerted by significant segments of workers who are primarily linked to highly concentrated economic activities that have developed in conformity with external models.

The disadvantages are felt primarily in the form of greater difficulties on the economic plane; in other words, a larger weight must be assigned to the "economic task." The positive conditions, on the other hand, yield a relative advantage in the political plane as the forces in favor of transformation confront much weaker social resistance and opposition than they would face in other, more economically advanced Latin American societies. This advantage applies only with respect to internal resistance, inasmuch as the most acute political opposition is in fact organized and carried out by external forces.[2]

These considerations suggest that an assessment of the economic viability of the various political proposals is essential. The definitive characteristics of the different strategies for future development are probably to be found in the answers each provides to five central questions of an economic nature: (1) What basic resources are available and how will they be utilized? (2) What pattern of life is sought for the majority of the national population? (3) How is the internal organization of each economic system envisioned? (4) What role is assigned to Central American economic integration? (5) Beyond the issue of regional integration, what international position should be adopted?

[2] In this respect, a comparison with the Chilean experience under President Salvador Allende's government would be useful. The first phase of economic evolution was very positive. Concurrently, however, internal political resistance to the transformation process grew to encompass wide segments of the population.

(1) In general terms, two factors highlighting the current importance of developing specific strategies for the use of basic resources are the relative scarcity of natural resources, which is a result of the irrational exploitation prevalent up until now, and the relatively large reserve of unutilized labor. There is an evident need to mount an enormous effort to protect, rejuvenate, and efficiently use land, water, forests, and hydroelectric resources as well as to recognize labor's extremely high productive potential and employ it intensively. These needs will not be met within the bounds of just any type of social organization. The Central American experience has repeatedly demonstrated the extent to which meeting these goals is incompatible with the global patterns of economic evolution that have prevailed in the region. The need to undertake this effort in turn legitimates proposals for much more profound transformations.

(2) In Central America, more than in other Latin American societies, the direct relationship between limited access to a diverse range of consumer goods and high levels of inequality is obvious. Using revenues from primary exports to finance the importation of consumer goods that cannot be produced internally in a reasonable time period has very high social costs. In any case, given the prevailing average income levels, only limited sectors of the population have access to this diverse set of consumer goods; a large portion of the population is marginalized in conditions of extreme poverty. If social inequalities are to be reduced by any reasonable amount with the goal of achieving minimal social stability while ensuring satisfaction of the most essential needs, national consumption patterns will have to be very modest. They must, however, be complemented by the provision of the necessary, fundamental social services. Given both actual levels of development of the productive forces and those attainable in the relatively short term, proposals for eradicating the most flagrant deficiencies in the whole population's living conditions, which have been inherited from the past type of development, are feasible. These goals cannot be achieved, however, if countries try to satisfy the much greater demands of those social strata that will fight for privileged positions. One of many considerations raised by observers of these cases thus pertains to the role of the middle classes, and particularly of the upper middle class, in the process of transformation.

(3) The same phenomena are manifest in the structural traits assumed by the economic system, in the relative weights of the various sectors of activity, and in the forms of articulation between them.

It is highly probable that in the foreseeable future, even in the midst of deep social transformations, the Central American economic systems will continue to be very "open." The external sector will occupy a significant place and there will be important fluctuations in agricultural exports as a result. The vital role of these exports, linked to the effort to supply a greater percentage of the internal demand for food from national production, could lead to much greater emphasis on the agricultural sector than is normally found in traditional views of Latin American development. The expansive tendency of the service sector, which has given it a relative weight in total national product completely disproportionate with the average levels of development, would also have to be reversed. Social services would be exempted from this reduction, however, since they must actually be expanded as the process of social transformation generates increasing demands for education and health care, as occurred in Nicaragua.

The typical patterns resulting from "import-substitution industrialization," in contrast, do not satisfy these objectives of providing the basic necessities at all. Central America's future industrial development, rather than diversifying consumption, should be closely coordinated with development in its agricultural sector, by processing agricultural goods and producing needed inputs and some of the components for productive equipment. It will also be linked to other sectors of activity and to providing, directly or indirectly, necessities for the urban population that have been assigned a high social priority. This degree of linkage will be greater, the higher the level of "standardization" achieved by the industrial sector.

In summary, it is clear that the type of economic structure needed will be very different from that prevalent in more developed countries of the region and from that which the Central American countries have tried to imitate in the course of their previous evolution.

(4) Although the essential features would not change, these conjectures about economic structure would have to be modi-

fied substantially, depending on the alternative chosen by the five countries: independent national development or joint development within the boundaries of a dynamic regional integration process.

In the past, the fruits of the Central American Common Market were enjoyed in large part by the large transnational corporations. Even so, the gains made from regional integration have left enduring marks. The economic links that have evolved have even resisted the contrary pressures exerted by transitory differences in crucial political situations, such as exist today in the economic relations between Nicaragua and the other countries of the region. In some way, economic integration appears to be a constant necessity for the five countries and is based as well on a common political aspiration. Social transformations are destined to increase. They will open up new prospects for this integration process, including the possibility that it will eventually extend far beyond commercial interchanges. Therefore, any vision of future development cannot escape the need to consider alternative schemes of either isolated national development or a common integrated development.

(5) Even if integrated development is attempted, the Central American economies' problem of insertion into the world economy will continue to be a key aspect in defining strategies for future development. This topic has not been analyzed very thoroughly, despite its obvious importance. Its complexity is suggested by the experience of Cuba, which began with conditions similar in various respects to those that may arise in the Central American countries. Some of the lessons to be drawn for Central America from the Cuban example concern the following: the implications of Cuba's transferral of part of its trade, and of economic relations in general, from the capitalist camp to the socialist camp; the influence that even its reduced portion of trade with nations outside of the socialist camp still exerts on the functioning of the internal economy; and external actors' continued participation in the economy through the transfer of capital and technology, facilitated by such instruments as Cuba's recently promulgated Law on Foreign Investment.

This type of strategic decision, of course, does not depend solely on the will of those who adopt it but also depends on prevailing attitudes in the international sphere. From this point of view, the efficacy of negative policies that attempt to obstruct the internal processes of social transformation taking place in Central America will be determined by those counterbalancing factors already mentioned. They include these economies' high degree of external dependence, on the one hand, and the relative simplicity of their most vital demands, on the other.

In the foregoing discussion of the wide range of possible options for future development, there was no intention of suggesting a "model of development" for the Central American countries (although this is a topic that must be considered in any proposal concerning Central America's future). This discussion is meant to illustrate how a given trajectory of past development, as well as some of the present circumstances, condition and determine the viability of alternative paths for the future.

The Central American societies will undoubtedly acquire new traits that will be consonant with the legacies received from the past and shaped by the present struggles that will open the way to the future—each with its own particular aspirations and hopes. Both aggressive and "friendly" external pressure will be added to challenges and tasks that are already great enough, as is occurring now. The depth of the transformations being undertaken, and the types of social organization directing them, will not fit into predefined molds nor will they conform to foreign desires or requirements. External judgments about their supposed radicalization should serve as an excuse neither for the hostility and aggression of some nor for the conditional solidarity of others. No external cooperation or solidarity can sustain itself with such ambiguities. Similarly, no political formula can fail to take into account some of the economic conditioning factors discussed here.

Dilemmas of the Nicaraguan Revolution

Xabier Gorostiaga

IN various debates in which United States colleagues have discussed the Nicaraguan Revolution, one encounters a plethora of questions and accusations, and a series of legalistic and formal interpretations arising from a mentality and culture created by a society of abundance, dominated by a strong spirit of individualism and a developed institutional apparatus. This study attempts to present the problematic of the Nicaraguan Revolution, underlining the tensions, paradoxes, contradictions, and errors experienced by a country trying to overcome underdevelopment and a dictatorial heritage, to survive in the international and regional economic crisis, and to create national independence in a small country situated in a strategic area of U.S. hegemony.

The goal here is not to provide answers or solutions, but rather to situate the Sandinist Revolution in the context of the difficulties and structural contradictions that surround it. This should allow international observers to make an honest and, insofar as possible, objective assessment of the first three years of the revolutionary process. An additional goal is to stimulate a constructive debate that might help overcome the impasse in negotiations between the United States and Nicaragua, and might also help avoid a regionalization of the armed conflict in El Salvador and Guatemala to the rest of Central America.[1]

The problematic will be presented in the form of dilemmas, in

[1] This goal seemed more important to us than a response to the list of accusations prepared by the State Department and repeated by Everett E. Briggs, Deputy Assistant Secretary of State for Inter-American Affairs. On other occasions this same list of accusations, in large part either distorted or totally false, has been reiterated by other U.S. officials. We consider that the method of accusations and counteraccusations does not

an attempt to capture the tensions and contradictions of a process of profound social and political, i.e. revolutionary, transformation. Identification of three major dilemmas may help to synthesize the problematic of the Popular Sandinist Revolution after three years: the internal dilemmas (economic, political, and national), the dilemmas sparked by the regional crisis, and those caused by the insertion of the Revolution into a critical international situation.

THE INTERNAL DILEMMAS OF THE SANDINIST REVOLUTION

The Economic Dilemma

How can the basic needs of the great majority of the population be satisfied, at the same time that a mixed economy is being maintained? How can this mixed economy, which is principally in private hands, be made to respond to the logic of the majority rather than to the logic of profit for capital?

This is a basic issue in the Sandinist Revolution. When private enterprise complains about the "poor business climate," it does so exclusively from the perspective of returns to capital. The people complain, on the other hand, about the poor climate in relation to private enterprise, which does not satisfy the needs of the great majority of them. This dilemma, then, springs from two different logics: a logic of the majority, based on the population-at-large; and another logic serving the interests of the owners of capital. How to satisfy these two needs that appear to be contradictory? This is a grave problem for the Revolution, and it has no easy solution. The fact that the Sandinist Revolution has maintained a largely privately owned economy for three years is an example of the enormous effort the Revolution is making to sustain this economic pluralism. The latest report of CEPAL on Nicaragua (July 2, 1982), appraising the tremendous flood damage at $356 million, noted that the state controlled 24 percent of the agricultural sector, 22 percent of industry, and 40 percent of commerce. The Sandinist Revolution has made it clear that the logic of the majority prevails

---

allow for dialogue, and even less for developing a constructive proposal, which is the purpose of these unofficial encounters. For a summary of Briggs's position, see Clint Smith's Afterword to this volume.

in this mixed economy, organized to benefit the people who won the victory against Somoza and the oppressive political-economic system that has historically dominated the country.

A "juxtaposed economy" describes a mixed economy where the public sector and the private sector coexist side by side. Both sectors maintain their own dynamic, and socially the public sector subsidizes the interests of the private sector. In the Sandinist model, there is a tendency toward the creation of a planned mixed economy (a mixed economy planned, at present, without a computer or technological and institutional resources). This planned mixed economy is subject to the logic of the majority, in which the private sector has meaning and purpose, and possibly a long-term strategic position as long as it accepts the logic of the majority and serves the basic needs of the people.

Economists speak of the "trickle-down effect" by which growth and goods are produced and then descend toward the lower sectors. The Sandinist Revolution searches for a contrary dynamic, a "trickle-up effect," from the bottom up, which first satisfies basic needs and then raises the goods of the economy upward toward the middle sectors, eventually arriving at non-essential consumption and private accumulation, once the basic needs of the majority have been satisfied. These two concepts respond to different logics: the logic of private accumulation and the logic of the satisfaction of the needs of the majority, with the subsequent initiation of social accumulation and the development of the productive forces that would overcome underdevelopment. The task in Nicaragua today is to overcome the juxtaposition of the two economic sectors, in order to create a planned and integrated economy, programmed according to the logic of the majority. Obviously, this model creates tensions, but is there any other way to overcome the dilemma?

It should be recognized that there are social forces in Nicaragua, and international forces as well, that want to eliminate the very dilemma itself. The supporters of the radical thesis consider a mixed economy to be unmanageable and push for a sudden leap toward a socialist economy. On the other side, there is a reformist position seeking to maintain a juxtaposed mixed economy that would not permit the achievement of the profound social changes for which the people have fought, changes that involve transforming social relations and the economic system.

The leaders of the Sandinist Revolution have repeatedly insisted that socialism is not constructed by decree and acts of force. The popular clamor for a socialist society, which prevails in Nicaraguan worker and peasant organizations, has been met with the pragmatism, flexibility, and political originality of *Sandinismo*. Sandinismo attempts to determine the type of socialism that would be both desirable and feasible, given the internal constraints generated by profound underdevelopment and within the regional and international contexts of the Nicaraguan Revolution. On the other hand, Sandinismo reaffirms the need to maintain and increasingly to develop a mixed economy consistent with the logic of the majority.

It is important to remember that the mixed economy in Nicaragua appeared not as the product of ideological formulas, but rather as an historical consequence of the special characteristics of the Popular Sandinist Revolution, which knew how to bind together a wide spectrum of society behind a project dominated by workers and peasants. On the other hand, it is also the fruit of realism, achieved after the disasters of an economy destroyed by Somocist corruption, the war, and the 1972 earthquake. The integration of Nicaragua into the Central American Common Market has supported the maintenance at the regional level of those links that favor the economic reconstruction of the country.

The mixed economy is made necessary by an additional set of factors such as the maintenance of political pluralism; national unity; maximum utilization of scarce technical and financial resources; minimization of the social costs of reconstruction; reduction of the risks of a possible international boycott; diversification of the structural dependency of the country; and the creation of a nonaligned economy in support of a policy of international nonalignment.

The accumulated experience of other revolutionary processes demonstrates the risks of a mixed economy as well as its positive aspects. In Nicaragua there is an awareness of the ambiguity of this solution, but the consensus is that a sufficiently stable balance can be achieved, in the long as well as the short term, through control of the financial system, by nationalizing foreign trade, and by gaining the support of labor organizations. This original solution seems to be possible in terms of the constellation of internal forces, but the situation is made more difficult when external economic and political forces try to use the internal tensions of the Sandinist model to destabilize the Revolution. The dilemma, therefore, remains in force after three years of the revolutionary process; if it should some day disappear, history will judge which factors facilitated the originality of the Sandinist experience.

The Political Dilemma

How can political pluralism be maintained while a response is being formulated to the expectations created by the massive popular insurrection against the dictatorship and the system of political-economic oppression? Popular power and demands for a change of structures and traditional political power in the country were obviously the goals that energized the insurrection.

Members of the private sector perceive that the new power structure affects their old political privileges, and they feel that this popular power is totalitarian rather than democratic. However, the private sector's formal political representation is greater than strict proportionality would dictate. For example, the degree of participation of private enterprise and representatives of the private sector within the Council of State does not correspond to their relative numerical presence in the country.

Of the fifty-one members of the Council of State, there are eleven opposition members (political parties and entrepreneurs) representing 21.6 percent of the total. Independent organizations (representatives of churches, leftist syndical organizations) have eight representatives, or 15.7 percent. The representatives of the Frente Sandinista de Liberación Nacional (FSLN) and associated mass organizations have twenty-five representatives, or 49 percent. The militant opposition to the Revolution, with about 22 percent of the representatives, is nevertheless overrepresented in relation to the statistical proportion of possible voters who would support them.

On the other hand, it is worth distinguishing between the opposition and discontent. There are those who are disappointed with the Revolution for not having fulfilled all the expectations created by the Revolution itself. These sectors would never vote for a rightist opposition, but would rather support a radicalization of the process that might fulfill their aspirations more rapidly. Not all the discontented in Nicaragua are on the right.

The political dilemma has been situated in a context of notable internal stability during these three years, in a Central America that has been in economic and political upheaval, and with an extraordinarily aggressive U.S. administration that has employed various means to destabilize the Sandinist process. Only the clear political hegemony of the FSLN has allowed for this balance among the diverse and contending internal forces, especially with the external destabilization that has amplified the tensions in Nicaraguan society. Most of these internal tensions could have been suppressed by the political authority established by the Revolution. Nevertheless, opposition groups not only continue to exist but, with outside help, have even increased their political presence.

At the international level, however, it is hard for the Sandinist model to be considered as pluralistic. The root problem lies in two different concepts of pluralism. In developed capitalist society the concept is based on the liberal vision of a society created under the ideological hegemony of the private sector and individual interests. In a country in the process of a social transformation, seeking to overcome inherited underdevelopment, dependence, and sociopolitical distortion, however, pluralism must be placed within the context of this process. In such cases, the collectivity must be the predominant interest. In the case of Nicaragua, this is the interest of a peasant-worker majority, which was the central force in toppling the dictatorship and which must also be the central force in overcoming underdevelopment. A new social power structure demands a redefinition, within its parameters, of the term *pluralism* and, above all, a qualitatively different participation in decision making, in cultural modes, in forms of exercising democracy, in distribution of property and income, and in the character and style of government in the new state. These changes in power relations, seen as totalitarian by those forces that enjoyed relative privilege in the previous regime, are perceived as an advance toward true democracy by those historically marginalized from the power structure.

The political dilemma remains very real. Since March 1982, when a state of national emergency was declared, in order to rally the country to the defense of the Popular Sandinist Revolution against the threats and real aggressions of recent months, internal political tension has become more acute. The opposition has been most hurt by the state of emergency, since they have suffered the most, chiefly from the temporary suspension of several guarantees of the Fundamental Statute and the Statute of Rights and Guarantees of Nicaraguans. The state of emergency is not a direct product of the Revolution, however, but rather a defensive measure that, as has been announced, will end as soon as negotiations with the United States begin and the causes of the external threat are eliminated.

Nevertheless, this political dilemma could explode, depending upon the internal and external forces of counterrevolution (mainly in Honduras and Costa Rica) and, above all, on the position taken in the future by the Reagan administration vis-à-vis Nicaragua.

How can political participation at all levels be maintained and increased while a political pluralism is also maintained that does not impede the social and cultural transformations demanded by a society in which the poor have acquired rights and civic power for the first time in their political history? How can all this be achieved without major social and political tension, encouraged from the outside?

The National Dilemma

How can Nicaragua become an independent and sovereign country, respected by the United States, in view of its location in an area strategically vital for U.S. interests?

After so many years of struggle, the Nicaraguan people have undeniably conquered the right not only to social justice, but also to national dignity. Nicaragua has once and for all ceased to be a "banana republic" and has begun to be a free and sovereign state. In this dilemma there is a contradiction between the recently acquired sovereignty and the strategic interests of the United States in an area over which the United States considers itself to have unchallenged hegemony. The existence of an independent and sovereign state breaks the absolute hegemony the United States seeks to maintain in the region. Besides, such independence sets a dangerous example. On the other hand, after such disasters as the crisis of Vietnam, the failures of U.S. foreign policy in different parts of the world, the international economic crisis, etc., the Reagan administration is trying to show in Central America, and especially in Nicaragua, that the United States is still the hegemonic world power. Here the collision takes place between Nicaraguan national sovereignty and the strategic interests of the United States in the area.

Anti-imperialism is a characteristic engraved on Nicaraguan nationalism in the wake of years of domination and subjection, and it is presently being reinforced by the aggressiveness of the U.S. administration. The building of an "outwardly oriented" national identity, with an independent and nonaligned presence in international forums, and the demand for respect in relations with more powerful countries go hand-in-hand with a new inwardly oriented national consciousness and dignity. The positive definition of this new national identity is based on the discovery of indigenous culture, on the creation of a new historical awareness, and on the construction of national institutions to overcome the colonialist underdevelopment that in 1979 left the country without institutions even minimally adapted to its national reality.

The natural effervescence of the nationalism recently experienced by the majority of the people is seen as subversive by those who not long ago considered Nicaragua to be the most comfortable part of their backyard. The main tension of the national dilemma thus centers on the fact that, for the first time in its history, Nicaragua feels like a sovereign nation equal to any country in the world and is unwilling to be disrespected or treated as a "subnation." In other words, if the United States can select and establish special relations with its friends, why cannot Nicaragua do the same? This is an obvious question, which nevertheless appears naive in the context of an international situation bordering on not-so-cold war. Despite the wide range and flexibility of the Popular Sandinist Revolution's international relations, the United States is unable to accept the new international position of Nicaragua, which only three years ago was its regional gendarme.

The Significance of the Dilemmas

The Popular Sandinist Revolution has confronted these three difficult internal dilemmas with pragmatism, realism, and flexibility. Does a magical solution to these tensions exist? Has the political opposition offered even one concrete proposal for their resolution?

The originality of Sandinismo is all the more significant when we realize that it arose after forty-five years of an iron dictatorship and a bloody war of liberation. The Popular Sandinist Revolution undoubtedly earned the international legitimacy and respect that the Reagan administration considers highly dangerous; it has become a reference point for the people of the region and throughout the Third World. This legitimacy and the presentation of a new model is what the U.S. administration is trying to destroy in Nicaragua. Nicaragua is a dangerous example, hard for an administration with such a simplistic vision of the international reality to manipulate.

Undoubtedly, there have been shortcomings, mistakes, and a lack of technical capability and human resources to resolve such complex dilemmas. It would be naive and dishonest not to recognize them or to learn from them, through healthy criticism. Nevertheless, when one analyzes the criticisms of both the internal and the external opposition to the Revolution that fail to acknowledge the achievements and emphasize only the mistakes, the lack of concrete proposals is evident. They are dilettantish criticisms that neither present alternatives nor deal constructively with the dilemmas inevitably at the root of the present problematic in Nicaragua.

THE DILEMMAS SPARKED BY THE REGIONAL CRISIS

The Popular Sandinist Revolution and the Central American Crisis

How can a social, political, and national transformation be undertaken within a region that is experiencing a profound political and economic crisis?

The Popular Sandinist Revolution is not taking place in a regional vacuum, nor is it being built on an island. Rather, it is occurring in a region that is profoundly integrated, politically and economically, and is simultaneously, at this moment, experi-

encing the greatest political and economic crisis in its history. At
the international level, the entire Central American region finds
itself in a profound economic recession, with a current account
deficit of $1.9 billion in 1981, resulting from the reduction of
the volume of exports and a dramatic deterioration in the terms
of trade. This has led to a massive indebtedness of the five countries in the region (a total regional debt of $11.5 billion in
1981), with an annual service on the public debt alone of $1 bil-
lion, and a capital flight from the region on the order of $3 bil-
lion in the last two years. The crisis of Central American integration, and protective measures in response to national crises,
have led to a regional recessionary spiral that impedes the appli-
cation of common solutions. Given this grave economic situation, the Reagan proposal for the Caribbean Basin appears
tragicomic.

The economic crisis is of a structural nature, exacerbated by
the international economic crisis that affects such open economies. Nevertheless, the decay of traditional political models and
the rise of new revolutionary political alternatives in El Salvador
and Guatemala, as well as the demonstration effect on the people of Honduras and Costa Rica, are the profound cause of a
crisis that has become unmanageable for local and international
power groups. Given these circumstances, how can a peaceful revolutionary transformation, at a minimal social cost, be
achieved amidst a regional political-economic crisis, especially
at a time when the Reagan administration has selected the area
as its battleground? All this, furthermore, takes place within the
framework of international tensions that affect the region: the
East-West tension; the tension between the Socialist International and Christian Democratic approaches, which must deal
with European as well as Latin American issues at the level of
Central America; and the conflict between the Latin American
subpowers (Mexico, Venezuela, and Brazil) that are intervening
in support of different interests in the region. The fact that the
phenomenon of the Popular Sandinist Revolution, the first revolution on the continent in the last twenty years, has taken place
amidst all this conflict pinpointed in Central America, clearly
creates difficulties and dilemmas of a regional nature.

The Sandinist Revolution, on the other hand, cannot help but
feel close to the struggles of the peoples of El Salvador and Gua-

temala, with whom the Nicaraguans share more than one hundred years of resistance against U.S. and oligarchic domination. How can this closeness be maintained simultaneously with a position of nonintervention in the internal affairs of those countries—a position that, if not maintained, could lead to a regionalization of the conflict, transforming all of Central America into a new Vietnam?

The Popular Sandinist Revolution and Yankee Aggressiveness

How can the Revolution be carried out in the Central American region during the incumbency of the Reagan administration? It is important to analyze this question as some members of Congress, such as Representative Tom Harkin, have done, and to try to visualize what Central America might be today without Reagan. It is possible that the Revolution would have maintained sufficiently cordial economic and political relations with the United States if the Nicaraguan proposal to negotiate and resolve some of these dilemmas had been accepted. It is possible that without the Reagan administration there would have been internal negotiations in El Salvador between the popular forces and the old Duarte regime, without having arrived at the elections that sharpened the Salvadoran dilemma. It is possible that without the Reagan administration there would be stable negotiations with Honduras, joint surveillance of the Honduran border, and control over the thousands of ex-Somocist *guardias* trained and financed by the Reagan administration. Without the Reagan administration several steps might have been taken in search of a joint regional solution, instead of the formation of the Central American Democratic Community, which has been a divisive factor.

These are not, however, anything more than hypotheses. We have a simplistic and militaristic U.S. administration with undeniable fascist traits, which make impossible the visualization of a peaceful negotiated solution in the region. The international rhetoric and propaganda of the United States tries to portray Nicaragua as the promoter of conflict and tension in the region. The United States is using the region to heighten the East-West conflict, even though the conflict comes from the United States to Central America, and not vice versa.

The fact that Nicaragua is currently laboring under a state of emergency is the product not of an increased radicalization or rigidity of the Popular Sandinist Revolution, but rather of threats and external aggression. At the beginning of 1982, the Revolution had plans for a project to reinforce national unity through a series of measures: laws to increase economic incentives, a law to promote foreign investment, the release of COSEP (Higher Council of Private Enterprise) prisoners, a law regulating political parties, etc. All this was ruined when on December 1, 1981, the Reagan administration approved the covert operations that took place in the first months of 1982, with repeated threats and attacks, costing the lives of two hundred Nicaraguans and creating major economic losses for the country.

It seems to be a contradiction, but these covert operations are currently public because they have been approved and publicly acknowledged by the highest leaders of the Reagan administration. Unlike the covert operations against Allende in Chile, which were always denied by the U.S. administration, these operations against Nicaragua are publicly supported. How can the Revolution demanded by Nicaraguans be implemented at the least social cost to the country and to the region, and at the same time deal with perhaps the most simplistic and aggressive U.S. administration of the century?

Alternatives of the Reagan Administration for the Region

What solutions can be seen for this regional dilemma? To synthesize, four scenarios can be postulated.

(1) The possibility of direct U.S. intervention, which was viewed as feasible in the month of March 1982, has currently become less likely because of opposition among the U.S. public (87 percent were opposed to such intervention, according to a *Newsweek* poll taken in May 1982). In addition, the international and Latin American opposition to such intervention has increased with the war in the Malvinas; this has also made U.S. intervention less feasible. The most important counterweight is the increased defensive capacity created by the Nicaraguan people themselves. Nevertheless, the possibility of direct intervention cannot be eliminated, inasmuch as logic and analysis have often, in the history of U.S. policy, been overtaken by irrationality.

(2) Indirect intervention, using groups of mercenaries and

Latin American troops, is seen as more probable. This possibility, too, has decreased because of the war in the Malvinas, which has, according to information from Great Britain, led to the removal of 250 Argentine advisors from the region and to a substantial change in Venezuela's policy toward the United States. In addition, U.S. support for Great Britain in the Malvinas has decreased the possibility of invoking the Inter-American Treaty of Reciprocal Assistance for an attack on Nicaragua. In this sense, the possibilities of a military intervention at the Latin American level also have been lessened.

(3) An attack by the Somocist *guardia* and from a group of countries in the northern triangle (Guatemala, El Salvador, and especially Honduras), however, remains an open possibility that could be used as a way out of the Salvadoran crisis in which Nicaragua would play the role of scapegoat.

(4) Increased escalation has, since July 1982, seemed the most probable alternative. It entails a set of combined activities destined to create a process of overall destabilization that might lead to the violent overthrow of the FSLN and the destruction of the Sandinist Revolution.

The Prospect of Increased Escalation

Economic destabilization. This includes the obstruction of financial flows by pressuring multilateral organizations, private banks, and governments still collaborating with Nicaragua. Regional, internal, and international economic crises facilitate in turn the creation of an economic crisis based on the shortage of foreign currency.

Internationally, the deterioration of the terms of trade, and especially the collapse of coffee and sugar prices and the serious floods that affected agricultural production, will lead to a foreign debt of over $500 million in 1982, which cannot be covered with capital flows, because of the financial boycott. This currency shortage will lead to a large decrease in industrial production and a substantial increase in urban unemployment, and will especially hurt Managua, where an increase in imported goods will induce a strong inflationary process. This economic crisis will continue moving toward its climax and have its greatest social impact probably at the same time that political and military pressures against Nicaragua are intensifying further.

Political destabilization. This will exacerbate the economic crisis and reduce the standard of living. The Nicaraguan opposition will try to organize a "march of the empty pots," repeating the various methods of popular protest used in Chile against Allende.

The ideological struggle will escalate, reaching new heights of tension. It can be predicted that religion and human rights will be at the core of this conflict. The Nicaraguan opposition, as well as international religious and political organizations, have turned Archbishop Monseñor Obando y Bravo of Managua into the "leader of the opposition"—another Archbishop Makarios, owing to the weakness of traditional opposition groups.[2]

The conflicts resulting from this political opposition will be internationally presented as a confrontation between the church and the Revolution.

In addition, the economic crisis will facilitate the rise of protests that could provoke tension and confrontation and would then be portrayed internationally as repression against the people. The armed activities in the north of the country, especially in the Miskito zone, will lead to the organization of an international propaganda campaign against Nicaragua, accusing it of intervention in Honduras and of violating human rights.

The $19 million that President Reagan allocated to the CIA on December 1, 1981, plus an international campaign to delegitimate and isolate the Sandinist Revolution (accusing it of religious persecution and violations of human rights) will create the conditions for the last step of the escalation.

Military intervention. This phase of the continuing escalation contains three parts.

(1) With the creation of the Central American Democratic Community, Nicaragua is being economically and politically isolated from its neighbors. The countries of the northern triangle (Guatemala, El Salvador, and Honduras) have been politically and militarily prepared for a confrontation with the Sandi-

[2] The daily *La Prensa* has continuously portrayed Monseñor Obando y Bravo in this fashion, as have the principal leaders of opposition parties and the most politicized embassies in Managua (United States, Venezuela, Spain, etc.). The ultraconservative U.S. church group, the Institute for Religion and Democracy (ICD), and Monseñor López Trujillo of the Latin American Episcopal Conference (CELAM), have helped to internationalize this image. The latest report of the Heritage Foundation (March 1982) also emphasizes the political role of Monseñor Obando y Bravo.

nist Revolution. The grave economic crisis in Costa Rica has enabled the United States to negotiate a financial pact with the government of President Monge, in exchange for stepped-up harassment against Nicaragua. General Torrijos's "accident" and the strange resignation of President Royo have meant the disappearance of *Torrijismo* in Panama and the loss of the Sandinist Revolution's closest ally in the immediate vicinity. The rightward shift of Panamanian politics and the increased role of the National Guard in the defense of the Canal are allowing U.S. troops in the Canal Zone to play a more active role in Central America and the Caribbean, especially with regard to Nicaragua and Cuba. In Mexico, the acute economic crisis and the shift to a more technocratic administration are likely to debilitate the country that has been the Sandinist Revolution's most important source of economic support over the last three years.

(2) Together with attempts to encircle Nicaragua, there is permanent harassment on its borders and internally from an opposition organized and financed to overthrow Sandinismo. The danger of aggression continues to require a diversion of scarce resources to defensive tasks and, above all, a concentration of the Revolutionary leadership's energies on questions of defense rather than on reconstruction. The economic and political deterioration caused by a prolonged defensive alert is intended to create the final conditions for the frontal attack.

(3) The arms buildup in the countries in the area, including, for the first time, Costa Rica; the continued U.S. military operations in Central America and the Caribbean; the intensification of border attacks that have produced over one hundred deaths in the months of June and July 1982; the initiation of aerial attacks; and the continued presence of U.S. war vessels in Nicaraguan territorial waters—all are creating the conditions for a frontal attack that can be foreseen as very nearly inevitable. "After Lebanon, Nicaragua" is the way the scenario is perceived from Managua.

Faced with the regional crisis and the progressive escalation of anti-Nicaraguan activities, the Sandinist Revolution has offered to negotiate with the United States, as well as with neighboring countries. In the United Nations General Assembly, in the Security Council, in various international forums, through

Mexico (and by other means) Nicaragua has presented a set of proposals that have been evasively received and even vetoed by the United States in the United Nations.[3] From the Nicaraguan perspective, it is ironic that the Sandinist Revolution is accused of being a threat, when it has tried, using all means and international forums, to negotiate a regional peace. Those who have accused it of being a danger to peace are the very ones who have rejected and vetoed these negotiations.

This regional dilemma creates a further problem in addition to the already numerous internal problems of the Nicaraguan process. When one listens to the proposals made for Nicaragua, one becomes aware of the lack of analysis about these structural problems which confront the young Revolution.

THE DILEMMAS DERIVING FROM THE INTERNATIONAL SITUATION

Nicaragua is a small and poor country, underdeveloped in productive and human resources. It is also a country extraordinarily dependent on and exposed to the international market, to which it must continue to be linked. Nicaragua cannot isolate itself. The problem is how to insert itself into the international division of labor without obstructing the social transformation and increased national independence that the Revolution seeks to create.

The political economy of the Nicaraguan government is based on the principle of diversifying the country's dependence on the United States, augmenting interrelations with Europe, Latin America, and the nonaligned countries, and initiating a new economic, diplomatic, and political relationship with the socialist countries. In the 1950's Nicaragua's economic dependence on the United States was immense. About 60 to 70 percent of all transactions took place with the United States. Currently, an attempt is being made to diversify these relations, making them more balanced and flexible. The economy must walk on "four legs": one-fourth of the total economic relations with the United States, one-fourth with Europe, one-fourth with Latin America and the nonaligned, and one-fourth with the socialist countries. Currently this final one-fourth is being established, but it is a

[3] In July 1982 the Nicaraguan government agreed to negotiate according to the terms proposed by the Honduran government, but very little has been achieved.

slow process: relations with socialist countries comprise from 5 to 7 percent of all international economic relations. Despite this flexibility in international relations, Nicaragua has been accused of being part of the Soviet bloc. Comandante Daniel Ortega's trip to the Soviet Union in May 1982 was portrayed by the U.S. press as a "definitive alignment" of Nicaragua with the U.S.S.R., yet the fact that another member of the junta, Sergio Ramírez, visited Spain, Austria, Holland, Sweden, Ireland, and Greece was played down in the international press. Even less notice was taken of the trip of Rafael Córdova Rivas, the third member of the junta, to Venezuela and Costa Rica. The Sandinist Revolution maintains its project of sovereignty and independence, which forms the basis for the establishment of relations with all countries. This is a structural necessity produced by the dependency, smallness, and underdevelopment of our country.

This structural dilemma in our international relations is complicated, however, by the fact that Nicaragua's friends from the non-core capitalist countries of Europe and Latin America, the so-called social-democratic or social-capitalist countries, have provided much less aid than the aggregate figures appear to indicate.

The magnitude of the destruction and decapitalization with which the Popular Sandinist Revolution has had to deal in its first three years is revealed by the figures. The total burden of $4,144 million[4] can be broken down into its components as follows: inherited foreign debt of *Somocismo*, $1,650 million (39.8%); losses due to economic inactivity, 1978–79, $1,246 million (30.1%); decapitalization and plunder, 1978–79, $518 million (12.5%); wartime destruction of physical infrastructure, $481 million (11.6%); service on foreign debt, 1978–79, $249 million (6.0%).

The non-core capitalist countries that have helped Nicaragua have not even covered half of what was lost in the war and related destruction. Their aid and financial support have not enabled the country to begin a process of development toward the new economy the country needs. It is relevant that of all the loans and donations received by Nicaragua, 49 percent comes from nonaligned countries of the Third World; only 32 percent

[4]CEPAL and the Central Bank of Nicaragua.

comes from the developed capitalist countries, and the remaining 18 percent from socialist countries, including Cuba. For those who would argue that the solution to the international dilemma of the Sandinist Revolution lies with the non-core capitalist countries, such as those ruled by social-democratic parties, it should be pointed out that these countries have offered nice words and have given symbolic backing, but they have not supported the Revolution to the extent that the country needs.

Among the socialist countries, it is important to note the extraordinary generosity and dedication on the part of the Cuban Revolution, despite its limited resources. The Cuban Revolution, in maintaining this solidarity, is taking bread from its own mouth, and this burden cannot be a permanent phenomenon. The socialist countries have begun to move closer to the Sandinist Revolution, but not yet close enough to provide substantial support. This lack of aid has structural explanations, such as the enormous geographic and economic distance separating Nicaragua from the European socialist countries, and their own economic difficulties—especially given the need to help Poland solve its economic, financial, and political crisis. Aid from socialist countries is further limited by technical problems, since Nicaragua, in the zone of influence of the United States, has predominantly U.S. technology to which the technology of the socialist countries cannot be easily adapted. The smallness of our market and the immensity of our technological underdevelopment impedes rapid conversion to a new type of technology.

Increasingly, a grave dilemma and a strange paradox become evident. The Reagan administration appears to be pushing Nicaragua toward the socialist bloc, as is manifest in terms of both economic aid and military affairs. U.S. officials imprisoned the Nicaraguan pilots who were in the United States to buy civilian helicopters, and they have repeatedly refused to sell arms to Nicaragua. On the other hand, the United States protested to France against its sale of a small amount of military equipment to Nicaragua. What is the object? The United States wants to keep the Popular Sandinist Revolution without an air force or navy while it arms Honduras and El Salvador disproportionately.

The United States, for its part, has cut off all economic aid, has pressured against multilateral loans in the World Bank and the Inter-American Development Bank, and has strongly pressured its allies not to give economic aid to Nicaragua. It pressured the Canadians to choose Honduras instead of Nicaragua for its concentration of economic aid to the region. It has also pressured Venezuela and other European countries to stop giving aid to the Sandinist Revolution. In addition, the Reagan administration has put pressure on private international banks to cease financing Nicaragua, despite the fact that, to date, our country has fulfilled all its international financial obligations, including the foreign debt contracted by Somoza.

Clearly, the Sandinist Revolution cannot accept this economic and military boycott and will look for resources wherever they can be found. U.S. pressure forces Nicaragua to seek shelter in the socialist countries. Thus, the big question, and the paradox, is: Could it be that the Reagan administration wants the Nicaraguan Revolution increasingly to align itself with the socialist bloc, in an attempt to delegitimize its originality and to prevent the success of this model of a mixed economy and political pluralism? Does the United States want to prevent the economic success of the Nicaraguan Revolution in order to demonstrate that it is impossible to maintain a popular and efficient economy? Does it hope, with this strategy, to delegitimize and to isolate those friendly countries in Latin America and Europe who have supported the Revolution?

To summarize: we thus have a major dilemma at the international level. Structurally, the Nicaraguan Revolution needs to remain open to the capitalist world, diverting some of its dependence on the United States to non-core capitalist countries. These countries, however, have not committed themselves to the Revolution to the extent necessary, and the socialist countries, which are in a bad economic situation, are unable to satisfy its needs. Besides, Nicaragua's small size and the geographic distance separating it from the socialist countries does not permit a strong economic bond with them. At the same time, the Reagan administration appears to be using pressure tactics to force the Sandinist Revolution, as a last resort, to move toward the socialist bloc. In this manner, the United States seeks to isolate the Revolution from Latin America and Europe.

With an analysis of these three dilemmas—internal, regional, and international—this paper has attempted to synthesize the large structural problems confronting the Sandinist Revolution.

In outlining the dilemmas, we have not tried to suggest solutions. Those will be provided only by the process itself. Some theoretical solutions can be sensed, but the real solutions will arise from the Nicaraguan people, organized in the process of constructing a new society and a new person. To the extent that greater popular participation, more self-criticism, and increased international solidarity develop, it will be easier to avoid errors and find the most efficient solutions to our problems and, likewise, to the entire Central American crisis.

The U.S. Debate on the Central American Crisis

Luis Maira

AFTER the Salvadoran elections for a constituent assembly on March 28, 1982, an optimism bordering on exultation characterized the behavior of the Reagan administration regarding the Central American crisis. Two months later, however, when revolutionary sectors recovered the initiative and the Farabundo Martí National Liberation Front (FMLN) forces reconfirmed their capacity to deliver serious setbacks to governmental military contingents, a return to pessimism and bewilderment could be observed.

These attitudes are illustrative of the Reagan administration's policies toward political processes in Central America. These policies are both globalistic and "short term" with regard to the crisis in the region. They fail to take seriously into account the profound national roots of the crisis, and they attempt to subsume it under the strategic confrontation between the United States and the U.S.S.R. As events since early 1980 have confirmed, such policies have led to the strengthening of hard-line attitudes and to the failure to recognize the extent of support enjoyed by revolutionary sectors and by those who do not share the position of the U.S. government. The result has been reflected in the search for solutions to the crisis that attempt to eliminate the influence of the revolutionary sectors in the several Central American countries.

We are convinced that, despite the winning of some tactical victories, current U.S. policies cannot lead to the building of a stable political system, capable of preventing the resurgence of social discontent and violence. The contemporary history of Central American society supports this contention. In 1932, the peasant rebellion in El Salvador, led by Farabundo Martí, was mercilessly crushed, at a social cost of more than fifteen thousand deaths. In 1934, after the elimination of Augusto César Sandino, the alternative of an autonomous, popularly based democratic regime in Nicaragua was suppressed. In 1954, the possibility of a democratic consolidation based on a moderate program of social transformation in Guatemala was ended with the overthrow of the constitutionally elected president, Jacobo Arbenz. In this way, oligarchies have had all political power in their hands for decades, and have been able to impose and remodel all development strategies. And where has this led us? Are the social forces that today besiege these regimes any different from those of the past that made similar demands?

Any solution to the Central American crisis that has a political dimension, and not just a military one, must take into consideration both the immediate political history of the most afflicted countries of the region, as well as the social aspirations and goals of the most dynamic forces in their respective societies. Similarly, for the government of the United States the interpretation of the political history of Central America has a fundamental importance for the concrete policies adopted and for the likelihood of their success.

In this context we will attempt to review the paradigms that predominate in U.S. analyses of the contemporary history of Central America, with the goal of establishing several tenets and conditioning factors, in both the political and the structural sense. Then, we will critique these visions and identify key elements that arise from the economy and society of the countries of the Isthmus. Without consideration of these factors, it will be difficult to achieve the establishment of a stable solution in the near future. Behind this exercise is the conviction that political options are born in the real history of each nation and are directly constrained by the development of its productive and social forces. This is a reality that neither the economic nor the material power of the capitalist world can change.

U.S. INTERPRETATIONS OF THE CENTRAL AMERICAN CRISIS

In theory, Central America should constitute one of the best-understood regions for U.S. diplomats. Washington's links with these countries go back to the first years of the twentieth century when the United States, guided by the policies of President Theodore Roosevelt, established the goal of creating an international extension of the vigorous domestic development of its own productive forces.

Over the years, however, Washington's policies in Latin America have resulted in an impressive succession of frustrations, many of which have repercussions in the current crisis. In our view, these frustrations have resulted from two concrete factors: on the one hand, the errors made in the different plans and options implemented by the State Department since the start of the century; on the other hand, the limitations of liberal and conservative political perspectives that serve as the poles around which diverse foreign policy proposals are formulated. These visions emphasize elements that to varying degrees are inappropriate for a comprehension of the political and economic processes of Latin American countries.

With regard to the content of U.S. policies, the Central American subregion has been a reflection of all the stages of international activism in the United States. Within the first imperial expansion, the larger Caribbean Basin was a priority area. Considered to occupy a prime position astride the world's commercial routes after the opening of the Panama Canal, the Caribbean became an "American lake" and came to play a geographical role similar to that which the Mediterranean Sea has had for centuries in European imperial disputes.

For the small countries of Central America, this fact had brutal consequences. In the course of a few years, they began to receive an increased flow of direct U.S. investments, located mainly in public utilities and in key agricultural sectors, contributing to the picturesque image of "banana republics," with which many analysts continue to identify them. At the same time, these countries began to feel the impact of the presence of the U.S. armed forces, which had its clearest manifestation in the "protectorate" regimes established with the direct participation of the U.S. marines, in the Dominican Republic, Haiti, and Nicaragua. For a long period, these countries were physically occupied by U.S. troops.

U.S. intervention in the Dominican Republic began in 1905, when a tax collector, designated by President Roosevelt and supported by U.S. marines, was imposed on the country to take charge of customs, collect taxes, and issue vouchers guaranteeing the payment of debts to foreign creditors. The situation worsened between 1916 and 1924, when about two thousand marines directly occupied the country, leaving only after the local government accepted a treaty institutionalizing the protectorate.

In Haiti the direct presence of marines helped to impose the treaty of 1915 that established the presence of a U.S. high commissioner as overseer of Haitian politics and economics. Beginning in 1924, a U.S. official took charge of the recently created Haitian Office of Internal Taxation, accentuating even further Washington's control over the country. Finally, in Nicaragua there was a military intervention with three thousand men and nine war ships in 1912, shortly after the imposition of agreements like the 1910 Dawson pact and the 1911 Knox-Castrillo convention. Again, in 1927, U.S. military forces occupied Nicaraguan territory, and remained there until 1932. It was against this intervention that Augusto César Sandino fought and won, becoming the principal national hero in Nicaragua's history.

Despite the fact that President Franklin Delano Roosevelt's proclamation of the "good neighbor policy" led to the removal of the direct U.S. military presence in Central America and the Caribbean, this occupation had a profound impact on the history of Central America. This must be taken into account in evaluating the present crisis, especially in light of the fact that there were a series of subsequent manifestations of intervention in this area: in Guatemala in 1954, Cuba in 1961, and the Dominican Republic in 1965.

No symbol could better illustrate the Central American perception of this (at times suffocating) presence of the U.S. interest than the partly mythical, partly real (especially concerning the activities of the United Fruit Company) images of the *Papa verde* (the Green Pope), drawn by the Nobel Prize-winning Guatemalan writer Miguel Angel Asturias during the 1950's. While it is true that the countries of Central America have changed and that they are no longer a collection of haciendas and agro-industrial businesses, a vivid feeling of distrust toward everything that comes from the United States has persisted. This is a deeply rooted and widespread cultural element of the populations of these countries.

Seen from the U.S. side, one can observe a peculiar situation. The behavior of the State Department and of administrations in Washington has demonstrated that, despite years of ties to the region, they have failed to comprehend the historical essence that explains the political and economic development of the states of the Central American Isthmus.

To a large extent, the severe crisis that currently wracks Central America is directly related to the prolonged support U.S. governments have given to authoritarian regimes there. The present situation has come about because a series of democratization and modernization projects of Central American societies were thwarted by force in the 1960's and 1970's. In Nicaragua, Pedro Joaquín Chamorro and other moderate opponents proposed the urgent replacement of the dynastic regime of the Somoza family. In response, they faced a series of repressions and electoral frauds, culminating in the open manipulation of the electoral process in 1974. In El Salvador, a reformist opposition bloc, in which the Christian Democratic party was the principal political force, clearly won the presidential elections of 1972 and 1977. In both instances, fraudulent manipulation by the government was followed by massacres of the population, closing the path to power of the opposition that had won at the polls. In Guatemala, the civilian government of university professor Julio César Méndez Montenegro was toppled by the armed forces before it could take power, under the pretext that the military needed to guarantee public order. Since 1970, four generals have occupied the presidency of the country. In both the 1974 and the 1978 elections, the opposition groups have charged that the electoral results claimed by the government are false. In recent years, as if attempting by force to stem history and make the present situation irreversible, the principal opposition leaders have been assassinated in the capital, in broad daylight, by paramilitary groups of the extreme right. In the elections of March 1982, the electoral fraud was so pervasive and obvious that General Efraín Ríos Montt staged a bloodless coup two weeks after the elections, rather than allow the official candidate, ex-minister of defense General Aníbal Guevara (proclaimed victor, contrary to all evidence) to take office. Here again, one can observe immediate support from the United States, despite the fact that Ríos Montt clearly cannot change the fundamental aspects of the system of power in Guatemala.

Many years ago, in one of his most penetrating works, Erich Fromm spoke of the necessity to give way to "anticipatory change" if the costs of "catastrophic change," which would inevitably result from the stubborn refusal to offer political participation to the new social forces accompanying modernization, urbanization, and productive change, were to be avoided.[1] U.S. policy makers for Central America, in divers administrations, have refused to accept the reality of these pressures and have preferred to maintain the seemingly low-cost alliances with authoritarian and conservative governments who proclaim their friendship toward the United States, their anti-communism, and their solidarity in the defense of Western civilization. In this manner, as Edelberto Torres Rivas, one of the foremost scholars of Central American events, has noted, reformism is gradually disappearing from the politico-ideological spectrum of the countries that are most crisis-stricken.[2] At the same time, the procedures of liberal democracy have lost all credibility in a subregion which, with the exception of Costa Rica, has never known stable liberal democracy.

This situation leads us to explore the ideological visions behind specific policy proposals for the region. In doing this, we want to underline that central to the present political crisis in Central America are interests that are perceived in contradictory fashion within the United States. This is true even within the teams charged with formulating official U.S. policy, as can be demonstrated by a careful review of the different analyses and documents produced in the State Department and the National Security Council. This impression is further corroborated if we consider the academic work of some of those principally responsible for the formulation of present Latin American policy within the Reagan administration.

There are two basic visions of the origins and development of events in Central America, visions that have generated fundamentally different policy options. They directly influence the making of decisions even though, in the majority of official ex-

[1] Erich Fromm, *May Man Prevail? An Inquiry into the Facts and Fictions of Foreign Policy* (New York, 1963).

[2] See Edelberto Torres Rivas, *Crisis del poder en Centroamérica* (San José, Costa Rica, 1981). See also Torres Rivas, "Síntesis histórica del proceso político centroamericano," in *Centroamérica Hoy* (México, 1975).

planations in which the decisions are presented, the ideological bases are not made explicit. This fact only makes it all the more important to pay attention to these matters in the academic sphere.

Although various attempts have been made at more complex analyses, the liberal-conservative dichotomy still dominates most scholarly discussion in this area.[3] Additionally, even though insufficient, these perspectives also continue to provide the principal criteria motivating the most recent policies. In the conservative camp, since the arrival of the Reagan administration, one can observe a set of works, produced in research centers controlled by the new U.S. right, that perform an orienting role similar to that of navigational maps in maritime transport, aiding the team that currently makes Latin American policy in Washington. If the radical perspective is excluded, since its influence in the interior of the state apparatus is null (it enjoys support only among some groups actively opposed to the policies of the administration), it is significant to note that the liberal and conservative visions are in consensus on a number of matters. Most important, both hold that the United States, by virtue of its power, has the right to intervene in the formulation of political options for countries located within its sphere of influence. What varies between the two views is the proposed substance of that intervention. The Republican right identifies more with oligarchic groups and military leadership in Central America; the liberals prefer an alliance with moderate and reformist sectors.

In order to present a fair view of these paradigms, we will draw on some works that have had real influence on those responsible for hemispheric policy, and which, like few others, clearly express the rationale behind both points of view. The authors represented are Jeane Kirkpatrick, Constantine Menges, Robert Pastor, and Federico G. Gil, Enrique A. Baloyra, and Lars Schoultz.[4]

[3] For one such attempt, see Abraham Lowenthal, "United States Policy Toward Latin America," in Julio Cotler and Richard R. Fagen, eds., *Latin America and the United States: The Changing Political Realities* (Stanford, Calif., 1974), pp. 212–35.

[4] Jeane Kirkpatrick, "The Hobbes Problem: Order, Authority, and Legitimacy in Central America," in *American Enterprise Institute 1980 Public Policy Week Papers* (Washington, D.C., 1981); Constantine Menges, "Central America and Its Enemies," *Commentary, 72*, no. 2 (August 1981), 32–38; Robert A. Pastor, "Our Real Interests in Central America," *Atlantic*, 250, no. 1 (July 1982), 27–39; Federico Gil, Enrique A.

The analysis of Gil, Baloyra, and Schoultz, a synthesis of the liberal literature on the crisis, attempts to show the uniqueness of the situations that Central American countries are currently experiencing, thereby avoiding a perspective tainted by the imperatives of the East-West conflict. The authors hold that it is crucial to recover an historical perspective within each country. "We believe," the authors emphasize, "that the origins of the contemporary forms of authoritarian domination are the direct or indirect result of the establishment of oligarchic republics during the bourgeois revolutions of 1870–1871."[5] This perspective is seen by them to be valid at least in the cases of Costa Rica (in an early period), El Salvador, and Guatemala. It is worth noting that in Costa Rica, on the one hand, the liberal revolution provoked a process of division of the land and the establishment of a wide sector of middle-sized landholders; in Guatemala and El Salvador, on the other hand, the simultaneous liquidation of the communal lands and the property of the Catholic Church inaugurated a process of concentration of agricultural property that, over time, converted the oligarchic and landowning sectors into a central political force in control of the state.

This model of political domination arising from the liberal uprising experienced a first challenge in the wake of the Great Depression of 1929, but the ruling sectors were capable of absorbing the pressures of changes in society by means of personalized dictatorial regimes. The authors, following the analysis of Spanish sociologist Salvador Giner, characterize these regimes, which in El Salvador and Guatemala contentrated on restoring public order, as "reactionary despotism." In the 1930's the conservative sectors won a temporary victory by pacifying peasants, workers, and students through repression, thereby avoiding any questioning of an economic model based on the export of primary products.

In this manner, the liberal view notes that the key to present events lies in the survival of exhausted political and economic models sustained for years by elites who have known how to preserve their power. Likewise, this literature insists that the current situation can be understood only if exogenous factors

---

Baloyra, and Lars Schoultz, "The Deterioration and Breakdown of Reactionary Despotism in Central America," written for the State Department, dated January 1981.

[5] Gil, Baloyra, and Schoultz, p. 11.

are not viewed as of primary importance in any analysis of the region.

Gil, Baloyra, and Schoultz assume that "reactionary despotism has deteriorated in Central America due primarily to endogenous factors and not as the result of economic instability and/or the machinations of international actors." This requires the placing of responsibility on the regimes' "inherent obsolescence and inability to adjust to changes brought about by modernization. . . . What is surprising is not that these regimes are deteriorating and breaking down, but that they lasted as long as they have."[6]

From this perspective, it is possible to identify the causes of the crisis, which

has not been brought about by the zealous actions of human rights activists and social reformers encouraged by the Carter administration, nor by subversive leftist elements acting as proxies for Havana or Moscow. . . . These elements did not invent nor are they responsible for the material conditions of life prevalent in Central America, which represent one of the structural causes of the present crisis. To be sure, neither poverty nor inequality . . . nor the low quality of life . . . are sufficient to bring about a crisis. But several factors—the proximate causes of the crisis—have helped politicize and mobilize people affected by the material and political conditions of reactionary despotism, and galvanized their resolve to destroy it.[7]

Onto a political stage that has for many years involved numerous elements of social disequilibrium, have entered additional and more immediate political factors: the work of social democrats and Christian democrats who, beginning in the 1960's, activated and politicized the socially subordinated sectors; the failure of electoral formulas and the constant fraud that surrounded elections; the new role of opposition and social mobilization assumed by the Catholic Church. Taken together, these factors explain how the political will of the opposition forces to unite and put an end to the present situation has been strengthened, and now involves the use of whatever means are necessary to achieve the liquidation of the current regimes.

From this internal diagnosis, the liberal perspective elaborates a clear U.S. policy stance. This policy must reject simple concep-

[6] *Ibid.*, p. 45.
[7] *Ibid.*, p. 55.

tions of security that lead to the "search for friends or enemies since these do not tend to be very permanent in politics." The government in Washington should begin by perceiving that the United States is viewed "as an obstructionist force by some of the actors who are trying to implement a process of democratic transition in their own countries, given the past history of United States initiatives toward those countries."[8] This perception has been exacerbated owing to the erroneous usage of certain terminologies: "The [State] Department insists on calling the Salvadoran Junta 'moderate' and the Sandinista government 'radical,' yet the Sandinistas have made a tremendous effort to fulfill foreign debt obligations contracted by Somoza—to God knows what ends—while the Salvadoran Junta has been 'unable' to prevent a massive loss of life."[9]

The natural conclusion of this perspective is that the Central American policy makers in Washington should change the criteria with which they judge current events, learning through an historical and structural understanding of the actual conflicts. For this, more diplomacy and less "crisis management" is necessary.

In a more recent work Robert Pastor, one of the most important aides to the Linowitz Commission (1976) and later in charge of U.S. policy toward Latin America in the National Security Council during the Carter administration, expounded some suggestive explanations along the same lines. In his view, "The instability of Central America stems from the region's socio-economic progress and political-military stagnation. (Access for all groups to the political process is one important reason Panama, Costa Rica, and Mexico have been able to escape the instability.)"[10]

Pastor clearly assumes that the phenomenon of political polarization is an element that stands in the way of a search for a solution to the problems of the region. This phenomenon is explained by diverse objective tendencies, but is in itself converted into the principal obstacle.

Population pressures, political obstructionism, military repression, and a severe economic depression—these are the medium- and long-term causes of instability; the tinder awaited the spark. The immediate

---

[8] *Ibid.*, pp. 6, 7.   [9] *Ibid.*, p. 10.
[10] Pastor, p. 28.

cause of the current instability in Central America was the Nicaraguan revolution, which traumatized the region. The left became bolder, the right more intransigent, and the middle more precarious. Polarization—the process by which the middle is forced to choose sides, flee, or die—gained momentum. Both the extreme left and the extreme right are committed to trying to make the political reality conform to their perceptions and propaganda—that there is no middle. The left claims that the choice is between the oligarchy and the people; the right, that it is between communism and Christian values.[11]

Pastor criticizes the ideological deformities with which the Reagan administration has defined U.S. interests (recall the famous statement by Secretary Haig on January 28, 1981, in which he affirmed that the battle against international terrorism will take the place of human rights among our priorities). Deeming the present opposition fronts both too broad and too incoherent, he proposes an alternative of negotiation in order to assure the predominance of the moderate sectors whose reconstruction and support he fervently recommends. Thus, for example, he argues:

In El Salvador the left is not a unified, coherent Marxist-Leninist movement like that of the Viet Cong but rather a heterogeneous umbrella over five guerrilla groups, hundreds of political organizations, and disaffected Social and Christian Democrats. Sincere negotiations aimed at forging a democratic alternative would naturally separate those who are interested in democracy but want genuine guarantees if they are to participate in elections from those who are interested in imposing a Marxist-Leninist dictatorship.[12]

Likewise, he feels that "the strategic challenge the U.S. faces in Central America is difficult precisely because it has less to do with traditional concepts of national security than previous challenges did, and much more to do with trying to influence the process of political change in a sensitive Third World environment. The time when the U.S. could bring political stability to the region is long past; all we can do now is contribute to the problem or to the solution."[13]

The conservative vision of Central American development is based on a completely different set of assumptions. It reflects

[11] *Ibid.*, p. 29. [12] *Ibid.*, p. 38.
[13] *Ibid.*, p. 39.

the pessimism of the U.S. radical right concerning democratic options in developing countries. This attitude takes the form of a total adherence to the theory of social modernization, as developed in the 1960's and best articulated in Samuel Huntington's *Political Order in Changing Societies*. According to this theory, a stable political order can accompany either a traditional or a modern social system, but political stability is difficult to achieve precisely in those societies en route to modernization. This is exactly where the conservative view situates the Central American countries, characterizing them as weak states whose governments lack true decision-making power and as situations in which civil society is composed of fragmented and opposing interests. These interests form large blocs that lack the power to impose themselves on society, thereby creating a situation of political deadlock. Prolonged political instability results from this deadlock, opening the door to external intervention by governments and extremist organizations that can then make pacts with, and eventually subordinate, domestic movements.

An excellent example of this train of thought vis-à-vis Central America can be found in the works of Jeane Kirkpatrick, current ambassador to the United Nations. As if she wished to place herself in diametric opposition to the liberal version, Ambassador Kirkpatrick notes that the father of modern authoritarian political theory, the Englishman Thomas Hobbes, provided the essential framework three centuries ago for the resolution of the contemporary crises in Central America. Kirkpatrick begins by insisting that policy makers should learn the fundamental lessons of Hobbes: "the primacy of order as the basic value of a political system without which no other value can be enjoyed."[14]

Kirkpatrick's particular bias develops around this premise. To understand current events in El Salvador (or earlier in Nicaragua)—countries affected by disequilibria and turbulence created by recent transformations—"it is, of course, necessary first to understand what kind of regime and what kind of society they are." These countries exhibit "continuing disagreement about the legitimate ends and means of government, pervasive distrust of authority, a broad ideological spectrum, privatization, low participation in voluntary associations, a preference for hier-

---

[14]Kirkpatrick, p. 135.

archical associational modes (church, bureaucracy, army), a history of military participation in politics, and *personalismo*." In these countries political regimes become unstable because of the weight of these factors, thereby preventing governments from controlling the political process. Thus, in El Salvador and in other Central American countries, "weak governments confront strong social groups, and no institution is able to establish its authority over the whole."[15] Given this picture, there are no legitimate forms of access to power, and each sector competes using all the means within its reach: "The church manipulates symbols of rectitude; . . . workers use strikes; businessmen use bribery; political parties use campaigns and votes; politicians use persuasion, organization, and demagoguery; and military officers use force." The military usually win out, violence becomes a permanent feature, and war becomes a constant possibility. Typically, however, "in traditional Latin politics competitors do not normally destroy each other. They suffer limited defeats and win limited victories."[16] This only further accentuates the instability of these regimes.

It is into this now routine pattern that the guerrilla enters, as well as groups trained by Cuba and linked to the plans and alliances of the Soviet Union. These forces use terrorism to destroy order, disorganize the economy and daily life, and demoralize the police and governments by demonstrating the latter's inability to protect personal security and maintain public authority. "With the arrival of the concept of terrorism as a *form* of revolution, the advent of the revolution need no longer await the masses."[17]

This scenario, in terms of specific policy options, presents the United States with some very concrete dilemmas of profound concern to neoconservative thinkers. In the first place, they argue, one must remain aware that Central America is today an internationalized region in which forces antagonistic to the U.S. national interest are at work. The Socialist International, the Catholic Church, and Cuba, all from different positions, have intervened and have helped destabilize these countries. Under Carter, an additional destabilizing factor was added: the U.S. government itself wanted to play a new role, seeking "internal

---

[15] *Ibid.*, pp. 128, 129. [16] *Ibid.*, p. 130.
[17] *Ibid.*, pp. 130–31.

reform, democracy, social justice—goods which even strong governments find it difficult to produce." [18]

This perspective of "internationalization" has also been taken, in a broader and more conspiratorial fashion, by Constantine Menges, in his work published in *Commentary* in August 1981. In his view, the role of external forces is almost determinate. These forces, despite their ideological diversity, act together to support the rise to power of the extreme left. Thus, he highlights the basic role fulfilled by "the presence of four international forces supporting the groups engaged in such revolutionary violence: first, Cuba and other Communist countries along with the regional Communist parties; second, Palestinian terrorists and some radical Arab states; third, Mexico; fourth, virtually all social-democratic governments as well as the parties that make up the Socialist international." [19]

Given that this is a heterogeneous coalition, Menges, presently a high official in the Latin American section of the Central Intelligence Agency, attempts to propose an explanation of this fact:

Why have Mexico and the social-democratic parties decided to join with Cuba in supporting Central American revolutions? The explanation can be found in the influence of a strong, radical-leftist faction within the PRI and most social-democratic parties; in a theory of politics in developing countries which emphasizes anti-imperialism and nationalism while ignoring democracy and rejecting any notion of possible danger from forming coalitions with Communist groups; in a hidden *Realpolitik* which assumes that timely help for leftist revolutionaries will be repaid in domestic social peace and future international influence; and in a partisan interest in weakening such domestic rivals as Christian Democrats.

During the last decade these factors in different combinations and strengths in Mexico and among many social-democratic parties and governments in Europe have produced what Carl Gershman has accurately described as an alignment with "anti-Western revolutionary movements in the Third World" which include, besides the totalitarian left in Central America, the PLO and other Palestinian terrorist groups and Marxist regimes and movements like SWAPO in southern Africa. [20]

The neoconservatives advocate the learning of a simple lesson

[18] *Ibid.*, p. 131.   [19] Menges, p. 32.
[20] *Ibid.*, p. 36.

if an effective policy is to be implemented. In cases of terrorist aggression with external support, of which the Central American countries are seen as examples, "a government's status depends, even more than usually, on its capacity to govern, to secure obedience, to punish those who disobey—in sum, to maintain order. Such a government can command obedience only insofar as it can secure acquiescence in its policies, can rely on habits of obedience, or can impose its commands by force and fear." To illustrate this solution for U.S. policy makers more graphically, Ambassador Kirkpatrick employs a concrete historical example proving that "the hero" is necessary to enforce order. In El Salvador, one such hero was

General Maximiliano Hernández Martínez, who governed El Salvador from 1931 to 1944, was minister of war in the cabinet of President Arturo Araujo when there occurred widespread uprisings said to be the work of Communist agitators. General Hernández Martínez then staged a coup and ruthlessly suppressed the disorders—wiping out all those who participated and hunting down their leaders. It is said that 30,000 persons lost their lives in the process. To many Salvadorans the violence of this repression seems less important than the fact of restored order and the thirteen years of civil peace that ensued.[21]

This perspective leads to the adoption of a policy that takes into consideration "the real elements of power," giving priority to the reconstruction of a stable order even if it has to be imposed by force, giving rise to new forms of authoritarianism. In the long run, the neoconservative writers tell us, political democracy is not a feasible model for all countries, especially those characterized by domestic entropy and subversive attacks by international communism. In such cases, it is advisable to perceive the U.S. national interest as leading to the decision to impede, by whatever means, the rise to power of any political coalition that threatens the continuance of the alliance between the United States and the countries of Central America. To achieve this goal, it is often inevitable that these countries continue to be led by dictators.

With President Reagan's inauguration in January 1981, the strategic perspective that forms the basis of the neoconservative view has clearly been imposed on the formulation of Washing-

[21] Kirkpatrick, p. 133.

ton's Central American policy. It is important to note that the
views of the advisors now working with the government have
been accepted with greater ease since they are more in line with
the predominant assumptions underlying State Department policy toward Central America.

A general criterion in the analysis of the specialists at Foggy
Bottom has been that Central American countries are increasingly less important in economic terms and more important in
terms of the national security of the United States. As early as
1977, the then Deputy Assistant Secretary of State for Inter-
American Affairs for Mexico, Central America, and the Caribbean, Sally Shelton, noted that, "Contrary to what the majority
of Latin Americans think, the economic interests of the U.S. in
Central America are fairly limited. Our total annual commerce
with the region is about 1.8 billion U.S. dollars, that is, less than
one percent of the foreign commerce of the United States. U.S.
investment in the area is approximately 700 million dollars, 0.5
percent of U.S. direct foreign investment. The region has no
strategic primary materials." [22]

Thus, at the heart of Washington's policy toward Central
America is the concept that none of the direct investments made
by U.S. corporations are very important, a fact reinforced by the
wide distribution of these investments in the various countries
of the region and by their diversified nature. For this reason, the
prediction of the negative effects that would be produced by the
"fall" of another country into the hands of anti-U.S. forces becomes the key consideration. In addition, within the Reagan administration an analysis that sees the situations in El Salvador
and Nicaragua as the best opportunities to initiate an effective
policy of global confrontation has gained strength.

This type of diagnosis, highly influential among the experts
who prepared the Republican party's foreign policy platform,
argues that, even if the countries of Central America are not
located in the region of the most direct U.S.-U.S.S.R. conflict
(which would be Africa and the Persian Gulf), they are nevertheless in a situation which is much more favorable to a U.S. victory. Such a victory would allow these countries to become ex-

[22] Sally Shelton, "Estados Unidos y América Central," *CIDE: Cuadernos Semestrales
Estados Unidos*, no. 6 (1979), p. 17.

amples with a favorable "demonstration effect" for the rest of the Third World.

Taken together, these assumptions and considerations concerning international politics explain both the high priority the Reagan administration has initially given to the Central American subregion, and the hard-line policies the administration has tried to implement. This perspective also holds the key to explaining many of the Reagan administration's failures in Latin America.

SOME KEYS TO UNDERSTANDING THE CENTRAL AMERICAN CRISIS

The description of these paradigms allows us to underline the fact that there exists a serious inadequacy in the analysis and understanding of the political processes in Central America on the part of U.S. specialists who have dealt with these issues and who have contributed to the decision-making process. This is particularly clear in the case of neoconservative experts, but it is also valid, in large part, for the liberal perspective, as is demonstrated by the erratic and incoherent policies of the Carter administration.

It is thus necessary to take into account the most important contributions of Central American social scientists, integrating into the analysis of the present situation a whole set of factors, in part historical and in part linked to the productive process. These factors are necessary in order accurately to situate and untangle the events that underlie the crisis and that make sense only if linked to the constraining tendencies and conditions produced in earlier historical epochs. The political history of the nations of the Central American Isthmus, like all political history, is conditioned by its immediate past. To attempt to build a peaceful solution that ignores this past is a capricious exercise destined for failure.

From this perspective, what are the most important of these factors?

The Dismantling of Reformist Projects

In the first place, it can be observed that the systematic elimination of all political options representing gradual change took place during the 1960's and 1970's. Many observers who have only recently studied the political problems of countries like Nicaragua, El Salvador, or Guatemala, are proposing the strengthening of the forces that represent reformist programs, and are located between oligarchic projects on the one hand and, on the other, the path of radical transformation and armed struggle supported by the left.

The problem is that these forces arose with considerable vigor throughout Central America during the 1960's and attempted to serve as potentially hegemonic alternatives that could replace the traditional dictatorships. Nevertheless, they were crushed by precisely those sectors dedicated to the defense of the established order. Thus, in those years, center parties were founded with the goal of effecting gradual and preventive change, and with the intention of competing electorally within the established legal system. Usually they were linked to international movements such as Christian democracy or social democracy and were able to mobilize intellectuals and middle sectors. They were even successful in gaining some influence among the peasantry and urban workers. These political forces assumed leadership in the fight against authoritarianism and were able to make alliances with parties of the left, in which the latter played a subordinate or complementary role. Such was the case of the Unión Nacional de Oposición (UNO) in El Salvador, which under the leadership of the Christian Democratic party won the elections of 1972 and 1977. Such was also the case with the alliance that supported the candidacy of General Efraín Ríos Montt in 1974 in Guatemala.

These forces usually had the backing of the Catholic Church and of some liberal sectors in the United States, particularly congressmen and leaders of the Democratic party. If the factors that gave rise to these reformist parties were weighted, the two that would emerge as the most important would be the program of the Alliance for Progress of President John F. Kennedy and the Second Vatican Council. Both events strengthened the idea that in developing countries economic and social reforms, and the consolidation of democratic mechanisms to assure greater popular participation among the most marginalized sectors of the population, were inevitable.

Centrist reformism, however, despite this consistent external support and undoubted electoral success, ended up being destroyed by two characteristic features of Central American politics: fraud and violence. By tampering with electoral results, oligarchic groups in power progressively demoralized the masses' faith in the feasibility of a peaceful electoral solution and created the conditions for the intensification of repression against the opposition. Then, through the open use of force, the leadership of even the moderate opposition forces who might have led a peaceful replacement of the dictatorship were eliminated. The most dramatic and well-known case was the assassination of Pedro Joaquín Chamorro in Nicaragua, in January 1978. But the country that has had the most systematic and overwhelming record is Guatemala. Shortly before the 1966 elections, a candidate for the presidency of the Revolutionary party, Mario Méndez Montenegro, was eliminated. In 1972, a Christian Democratic party deputy in congress, Adolfo Mijangos, was assassinated. More recently, as the two most important center-left groups in Guatemala began to form links with the Socialist International, their two most important leaders were killed by commandos of the extreme right: Alberto Fuentes Mohr of the Democratic Socialist party, in 1978, and Manuel Colom Argueta of the Frente Unido de la Revolución (FUR), in early 1979.

Thus, though a peaceful and reformist political solution might appear appropriate in theory for the majority of Central American countries, such a strategy is virtually inapplicable because of the political development of these countries. The facts show that during almost two decades the forces of the right have eliminated any political space occupied by centrist parties. These parties have ended up caught in a societal polarization that pushed them into membership of large blocs dominated today by the left.

The prestigious U.S. newspapers (recall the editorials in the *Washington Post* and the *New York Times* after the fall of Somoza) as well as liberal circles in Washington frequently insist on the need to support reformist political coalitions in the countries of Central America. Such coalitions are presented as an alternative to the triumph of radical groups, the most feared of all the various possible outcomes. The problem is that the present strength and legitimacy of leftist coalitions has been the result of the very intransigence and methods of traditional oligarchic leaders. For this reason, attempts to dissociate reformist parties from revolutionary organizations is seen by the moderate forces themselves as a way of shoring up the dictatorships in power. Revolutionary leaders see such attempts as a tactic that will favor counterrevolutionary forces when authoritarian regimes have finally been defeated.

One of the major lessons of Central American political events is that there is only a limited time available for the implementation of peaceful and gradual reforms. In Nicaragua, El Salvador, and Guatemala, the time has expired. The "reasonable reformism," as Edelberto Torres Rivas once called it, was an alternative of the 1960's or the early 1970's. In the 1980's, such a solution lacks the requisite political space and conditions.

The Role of the Armed Forces

A second factor distinguishing the recent period is the armed forces' assumption of an institutional role. This has enabled the military to overcome traditional military *caudillismo* and has allowed them to exercise a type of co-government with the most vigorous civilian nucleus of the Central American bourgeoisie.[23] For decades, Central American political systems were highly unstable, partly because of the ease with which military leaders, supported by a fraction of the military under their command, rose to power. In the everyday and literary language of Central American countries, the term *madrugonazo* (daybreak coup) was used to denote these seizures of power. They were characterized by the transitional nature of their political legitimacy, and their effects were often precarious owing to their lack of permanent and organized social or military support.

This mode of seizing political power and this type of leadership have disappeared in recent years. After the Second World War, the armed forces became more professionalized, and military leadership became increasingly collective. In this way, the power of *caudillos* was ended and was passed to army generals who exercise power in the name of the whole institution, and whose decisions are made through the regular and permanent organs of their institution. Contrary to what one might expect,

[23] For an early and lucid analysis see M. Costa Pinto, *Nacionalismo y militarismo* (Mexico, 1969).

however, this increased professionalism has not been a factor leading to flexibility for political systems, nor has it helped to modify productive structures, or to foster social change, despite the obvious inequality and injustice in these societies.

In our view, the explanation of this phenomenon is linked to the historical evolution of Central American countries, beginning with their independence. After the initial predominance of conservative projects and parties in the Isthmus immediately after the breaking of links with the Spanish Empire in 1823 (which led to the establishment of conservative governments like that of Rafael Carrera and Vicente Cerna in Guatemala, José María Medina in Honduras, Francisco Dueñas in El Salvador, all of whom shared the goal of destroying the unification project of Francisco Morazán, aimed at supporting the autonomous expression of the diverse national states), a widespread liberal reform movement took place. After initially proposing a political model of representative democracy, the leaders of the movement came to identify themselves with the existing power groups and worked for the reestablishment of the interests of the oligarchs. As Ciro Cardoso and Héctor Pérez Brignoli have correctly pointed out, "Far from a democratization that might have led to broad popular participation, the liberal reform created the solid foundation for an oligarchic republic and assured political stability through authoritarian mechanisms." [24]

This liberal revolution took place almost simultaneously in Central American countries in the early 1870's (J. Rufino Barrios was president of Guatemala in 1871, Céleo Arias in Honduras in 1872, and Rafael Zaldivar came to power in El Salvador in 1875). Because of its exhaustion in the following decades, however, it not only failed to implant a new institutional model along U.S.-European lines; it further exacerbated the constant disputes among political elites and favored the consolidation of a political structure based on agricultural exports. This structure led to a strong Central American dependency on the principal capitalist centers who were imposing, alternatively, cycles of coffee and bananas.

In the distortion of the liberal project, one can find an important part of the explanation of the active political role of Cen-

[24] Ciro Cardoso and Héctor Pérez Brignoli, *Centroamérica y la economía occidental,* 1520–1930 (San José, Costa Rica, 1977), p. 296.

tral American militaries and the reactionary character of their operation and programs. The group of military dictators who took power after the capitalist crisis of 1929 (among whom the most important were Jorge Ubico in Guatemala, Tiburcio Carías in Honduras, Maximiliano Hernández Martínez in El Salvador, and Anastasio Somoza in Nicaragua) imposed traditional authoritarian regimes that ended a liberal utopia never resolutely pushed by its own supporters.

During this period there was a strengthening of the political wedding between the army and the oligarchy. Together they exercised a functional coadministration of power, excluding the middle and popular sectors from any political participation and leading to the accumulation of multiple tensions that have exploded in the current revolutionary crisis. Naturally, when political and social modernization demand it, the political power of the military becomes increasingly more institutionalized and less personalized. But in any case this new leadership represents the tradition of minority alliances that will often be readjusted, but never abandoned.

New Forms of Organization of the Left

To these political factors must be added the appearance (also conditioned by the historical experience of recent decades) of new forms of organization within the leftist camp. The course of the struggle against authoritarian regimes in the most convulsed countries of Central America has led the revolutionary left to abandon two organizational mechanisms of the past: the traditional political party and the *foquista* guerrilla movement. Both mechanisms had led the Central American left to defeat after defeat by their failure to take into account the contemporary political situation and by their lack of political creativity in opposing military governments.

The left's work through partisan structures, of which the activity of communist parties linked to the Communist Party of the Soviet Union (CPSU) is a prototype, had attempted to impose on the Central American reality a series of analyses applicable to part of the international working class movement, but completely inappropriate for any of the countries of the subregion, given the unique behavior of fundamental social forces in this area of the world. Thus, for example, communist parties tried to create a "working-class hegemony" in circumstances in which the weakness of this part of the labor force in the productive organization of society prohibited such a strategy. They attempted to support political organizations representing the new factions of the national bourgeoisie without realizing that these factions had close links with oligarchic sectors, disqualifying them from leading any process of social change. And, above all, they tried to promote the creation of broad political fronts within the electoral system because they were convinced that only the building of a social majority would lead to the establishing of democratic and progressive governments.

On the other extreme, based on a fairly rigid reading of the lessons of the Cuban Revolution, guerrilla movements appeared in the 1960's. Their strategy was based on the conviction that the initiation of revolutionary transformation did not automatically arise out of situations of misery and exploitation, but that revolution would be possible if an external force acted as a catalyst for the existing contradictions within the countries of Latin America. Thus, attempting to develop rural guerrilla tactics, nuclei of dissidents from the historic left formed insurrectional *focos*, hoping to spark the confrontations that would detonate a widespread rebellion. These experiences took place in the second half of the 1960's in Nicaragua and, above all, in Guatemala. Naturally, a concept of this type failed to take into account the activity and work of the masses. Although they were to be an auxiliary to the military task, they were not the center of the revolutionary process, at least in its original phase.

The defeats experienced by one current and another did serve to prepare the political synthesis that took place in the mid-1970's. In this synthesis, the rise of a social movement that adopted the form of a coordinating front of popular struggles was the fundamental feature. In both Nicaragua and El Salvador, the frontal attack against authoritarian regimes has been based on this new reality. There has been an attempt to overcome political action perceived as the exclusive task of party elites. There has been a rejection of military struggle that is not linked to mass struggle. Instead, there has been a recognition of the diversity and complexity of the popular movement, and attempts have been made to develop and coordinate it through sociopolitical fronts. In this manner, the questioning of the established system and the demand for a democratic regime have become profoundly rooted at the base of civil society. Military activity is thus complementary to the social struggle and is carefully coordinated with it. The strong links between the political forces undertaking different types of political activity within the popular movement and the specifically military organizations bear this out.

This new organic reality is a key to understanding the vitality the revolutionary process has gained in recent years in the most turbulent countries of Central America. The activity of the Sandinist Front and the subsequent work of Salvadoran organizations such as the Bloque Popular Revolucionario and the Unified Popular Action Front (FAPU), which played a decisive role in the creation of the Democratic Revolutionary Front (FDR), exemplify the efforts to link political and military participation. What is sought is to synchronize permanently the task of organizing and articulating the demands arising from the popular movement with military actions and insurrection.

This synthesis of the social and the military, absent in earlier stages of the struggle of the Latin American left (at least to the degree that has currently been achieved), has naturally been aided by the political experience of Nicaragua, El Salvador, and Guatemala. In these instances military and oligarchic leaders have blocked any political solution based on respect for electoral mechanisms and for the implementation of the social reforms that can no longer be delayed.

The Nature of the Working-Class Movement

It is also important to consider the development of the working-class movement in Central America.[25] We have noted that workers' organizations were unable to play the same decisive role as in more advanced social formations because the process of industrialization in Central America has been both late and incomplete. Nevertheless, on a smaller scale, such organizations have had an important development in recent decades and have influenced the entire subregional political picture. As a

[25] On the Central American labor movement, see Mario Posas, *Luchas del movimiento obrero Hondureño* (San José, Costa Rica, 1981); Vladimir de La Cruz, *Las luchas sociales en Costa Rica* (2nd ed., San José, Costa Rica, 1982); and CIERA, *Estado y clases sociales en Nicaragua* (Managua, 1982).

consequence, in the past thirty years the popular movement in Central American countries has increasingly become more urbanized. This has resulted from a process of import substitution that, however precarious, has produced a certain industrial base, a growth in state activity, and a continuing expansion of the financial sector.

The behavior of authoritarian governments has been the essential element defining the options of this working-class movement. These governments have not only viewed the rise of trade unions with suspicion, but have attempted to limit and repress them as soon as they formulate any demands. Thus, because the central political authorities have handled even the most elemental demands as "subversion," the politicization and radicalization of the working-class movement has almost inevitably resulted.

In this manner, working-class and peasant organizations in all the Central American countries (with the exception of Costa Rica) have not enjoyed the options present in developed capitalist societies—choices between reformist and revolutionary alternatives "within the system." It has not been possible to conduct their work within the rules of the game. From its birth, the working-class movement in Central America has thus been strongly politicized and has formulated its options and programs in sharp opposition to the U.S. corporations, which have almost always appeared alongside the government of the United States as props for authoritarian regimes.

The Rise of the Popular Church

Among the institutions constituting the structural base of traditional authority, there is one—once a veritable pillar of the oligarchical order—which has undergone a dramatic change: the Catholic Church.[26] This change is not unique to the Central American church; it appears to be a continental phenomenon. In Brazil, for example, an important sector of the church hierarchy has taken part in a program of social change, and the grass roots movement of Christian communities has played a

---

[26] Nicaragua was the first revolutionary experience in Latin America characterized by the massive participation of Christians (as religious believers). See, for example, Instituto Histórico Centroamericano, *Fé Cristiana y revolución sandinista en Nicaragua* (Managua, 1979), and Pablo Richard and Guillermo Melendez, eds., *La iglesia de los pobres en América Central* (San José, Costa Rica, 1982).

crucial role in the process of democratization. However, this phenomenon did not simply burst onto the scene. As far back as 1969, the Rockefeller Report on the Americas noted that one of the most alarming symptoms of the Latin American political panorama, as far as the United States was concerned, was the radicalization of important sectors of the Catholic Church, and of other Christian churches. "The sword and the cross," reported President Nixon's special envoy, "have constituted the basis of traditional power for four centuries. Now, they tend to act in the opposite manner."[27] At the same time, the Rand Corporation prepared an extensive report on the political function of the Catholic Church and possible changes in it.[28] This was sparked by the fact that within a very few years the commitment of priests and lay persons to revolutionary movements had grown significantly.

There are original elements, nevertheless, in the political participation of Christians in the Central American crisis. To begin with, there has been a clear political commitment over a broad segment of Catholic masses who have taken a position of active involvement within the organizations of the left, including those resorting to armed struggle. This has been clear in the work of the Frente Sandinista de Liberación Nacional (FSLN) in Nicaragua, in the Bloque Popular Revolucionario in El Salvador, and in the Ejército Guerrillero de los Pobres in Guatemala. In the Salvadoran case this option has been even more significant because many of the popular organizations formed by the church itself as part of its attempt to apply the social doctrine of Vatican Two (e.g., the Federación de Campesinos Católicos, FECCAS), have joined the fight for democratization, and subsequently the armed actions against the government.

The political activity of these groups has been linked to the radicalization of many of the priests who work in rural areas, share the same peasant origins as the rest of the combatants, and suffer the severe living conditions of the countryside. They have experienced the effects of repression; the considerable number of assassinations of church members is proof of this.

---

[27] *Rockefeller Report on the Americas* (Chicago, 1969), p. 31.
[28] Luigi Einaudi et al., *Institutional Development in Latin America: Changes in the Catholic Church* (Santa Monica, Calif., 1961).

The assassination of the rural priest Rutilio Grande has become a symbol of this phenomenon.

In this fashion the so-called popular church constitutes a serious sociological reality in Nicaragua, Honduras, El Salvador, and Guatemala. It has converted priests and nuns, working among the masses, into advocates for strong pressure on the hierarchy—trying to force church leaders into adopting positions favorable to the popular struggle. The behavior of the Episcopal Conferences reflects an uneven sensitivity to these demands, but, compared with the monolithic conservatism that prevailed until recently, the break with unconditional support for dictatorial governments is an advance favoring the democratization process. In some instances, as was the case with the archbishop of San Salvador, Oscar Arnulfo Romero, the commitment has expanded and has increased even further the role of the church in the Central American crisis. This involvement was crucial in the decision by Salvadoran extreme rightists to assassinate Romero in March 1980.

It is important, however, to emphasize that this new phenomenon of a wide range of Central American Christian sectors in support of the political forces of the left has not been the work of the hierarchy. Rather, it has resulted from decisions at the base, creating serious problems of legitimacy for the hierarchy when the hierarchy attempts to side with traditional sectors in opposition to the political activity of its followers.

The majority presence of popular Christian sectors in the struggle for democracy in Central America has added a new ideological and ethical force to the political organizations of the opposition. The views of man and the world that Christians bring to the revolutionary struggle, as well as their willingness to provide clear testimony of their ideas as part of the cause they have embraced, have given strength to revolutionary organizations, and this is one of the keys to understanding the surprising support for these organizations in peasant communities and urban centers.

In the contemporary history of Latin America, Christian-inspired groups have, on numerous occasions, shown a political commitment to the leftist camp. This is the first time, however, that the majority of the Catholic masses in a revolutionary

situation have resolutely acted on the side of those proposing profound transformations, thereby lending them religious
legitimacy.

Recent Changes in the Productive Structure

It is essential to consider, finally, the complex economic process experienced by Central American countries in the postwar
period. There are a number of significant political consequences
that derive from the present situation. We will summarize their
most influential features.[29]

In the first place, it is necessary to assess the rapid pace of
modernization in Central America due to the expansion of the
productive forces of the several countries. In the postwar period, few subregions have experienced such drastic changes in
terms of rapid urbanization and industrialization. This has led
to a change in the class structure, new patterns of consumption,
changes in life expectancy, and new social aspirations for a wide
range of sectors. As in other areas, modernization has had the
political effect of altering the perception that misery is the result
of fate, that exploitation or repression are normal forms of the
exercise of political power. This awareness has profoundly challenged the legitimacy of oligarchic and authoritarian political
systems.

In Central America, however, the process has been accentu-
ated. If one reviews the major comparative economic studies of
Latin American countries (for example, the yearly reports of the
U.N. Economic Commission for Latin America, ECLA), it can
be observed that the nations of the Central American Isthmus
have grown at a fairly dynamic rate: in the 1960's and the first
half of the 1970's growth has ranged from 5 to 8 percent per
year in the different countries. But the fruits of this development
have not favored the majority of the population. Instead, they
have ended up in the hands of the most economically powerful
sectors, as a result of the deliberately concentrating character of
prevailing economic models. Thus, this increased wealth, rather
than representing a dynamic factor for the fulfillment of centuries-

[29] For a useful overview of the development of the Central American economies, see
Gert Rosenthal, "Principales Rasgos de la Evolución de las economías centroamericanas
desde la posguerra," in CECADE/CIDE, *Centroamérica: Crisis y política internacional*
(Mexico, 1982).

old needs of the majority of the population, has been converted into an element that exacerbates social differentials and worsens the living conditions of the poor.

Generally speaking, all policy options that might point to popular participation or equality have been deliberately excluded from the developmental strategies of Central American political regimes. The clearest example of this general tendency, as Jorge Arturo Reyna has demonstrated in his recent work *Honduras: Cambios o violencia*, has been the process of Central American integration. When the so-called Central American Common Market was put in motion in 1960, the objective was to offer larger markets for existing industrial production, improving economies of scale.[30] In addition, there were plans in subsequent years to expand the list of products destined for consumption by the middle and upper classes of the five countries of the Isthmus. This decision was consciously designed to avoid any profound industrialization that might offer these countries real opportunities for productive specialization. No attempt was made to emphasize products that might permit the incorporation of the most backward economic sectors into the consumption of the goods being generated.

This market, despite its name, constituted more of a free-trade zone. It therefore had limited dynamism and provided the basis for an intensive penetration of foreign capital, especially from the United States, thus further accentuating the tendency toward a denationalization of the economies of the subregion. Likewise, a paradox was exacerbated. Although the volume of foreign investment in Central America represented only a very limited percentage of the overall interests of the United States, these investments nevertheless had an enormous, and negative, local impact.

Economic growth, on the other hand, and the concomitant modernization, also failed to displace oligarchic groups. On the contrary, the dominant classes expanded through a reactionary political alliance between new and old capital. There was a joint effort to defend the interests and privileges they had come to share. (This is one of the reasons why the Communist parties' policies of allying with the "most dynamic sectors of the bour-

[30] Jorge Arturo Reyna, *Honduras: Cambios o violencia* (Tegucigalpa, 1982).

geoisie" never worked.) Given this situation, oligarchic groups linked to coffee or banana production participated with bankers and those involved in inefficient import substitution industries. This is particularly evident if we observe, for example, the behavior of the entrepreneurial elite in San Salvador (considered to be the economic capital of the Common Market) during the 1960's. In other cases, such as Guatemala, the armed forces became an entrepreneurial force through a massive process of corruption. Obviously, in this entire process Nicaragua presents characteristics that are unique, owing to the strictly dynastic nature of the economic concentration organized by the Somoza family.

A significant economic factor that appeared in the 1970's helped to slow down the pace of development: the energy crisis. None of the Central American countries was an oil producer at that time, and the quadrupling of oil prices after the Yom Kippur War in 1973, as well as the subsequent chaos in the energy market, was a factor narrowing the room for maneuver of Central American governments. This tended to increase foreign indebtedness and had a negative effect on the balance of trade. If to this we add the impact on the region of the economic crisis in the core countries, we can more easily understand how the wave of revolutionary activity in Central America has coincided with a loss of the economic dynamism of past decades.

In Central America there was a shift from a dynamic but concentrating development to a contraction of productive activity that further deteriorated the living conditions of the majority of the population. Needless to say, when the economic crisis occurred, the dominant sectors attempted to transfer its costs to the popular sectors without accepting any sacrifice of their own income, savings, or standards of living.

In our view, the factors we have outlined form both an explanatory background and a series of constraints for possible solutions to the Central American crisis. In general, it can be argued that none of these factors enters into the explanatory frameworks employed by liberal and conservative sectors within the United States. They have been especially ignored by the Reagan administration's policy toward Central America. This policy has rested on a strategic perspective, the result of which has been an attempt to manipulate, in the short term, the major events of the crisis, country by country. This manipulation has clear limits. Employing this short-term perspective, the government in Washington can achieve some specific victories. On the other hand, it will have a hard time resolving the revolutionary challenge now present in Central America.

U.S. Policy Options in Central America

William M. LeoGrande

THE eruption of political turmoil in Central America over the past two years poses a profound challenge to the United States. Earlier policies aimed at preserving a congenial status quo in the region are no longer adequate to the task. A new policy is needed—one that effectively advances the interests and values of the United States in a period when the Central American region is undergoing profound social and political changes. The key to formulating such a policy is a clear understanding of the basic processes that have produced political instability in the region.

From the colonial period to the mid-twentieth century, the nations of Central America experienced similar patterns of development. Land grants from the Spanish Crown installed small landed elites at the apex of all these societies. From their position of economic privilege, these elites were able to dominate politics and use the apparatus of the state to defend their social and economic interests. Throughout the region, their power served to perpetuate economic underdevelopment, social inequality, and political oligarchy.

For decades, the oligarchic systems were relatively stable. Despite sporadic peasant revolts, such as the Salvadoran insurrection of 1932, the rural population lacked the political awareness and organization necessary to be a consistently potent political force. Regional stability was also reinforced by the United States. As the United States emerged as a world power at the turn of the twentieth century, it developed major economic and strategic interests in Central America. The desire to protect

U.S. investments and the need to defend the Panama Canal produced in Washington a clear preference for stable, friendly governments in Central America—a preference that Washington was willing to enforce by military intervention if necessary. The power of the United States was such that U.S. ambassadors in the region could and often did act as proconsuls. As Washington exercised its influence in favor of stability, it inevitably came to be identified as an ally of the landed oligarchs.[1]

In the decades after World War II, the foundations of Central America's oligarchic systems began to erode. The process of economic development that gathered speed in the 1950's and 1960's had profound and irreversible social consequences: the building of industries produced new social groups, white collar and blue collar urban workers; the extension of transport produced a truly national society from previously isolated rural communities; and the expansion of education and communications produced a citizenry more aware of its place in the nation's social structure, the shortcomings of that structure, and potential alternatives.

Not surprisingly, these social changes had political correlates. The growing middle class, the newly emerging urban working class, and even the traditional peasantry began to see political action as a means to redress the severe inequities of the oligarchic system. Of course, there were differences, from one nation to another, in the depth and timing of this crisis in the legitimacy of the old order. But throughout the region the basic dynamics of the crisis were the same.

The landed elites responded to demands for democracy and social justice with intransigence. Rather than risk a diminution of their privilege, they chose to defend the bastions of the old order by political force. The United States, fearful that fundamental change might open the door to communism in the Americas, enlisted on the side of the oligarchs. In Guatemala, it went so far as to help depose a government of radical reformers, thereby reconstituting the old order on a new foundation of military rule.[2] Except in Costa Rica, the forces of reform were

[1] Richard Millet, *Guardians of the Dynasty* (Maryknoll, N.Y., 1977).
[2] For the story of the U.S. involvement in the 1954 coup in Guatemala, see Stephen Schlesinger and Stephen Kinzer, *Bitter Fruit* (New York, 1982).

everywhere throttled by the political might of the oligarchs and their allies in Washington.

The efforts at reform that characterized the opposition in Central America during the 1960's and 1970's were defeated by a combination of electoral fraud and political repression. The failure of reformism only exacerbated the crisis of legitimacy by convincing opponents of the old order that it was impervious to peaceful change. In Nicaragua, El Salvador, and Guatemala, the exhaustion of reformism was quickly followed by the growth of armed oppositions bent on destroying the old order rather than modifying it. The radicalism of the armed groups intensified the fear and resistance of the oligarchs, producing an ever-deepening spiral of political violence. The brutality of the armed forces, often aimed indiscriminately at whole social groups (e.g., peasants, intellectuals, clerics), served only to further delegitimize the existing regimes and bring new recruits to the guerrillas. The predictable outcome, as events in Nicaragua illustrated, was the collapse of the old order in the face of virtually universal popular opposition.[3]

For the defenders of the old order, the United States represented the last real hope of averting defeat. By the late 1970's, however, the United States was no longer prepared to serve as an uncritical ally of Central America's elites. Policy makers in Washington were torn between a traditional concern for stability and a growing revulsion at the brutality Central American regimes were using against their own citizens.[4]

In the wake of the Nicaraguan Revolution, the Carter administration sought to devise a new regional policy that would promote reformism and reduce the abuses of human rights while simultaneously undermining the political support of the armed insurgents. This policy was grounded in the assumption that the pressures for change in Central America had become irresistible. The old policy of supporting the "right" (i.e., the traditional elites and their military allies) was fruitless; it could nei-

[3] On the growth of revolutionary opposition in Nicaragua, see *Nicaragua: A People's Revolution* (Washington, D.C., 1980); on El Salvador, see Tommie Sue Montgomery, *Revolution in El Salvador* (Boulder, Colo., 1982); on Guatemala, see Marlise Simons, "Guatemala: The Coming Danger," *Foreign Policy*, no. 43 (Summer 1981).

[4] On the development of U.S. human rights policy, see Lars Schoultz, *Human Rights and United States Policy Toward Latin America* (Princeton, N.J., 1981).

ther contain nor resolve the growing regional crisis. Worse still, clinging to the old policy would tie long-term U.S. interests to regimes with little chance of long-term survival.[5]

To manage the process of regional change, Carter sought to revive the political "center" of moderate, reformist democrats, while opposing both the traditional right and radical left. But, as the administration's experience with El Salvador and Guatemala demonstrated, the difficulties with this strategy were legion. In El Salvador (as in Nicaragua and Guatemala) the center reached its political zenith in the early and mid-1970's. Its subsequent decline, precipitated by the failure of reformism, accelerated under the hammer-blows of repression so that by 1979 few centrists remained in the center.[6] Reversing the polarization of politics enough to create a viable center proved to be an impossible task. In both El Salvador and Guatemala, the political initiative continued to rest with the right and the left. Only in Honduras, where the spiral of escalating violence and polarization had not yet begun, did the Carter administration have any real success in advancing the cause of peaceful evolutionary change.

The Reagan administration came to office with a Central American policy that was, rhetorically at least, hostile to Carter's reformism.[7] Reagan de-emphasized human rights, promised to increase military aid to regimes threatened by insurgency, and cast the region's crisis in stark cold war terms. By implication, the United States appeared ready once again to enlist on the side of the old order in Central America. However, regional, global, and domestic realities have limited the administration's ability to pursue such a policy. Although it remains skeptical of social reform, reticent to stress human rights, and more willing than its predecessor to dispense military aid, it has been unable to ignore completely either reform or human rights. Congressional concern over the administration's preference for military measures has produced legislative limits on its actions in both El Salvador and Guatemala. The administration's re-

---

[5] For a full explication of this policy, see "Statement by Assistant Secretary of State Viron P. Vaky Before the Subcommittee on Inter-American Affairs, U.S. House of Representatives, September 11, 1979" (Washington, D.C., Department of State, 1979).

[6] Montgomery, *Revolution, passim.*

[7] The classic statement of this policy is Jeane Kirkpatrick, "Dictatorships and Double Standards," *Commentary*, 68, no. 5 (November 1979), 34–45.

sponse thus far has been to try to circumvent such limits rather than seek an alternative policy responsive to congressional concerns.

COEXISTING WITH NICARAGUA

Three years after the Sandinists' victory over Anastasio Somoza's National Guard, the Nicaraguan Revolution is still struggling to define the contours of its political and economic future. The United States is still struggling to define both its relationship to the new revolutionary government and, implicitly, the tolerable limits within which Washington will accept ideological heterogeneity in Central America.

Despite the Carter administration's best efforts, the collapse of the Somoza regime left the Sandinist National Liberation Front (FSLN) as the dominant political force in Nicaragua. The nine-member national directorate of the FSLN functions as the *de facto* executive power. Sandinists comprise a majority of the governing junta and the quasi-legislative council of state. They also hold all the key ministerial portfolios, including state security and the armed forces. Despite this near-monopoly of important political resources, the Sandinists have not moved to turn Nicaragua into "another Cuba." By retaining a significant degree of political pluralism and a mixed economy weighted toward the private sector, they have tried to preserve the unity of the multi-class coalition that overthrew Somoza. This has not been an easy task, and the FSLN has not been entirely successful at it.[8]

The Sandinists' pragmatic policies are the product of both domestic circumstances and international alignments. The FSLN itself is by no means ideologically monolithic—a fact too often overlooked in the United States. In order to build a movement powerful enough to defeat Somoza, the FSLN intentionally broadened its ranks in the late 1970's to encompass elements of the social democratic and Christian left.[9] The success of this strategy produced a movement that is by no means uniformly Marxist, let alone Marxist-Leninist, in its orientation.

[8] On postrevolutionary policy in Nicaragua, see George Black, *Triumph of the People: The Sandinista Revolution in Nicaragua* (London, 1981); Thomas W. Walker, ed., *Nicaragua in Revolution* (New York, 1982).

[9] William M. LeoGrande, "The Revolution in Nicaragua," *Foreign Affairs*, 58, no. 1 (Fall 1979), 28–50.

The FSLN's relationship with the private sector has been the central dynamic of Nicaraguan politics over the past three years. In a polity still without clear institutional procedures, the FSLN and the private sector confront one another in a fluid, ongoing clash of power and influence. The FSLN controls the state; the private sector controls most of the economy. The FSLN is anxious to secure the private sector's cooperation in the task of economic recovery; the private sector is anxious to secure greater influence within the emerging political system. Thus there exists an uneasy symbiosis that erupts periodically in political crisis as one side tests the resolve of the other. Thus far, such crises have always abated as a result of discussions or negotiations between the two contenders, but the potential for deeper conflict is obviously acute.

Within the Sandinist leadership, the pragmatists have thus far been able to contain the ideologues who prefer a new Nicaragua modelled on Cuba. This containment has been possible because the task of economic recovery has held the highest priority, and economic recovery requires the cooperation of the private sector. Containment also requires substantial external economic assistance, which has been coming largely from Western nations (e.g., Mexico, Venezuela, Western Europe). A sharp radicalization of the Revolution, including an end to pluralism and the expropriation of the private sector, would most likely put an end to such external aid. The Soviet Union has shown no eagerness to provide Nicaragua with the sort of aid it needs to keep the economy functioning.[10]

In early 1982, however, the issue of national security emerged as a priority equal to economic development. The emphasis on national security has been prompted by a high perception of threat and has led to an unprecedented expansion of Nicaragua's military capability. The FSLN's fear of being attacked is by no means totally unfounded. Former members of Somoza's National Guard have launched scores of attacks on Nicaraguan border areas from base camps in Honduras—camps that the Honduran armed forces either cannot or will not control. Tensions with Honduras itself have been high.

The Reagan administration's cold war rhetoric, its suspension

[10] *Washington Post*, May 10, 1982.

of economic aid to Nicaragua, its efforts to block multilateral aid, and its reported covert operations against the Sandinists have all served to exacerbate the FSLN's fears that Washington is intent upon destabilizing their government. From Managua, the threat appears real enough to warrant defensive preparations. Since most of Nicaragua's arms come from the Eastern bloc, an expansion of military capabilities inevitably strengthens Nicaragua's relations with Cuba, the Soviet Union, and Eastern Europe.[11]

If the need to bolster national security comes to overshadow the need for economic recovery, the prospects for pluralism in Nicaragua will diminish accordingly. To build its economy, Nicaragua must rely upon the West, but to defend itself it must rely upon the East.

The Reagan administration's objective in its policy of hostility toward Nicaragua is difficult to decipher. Perhaps the aim is to destabilize Nicaragua to the point that the FSLN can be ousted by its internal opponents. Given the FSLN's control of the armed forces and its level of organized popular support, however, this outcome seems extremely unlikely under any circumstances. Perhaps Washington's strategy is simply to set the stage for direct intervention, but both hemispheric and domestic opposition to such action would be overwhelming. In the wake of the Malvinas crisis, it is doubtful that the United States could find any Latin American country willing to endorse or participate in such an undertaking.

The policy of hostility may simply be aimed at intimidating the Sandinists in the hope that fear will lead them to change policies the Reagan administration finds objectionable (e.g., their policy toward El Salvador, their relations with Cuba, and their domestic strategy). If this is Washington's intent, it is likely to be counterproductive, just as it was in the early 1960's when applied to Cuba.

Finally, it may be that Washington has decided that Nicaragua is already irretrievably "lost" and that the best policy is one that makes a negative example of the Sandinist Revolution. If this is the objective of the United States, then the policy of hos-

[11]On March 9, 1982, the Central Intelligence Agency and Defense Intelligence Agency gave a joint press briefing detailing the Nicaraguan military buildup. The text of the briefing is in the *New York Times*, March 10, 1982.

tility is designed intentionally to produce a radicalization of the Nicaraguan Revolution. If Nicaragua follows a Cuban path of development, it will lose its international financial support from the Socialist International and the multinational lending agencies; it will suffer economically from the departure of the managerial skills of the private sector and from the difficulties of planning a backward economy; and it will "prove" the Reagan administration's contention that moderate democrats are inevitably the losers in coalitions with radical revolutionary forces. This could well strain the alliance in El Salvador between the political forces grouped in the Democratic Revolutionary Front (FDR) and the guerrilla forces grouped in the Farabundo Martí National Liberation Front (FMLN), and prevent the emergence of a similar coalition in Guatemala. Instead of being a new example and inspiration for those who desire to build a democratic socialist society, Nicaragua would become simply "another Cuba."

Apart from such Machiavellian calculations, a radicalization of the Nicaraguan Revolution is not, in fact, in the interests of the United States. To prevent such a development, Washington ought to be reinforcing Nicaragua's economic ties with the West rather than trying to sever them, and trying to reduce the Sandinists' perception of external threat rather than exacerbating it. A Marxist-Leninist Nicaragua militarily aligned with and dependent upon the Soviet Union would be the worst possible outcome for the United States, yet it is precisely the outcome being made most likely by Washington's current policy.

SEARCHING FOR A SOLUTION IN EL SALVADOR

Today, the Central American crisis is most acute in El Salvador. The political roots of the current conflict trace back to 1972 when the military government robbed the reformist Christian Democrats of electoral victory by a fraudulent ballot count. Radical opposition, some of it armed, grew rapidly over the next few years, and the government responded with repression, thus setting off a familiar spiral of violence and political decay.[12]

During the summer of 1979 the Carter administration, in line with its policy of promoting reform and bolstering the political

[12] Montgomery, *Revolution*, pp. 119ff.

center, urged the Salvadoran military regime to ease the level of violence. President Romero refused, and in October he was ousted by progressive military officers who promised the sorts of reforms favored in Washington.[13]

The new government quickly incorporated civilian leaders of the moderate opposition and even suggested its willingness to reach some accommodation with the armed opposition. It promised the eventual creation of democratic institutions and significant social reforms designed to break the economic dominance of the nation's landed oligarchy. Unfortunately, the October government proved to be incapable of carrying out its promises—a failure due primarily to the internal politics of the Salvadoran armed forces. The military, which had historically governed in ways congenial to the landed oligarchy, was by no means united in its enthusiasm for reform. From October to December 1979, the reform efforts of the civilians and progressive officers were blocked at every stage by the rightist officers. The result was governmental paralysis.

The October government's inaction alienated the armed opposition, which gave up on any possibility of working with the new regime, and the mere suggestion of reform terrified the oligarchy, which proceeded to escalate the violence of the "death squads." Amidst this worsening violence, the civilian members of the government sought a showdown with the officers, demanding that reforms be implemented. The armed forces refused, the civilians resigned, and the government moved sharply to the right.

U.S. policy did not change, however. The Carter administration ignored the new political complexion of the Salvadoran regime, acting as if it were still dealing with a moderate, centrist, reformist government. The willingness of the Christian Democrats to participate in the new regime and the eventual passage of limited reforms under intense pressure from Washington gave some credence to this characterization. On one fundamental issue, however, the governments of October and January were distinctly different. The October government had been willing to open a dialogue with the armed groups, with the goal of eventually ending El Salvador's political crisis by accommodation.

[13] William M. LeoGrande and Carla Anne Robbins, "Oligarchs and Officers: The Crisis in El Salvador," *Foreign Affairs*, 58, no. 5 (Summer 1980), 1084–1103.

The government of officers and Christian Democrats had, as its first priority, the defeat of the armed opposition, both politically and militarily.

Through 1980 and early 1981, the "moderate" facade of the Salvadoran government slipped inexorably away. The level of official violence against noncombatants escalated dramatically, rather than receding as the Christian Democrats promised it would. The reforms stalled in the face of obstruction from within the government and resistance by the oligarchy. And within the armed forces, the rightist officers consolidated their hold on power by removing the progressive officers from command positions. The rightward shift of the regime was chronicled through an ongoing stream of Christian Democratic resignations.

The political center, which the Carter administration hoped to promote, ended up split by the polarization of politics. When Reagan came to office, the center-right was in the government but had little discernible influence over policy, while the center-left was in alliance with the guerrillas.

The Reagan administration's initial policy toward El Salvador was more military than political in its orientation. A sharp increase in military aid was authorized and, in a reversal of Carter's policy, the aid was no longer tied to human rights or progress in the reform program. The crisis in El Salvador was posed in cold war terms: "a classic case of indirect armed aggression by communist powers," according to the State Department White Paper justifying the new policy.[14] Whether intentionally or not, this new policy had the effect of further undermining the influence of the Christian Democrats who, without any significant domestic constituency, relied upon the support of the United States for their survival in the governing coalition. The right in the Salvadoran armed forces was led to believe that the United States supported their drive for a military victory against the guerrillas, and the new U.S. policy was soon followed by a series of major offensives by the army.

The tragedy was that this policy subverted any hope for a negotiated solution to the civil war in early 1981. The failure of the guerrillas' January 1981 offensive convinced the Democratic Revolutionary Front, the opposition coalition of left and center-

[14] *Communist Interference in El Salvador*, Special Report no. 80, February 23, 1981 (Washington, D.C., Department of State, 1981).

left, that they could not win a quick military victory. It also convinced the international supporters of the FDR (Nicaragua, Cuba, Mexico, and the Western European social democrats) that a negotiated solution was preferable to continued conflict.[15] The unwillingness of the United States to endorse any sort of negotiations, and its willingness to supply the Salvadoran armed forces with the arms to wage counterinsurgency war meant, however, that negotiations were impossible.

As an alternative, the United States put forth the idea that elections in March 1982 would constitute a "political solution" to Salvador's crisis. The FDR-FMLN was invited to participate in these elections, on the condition that they first lay down their arms. The left refused, on the grounds that the necessary conditions for holding free elections did not exist. Since 1979, some 30,000 Salvadoran civilians had been murdered by the government's security forces and the paramilitary death squads on the mere suspicion that they might be sympathizers of the left. Moreover, in 1980 the entire leadership of the FDR was kidnapped by a death squad while meeting inside El Salvador. A few days later, their mutilated bodies were found. In light of this history, the FDR-FMLN feared that its electoral petitions and candidate lists would become death lists, and that open campaigning in areas controlled by the government would be impossible. Finally, since El Salvador had never had an honest election, the left doubted that elections designed and administered by its opponents would produce an honest result.[16]

The constituent groups of the FDR-FMLN were divided, however, on what policy to adopt toward the elections. Some groups called upon their supporters to boycott them; others called for voters to deface their ballots (which some 11 percent did). Some groups threatened to disrupt the elections with a military offensive; others promised to simply ignore them. No common strategy was ever arrived at, with the result that none of the strategies proved effective.

The elections were held as scheduled, with a larger turnout of voters than anyone anticipated. Although the Christian Demo-

---

[15] On the attitudes and policies of various external factors, see Richard Feinberg, ed., *Central America: International Dimensions of the Crisis* (New York, 1982).

[16] The FDR-FMLN position on the elections is outlined in an op-ed piece by FDR leader Rubén Zamora in the *Washington Post*, March 21, 1982.

crats won a plurality of the vote, the rightist parties captured a majority between them and immediately formed a coalition to control the Constituent Assembly.

The Reagan administration seized upon the heavy turnout to justify its opposition to negotiations between the government and the FDR-FMLN, calling the election results a "repudiation of the left." Other observers interpreted the turnout as a vote for peace, and still others saw the result as nothing more than an effective effort at voter intimidation.[17] Whichever interpretation is most accurate, there is no doubt that the election's outcome stiffened the Reagan administration's opposition to any sort of negotiated settlement to the war.

Yet the elections did not move the war any closer to conclusion. Any effort to decipher the meaning of the elections must begin with the fundamental, irreducible fact of Salvadoran political life: the political community of that nation is deeply polarized between two opposing camps locked in civil war with one another. The elections were held among the political groups on only one side of this fundamental cleavage. From the outset, it was impossible for such a truncated electoral process to produce a "political solution" to the war.

The elections did, however, rearrange the balance of forces among the groups on the right, with potentially far-ranging consequences. The coalition formed by the extreme-right party ARENA and the rightist PCN has returned to power the traditional elites who ruled El Salvador before 1979. The Christian Democrats have lost what little influence they had prior to the elections, and even the politics of the armed forces have shifted to the right with the removal of Col. Gutiérrez, who was widely regarded as a Christian Democratic supporter. Only intense pressure from the U.S. embassy and the threat of a military coup prevented the complete expulsion of the Christian Democrats from the government.[18] True to their campaign promises, the rightist coalition began immediately to dismantle the agrarian reform begun by the Christian Democrats.

Ironically, the very elections that the Reagan administration so loudly celebrated produced an internal alignment of forces in

[17] *New York Times*, March 30, 1982.
[18] *Washington Post*, April 23, 1982.

El Salvador that further limited the policy options of the United States. With the far right in power, the administration could no longer defend its policy as one of supporting the moderate center against extremes of right and left. With the reforms of 1980 in danger of being reversed, it was also hard-pressed to claim it was supporting an evolutionary strategy of social change. Furthermore, the new Salvadoran government showed no improvement on the human rights record of its predecessor. Thus, all the purported policy objectives of the United States were undercut by the March elections.

Now that the rise of the far right has ruled out any hope of gradually winning the loyalty of the Salvadoran people to the new government and thereby defeating the FDR-FMLN politically, only two solutions remain for the crisis in El Salvador: a military solution, in which one side or the other wins a full military victory, or a politically negotiated settlement between the government and the opposition. The Salvadoran army does not appear to have the military capability to defeat the guerrillas, and the Reagan administration does not appear to have the political capability of involving itself in El Salvador to the extent that would be required to produce a military victory on behalf of its client. Thus, a negotiated solution is still the best available option for the United States, although the rise to power of the far right makes such a solution vastly more difficult to obtain.

THE EXPANDING WAR IN GUATEMALA

The growing crisis in Guatemala may ultimately pose a greater challenge to the United States than the insurrections in either Nicaragua or El Salvador. It is in Guatemala that the economic and strategic stakes are highest and the political dilemma most intractable. The United States has substantial economic interests in Guatemala (over $200 million in investments), far more than in any of the other Central American states now in crisis. Guatemala's size and strategic position on Mexico's southern border give it a geopolitical importance exceeded in Central America only by the Panama Canal.

The United States also has a long history of intimate involvement in Guatemalan politics. In the three decades since the CIA sponsored the ouster of the Arbenz government in 1954, the

United States has been a pivotal actor in Guatemala's internal affairs.[19] The growing political crisis in Guatemala today is, therefore, a much more direct legacy of past U.S. policy than are the crises elsewhere in the region.

The political trajectory of Guatemala over the past two years is strikingly similar to the polarization experienced in neighboring El Salvador. Where the situations in these two countries diverge, it is usually in ways that make the prospects for peaceful change more bleak in Guatemala. Without gainsaying the repressive policies of either Somoza or the pre-1979 Salvadoran military government, neither of those nations underwent the trauma experienced by Guatemala between 1966 and 1974. During those years, the armed forces conducted a concerted and ruthless campaign to rid the nation of "subversives"—a campaign that took the lives of some 20,000 people, most of them peasants. This campaign, supported with U.S. military aid and advisors, demolished not only the small political groups of the radical left, but most of the moderate political parties as well. In 1974, the army delivered the *coup de grâce* to reformism by fixing the presidential election to prevent a moderate general, Efraín Ríos Montt, from coming to power. As in El Salvador, the combination of frustrated reformism and official violence produced a rapidly growing armed opposition to the regime.

When the Carter administration introduced its human rights policy in 1977, the Guatemalan government reacted angrily by refusing to accept further U.S. military assistance. Nevertheless, pressure from Washington did seem to have some initial effect. In 1978, there was a brief political relaxation as the armed forces sought to bring the Christian Democrats into the government in order to broaden its appeal. The conservative views of the Christian Democrats did not noticeably alter the ideological coloration of the regime, but even this small opening in the political process stimulated other opposition forces. The reaction of the right was swift; the political opening closed and, in the first three months of 1979, the two most popular civilian leaders of the moderate opposition, Alberto Fuentes Mohr and Manuel Colom Argueta, were assassinated by death squads.[20]

The effect of these assassinations and the scores more that fol-

---

[19] Schlesinger and Kinser, *Bitter Fruit*.
[20] Simons, "Guatemala."

lowed were reminiscent of the effect Chamorro's assassination had in Nicaragua. The moderate opposition was left demoralized and leaderless, the guerrilla armies of the left gained new adherents, and hopes for evolutionary change faded further.

The level of political violence in Guatemala has escalated over the past two years, but it has not stemmed the growth of the revolutionary opposition. On the contrary, the regime's indiscriminate use of violence against the rural population, most of whom are Indians, has for the first time given the guerrillas a base of popular support among the Indian population.[21]

The Carter administration had no success with Guatemala because it could find no moderate center strong enough to pose a credible alternative to the existing military dictatorship, and it could find no elements within the regime willing to yield to U.S. pressures for reform. The Reagan administration faces this same dilemma, though it is more willing to restore military aid to the current regime despite its brutality. As in the Salvadoran case, the Guatemalan armed forces will have no incentive to moderate their human rights abuses or begin the process of reform so long as they sense that the United States is willing to underwrite their quest for a military victory. Yet if the history of Guatemala proves anything, it proves that the popular pressures for change in that country cannot be contained by force of arms. Twice before—in 1954 and 1974—the military has won clear victories over the opposition by the use of military force. Now, less than a decade later, the regime is faced with a guerrilla opposition stronger than any it has faced before. The political crisis in Guatemala is simply not amenable to military solution, and no amount of bloodshed will ensure long-term stability.

The March coup that ousted Lucas García and installed Ríos Montt in power has not changed the basic realities of Guatemalan politics. Assuming that Ríos Montt can consolidate his position (an assumption that is by no means certain, given the factionalized character of the Guatemalan military at this juncture), and assuming that he is earnest in his promises to end corruption and human rights violations, he is nevertheless limited in his ability to bring about fundamental changes in the midst of the current crisis.[22]

[21] *Ibid.*
[22] *Washington Post*, July 19, 1982.

As yet, Ríos Montt has said nothing about undertaking the sorts of social and economic reforms that would be essential in any effort to avert further warfare, nor has he shown any inclination to negotiate with the guerrilla forces. On the contrary, his reputation as a loyal officer, committed to the military as an institution, does not suggest any openness to negotiations. Thus, there will be little he can do other than to continue prosecuting the war—an agenda that will make any improvement in human rights conditions, particularly in the countryside, difficult to achieve.

In light of this, it would be dangerous for the United States to enlist wholeheartedly with the new Guatemalan government, resuming military assistance and thereby linking U.S. interests with a government that is both precarious and as yet unwilling to undertake the kinds of policies likely to produce an end to the Guatemalan civil war. Unfortunately, the Reagan administration seems intent upon following precisely that hazardous route.

THE OPENING IN HONDURAS

Honduras has thus far avoided the political turmoil and polarization that have swept through Central America. In Honduras, the poorest and most backward nation in the region, the pace of economic development and modernization has been slower over the past three decades than in neighboring countries. At the same time, the Honduran government has reacted to pressures for reform with much less brutality and intransigence. Though the military has ruled since 1963, it has been willing to tolerate organized dissent from political parties, trade unions, peasant leagues, student groups, and the press. There have been no waves of intense and indiscriminate official violence, no plague of "disappearances," and no death squads. In the early 1970's the military government undertook some limited reforms, including the redistribution of land, in order to avert the growth of unrest among the peasantry.

The Honduran government's conciliatory and tolerant attitudes are atypical in Central America. In part, they stem from the absence of a powerful landed oligarchy in Honduras. Agriculture, and therefore the economy as a whole, have long been dominated by U.S. agri-business firms rather than a domestic elite. Unlike the governments in Nicaragua, El Salvador, and Guatemala, the Honduran state has not served primarily as the guardian of oligarchic interests; rather, it has been a channel of upward mobility for state officials who use their posts to enrich themselves by corruption. The result is a regime that, though unsavory and illegitimate, has not catalyzed significant polarization of the political system or armed opposition. This is not to say that the regional crisis has passed Honduras by—only that it is at a much earlier stage of development there, and thus is far less acute.[23]

For all these reasons, Honduras seemed to offer the brightest prospect for a successful "centrist solution" of the sort envisioned by the Carter administration. At the urgings of the United States, the Honduran armed forces held elections in 1980 and 1981 that produced a successful transition to civilian rule.

This transition to democracy, widely regarded as the best and perhaps the only way to avoid the growth of insurgency, has by no means been consolidated. The armed forces still command a major share of political power and contain some officers who would prefer a return to military rule, even if it means increasing repressive violence against opponents.[24] If these hard-line officers should come to predominate in the army, Honduras's democracy will be short-lived. The country would then suffer the same process of polarization and spiralling violence as its neighbors have endured. The policy of the United States should aim at helping to consolidate Honduran democracy by clearly and unequivocally warning the armed forces that good relations with the United States depend upon the maintenance of democratic civilian rule.

The greatest danger for Honduras is that it will be swept up in the tides of political conflict in surrounding countries, particularly Nicaragua and El Salvador. On this score, U.S. policy has been less than helpful. Both the Carter and Reagan administrations cast Honduras in the role of regional armory—the one "island of stability" through which the United States could increase its military presence in the region without provoking

[23] *NACLA Report on the Americas*, special issue on Honduras, 15, no. 6 (Nov.–Dec. 1981).
[24] *New York Times*, September 1, 1981.

sharp international or domestic opposition. It is a role that Honduras's fragile democracy may not be strong enough to sustain without fracturing. The Reagan administration has even gone so far as to utilize Honduras as a base for covert action against the Sandinist government in Nicaragua, thus greatly magnifying the danger of war between the two nations.[25]

It would be particularly tragic if the one country in addition to Costa Rica in Central America that seems to have a chance to avoid civil war should squander its chances by being enticed into the conflicts of the surrounding states. If the intention of the United States is to use Honduras as an instrument of U.S. policy in Nicaragua and El Salvador, Washington should recognize that it is wagering the future of Honduras as well.

ELEMENTS OF A REGIONAL POLICY

Formulating policy in the midst of crisis is always difficult. Normal patterns of political interaction and relationship are ruptured, uncertainty mounts as reliable information becomes scarce, and events always outpace the ability of policy makers to plan for them. When past policy has been oriented toward preserving the status quo, the disruption that comes with crisis seems threatening as well as unpredictable. Policy makers are then tempted to fall back on familiar responses, pursuing them with a vengeance even if they show little sign of producing the desired results.

The depth of the crisis in Central America and its complexity makes such routinized responses very dangerous for the United States. A reformulation of U.S. policy for Central America must begin with an unemotional assessment of U.S. interests in the region, whether they can be safeguarded independently of the survival of rightist military dictatorships, and whether the emergence of revolutionary governments necessarily poses a critical threat to them.

It may be that the traditional U.S. goal of regional stability can no longer be attained in Central America by supporting traditional elites. It may be that the revolutionaries are less the enemies of democracy and human rights than are the military regimes fighting against them. And it may be that less direct U.S.

[25] *Washington Post*, March 10, 1982.

involvement in the region's political and military conflicts offers the best hope of safeguarding U.S. influence and interests.

The most sensible general strategy for the United States to pursue in Central America today is one that seeks to reduce the level of internal violence and the potential for international conflict in the region. This implies a policy in which diplomacy and economic assistance are the principal levers of influence, and military assistance is minimal. In Nicaragua, the United States should try to improve bilateral relations by restoring economic assistance and offering to help reduce tensions on the Nicaraguan-Honduran border. In the case of El Salvador, the United States should join the growing international consensus in favor of a negotiated solution to the civil war and should do its utmost to convince the Salvadoran armed forces to enter into a dialogue with the FDR. In Guatemala, the United States should resist the temptation to increase military aid to the rightist military regime. The withholding of such assistance constitutes the only lever of influence that Washington has to push the regime into some sort of political accommodation that can avoid full-scale war. In Honduras, the United States should make clear to the armed forces that it supports the electoral transition to civilian rule and that U.S. military aid does not constitute an endorsement of either military government or regional intervention.

These are the sorts of policies that offer the best hope of restoring regional stability to Central America, and doing so in a way that benefits the people of the region. In the pursuit of such policies, the United States would enjoy wide support both in Latin America and among our European allies. The greatest danger to the United States in Central America today comes not from the Cubans' support of the FDR in El Salvador, but from a lack of vision in Washington—an apparent unwillingness to look beyond policies of the past, even though they no longer serve us.

Mexico in Central America: The Difficult Exercise of Regional Power

Olga Pellicer

MEXICO'S ROLE in Central America during recent years has prompted analysts of foreign affairs to proclaim the emergence of a "regional power" whose diplomacy poses a counterweight to the influence exercised in the area by the United States and, to a lesser degree, by Cuba and Venezuela.

Although under the terms of the San José energy agreement Mexico established an economic presence of previously unknown proportions in Central America,[1] the most conspicuous part of its role has been related to political concerns. This is understandable; Central American history currently hinges on the issue of political transformation. It is difficult, if not impossible, to reflect on the development of the region without considering at the outset the problem of power and the legitimacy of the ruling class. In Central America, debate centers upon the possibility of achieving social change without either provoking an American intervention, which would repeat the tragic events in Guatemala in 1954, or reinforcing a power structure whose internal contradictions and repressive practices perpetuate instability, increased American military involvement, and prolonged guerrilla warfare. Only political change can create stability in Central America. Mexico's action must be viewed in this context, and its significance will thus depend on the effect it has upon the process of political change.

---

[1] By the terms of this agreement, Mexico and Venezuela commit themselves to supplying up to 160,000 barrels of petroleum daily to the nations of the Central American Isthmus, Santo Domingo, Jamaica, Haiti, and Grenada. Seventy percent of such sales are to be made at current international market rates; the remaining 30% is to be sold on credit, to be paid in five years at an interest rate of 4%. This credit may be extended to a period of twenty years, with an annual interest rate of only 2% if it is applied to priority development projects in the buyer-nations.

The Mexican government cannot be expected to bring about structural changes that lead Central America in the direction of socialism. That role, if it belongs to any nation, belongs to Cuba, and the political cost of such action is so high that it seems improbable—despite American assertions to the contrary—that Cuba's leaders are disposed to undertake it. What is expected of Mexico, based on its government's interest in the ideology of revolution and its traditions in foreign policy, is a different role: that it act as a force to inhibit American interventionist tendencies; that it support revolutionary governments; and that it promote the establishment, in the region of Central America and the Caribbean Basin, of an international order that would permit the coexistence of regimes with a plurality of ideological, economic, and political orientations.

Mexico's credentials for this role include, to begin with, the capacity for dialogue with the revolutionary forces in Central America that have frequently found asylum there and, secondly, its good relations with the United States. It is correctly believed that the interest of American leaders in maintaining good relations with Mexico makes the opinion of the Mexican government important in the formation of American policy toward Central America. However, it is not easy for a world power to include the voices of so-called regional powers in its decision-making process, particularly when the regional powers try to follow an independent political path. Mexican action has perhaps inhibited more decisive American intervention in Nicaragua, but it has not succeeded in bringing about a negotiated solution to the civil war in El Salvador, the opening of a dialogue between the United States and Cuba, or the normalization of relations with Nicaragua. It is too soon, though, to reach definitive conclusions about the significance of Mexico's actions in Central America. In an atmosphere of accelerated change, both internal and external, diverse factors will affect the area in the near future.

MEXICO'S POLITICAL ACTION IN
CENTRAL AMERICA: A SUMMARY

Mexico's political action in Central America has taken three distinct paths in recent years: (1) support for the Sandinist government in Nicaragua; (2) attempts to achieve a negotiated solution to the civil war in El Salvador; and (3) global initiatives in support of mechanisms to relieve tensions in the area and open the way for coexistence among regimes of different kinds.

Mexico's most important commitment to the Sandinist movement was marked by its break with the regime of Anastasio Somoza in May 1979. It is difficult to assess the influence of this decision on the subsequent military confrontation. Doubtless, the action taken by Mexico precipitated the international ostracism of Somoza and created the circumstances in which it became unproductive to seek, by means of the Organization of American States, some collective action that would obstruct what was already visibly a Sandinist victory. Shortly afterward, Mexico expressed its support for the Sandinist government of reconstruction, playing a key role in the knotty problem of renegotiating the Nicaraguan public debt. In this capacity, Mexico not only provided technical assistance but also vouched for the Sandinist government during the early stages of negotiation. This marked the beginning of a policy of cooperation with Nicaragua that has made Mexico one of the most important supporters of that country's revolution. Thus, according to the U.N. Secretary General's report on assistance to Nicaragua, between 1979 and 1981 Mexico donated, in cash and in kind, a total of $39,509,900, an amount exceeded only by Cuba. Mexico contributed approximately 21 percent of the total aid received during that period. As for bilateral loans granted to Nicaragua in that period, Mexico granted $72,900,000, exceeded only by Libya; it accounted for 14 percent of the total sum loaned bilaterally to Nicaragua.[2]

Thus, Mexico's economic support of Nicaragua has been steady; its effort to lessen hostility against the Sandinist government, however, has not been as fruitful. The most important efforts in that regard have been made vis-à-vis the United States; for example, it is worth remembering the position of the Mexican president on the occasion of Secretary of State Alexander Haig's visit to Mexico in November 1981. Several days prior to the visit, López Portillo made his position clear by announcing to American television reporters what he would tell Haig: that it would be "a gigantic historical error to decide in favor of Amer-

[2]United Nations, *Assistance to Nicaragua: Report of the Secretary General* (A/36/280; New York, November 5, 1981).

ican intervention in Cuba or Nicaragua." The firm tone of this statement, and the proposals made to Haig concerning the necessity of a "verbal truce" to minimize the Central American tensions caused by the U.S. government's indictments of Cuba and Nicaragua, gave some idea of the Mexican government's commitment to defending Nicaragua in talks with American representatives.[3]

The second main theme in Mexico's political action toward Central America concerns the search for a negotiated solution to the civil war in El Salvador. The Mexican government's interest in Salvadoran affairs deepened at the beginning of 1981, following three events: the rapid decay of the government that had emerged after the military coup of 1979, growing opposition to that government, and the shift in American policy toward El Salvador following the inauguration of President Ronald Reagan.

It is important to remember that toward the end of 1980 Mexico received various Salvadorans who had been a part of the junta headed by Napoleón Duarte and who had subsequently left El Salvador, convinced that the junta did not hold real political power, that this power now rested in the hands of the military. Their statements to the Mexican press, and information they released concerning violence and repression exercised by paramilitary forces in El Salvador, coincided with the emergence of new opposition groups in conjunction with the grass-roots acceptance of the revolutionary movement in El Salvador. The best example of this was the formation in Mexico in January 1981 of the Diplomatic-Political Commission of the Democratic Revolutionary Front. Even as the scope of the Salvadoran conflict was widening, the new Republican administration in the United States began to outline its policy hinged on the idea that the revolutionary struggle stemmed from communist subversion backed by Cuba and the Soviet Union; in response, a massive program of military and economic aid was launched to assist the junta led by Duarte.[4]

[3] The dominant note of Haig's visit to Mexico was the discussion of Central America, a topic avoided in previous meetings of López Portillo and United States representatives. Cf. the Mexican press on November 24–25, 1981.

[4] It would take us too far afield to attempt here a summary of the origin and characteristics of the Reagan administration's policy in Central America. There already exists an abundant literature on the subject. Among publications in Spanish, see Luis Maira, "La política latinoamericana de la administración Reagan; del diseño armonioso a las

The American position elicited a number of responses from the Mexican government; in the first place, Mexico found unacceptable the ease with which certain factors were excluded from the analysis of the situation in El Salvador, namely the decay of the junta and the actual power exercised by the more repressive military factions. Second, the Mexican government viewed with apprehension the return to a view of international relations characterized by emphasis on the East-West conflict and the consequent reduction of weaker nations to the role of mere "spheres of influence" of the world powers. Finally, Mexico asserted that military aid to the junta would prolong, without resolving, a bloody confrontation whose level of violence has few precedents in Latin American history.

Throughout the first half of 1981 it was not yet clear what path Mexico would take to influence events in El Salvador. It seemed that, somewhat constrained by its adherence to a policy of nonintervention, the Mexican government would limit itself to supporting the right of the Salvadoran people to self-determina-tion. However, the military stalemate between opposition forces and the Salvadoran army supported by the United States, in addition to the growing possibility of an international confrontation, indicated the need for more decisive action by the Mexican government. Mexico decided to present a communiqué jointly with France to the Security Council of the United Nations, calling for an end to the violence in El Salvador by means of negotiations that would recognize the legitimacy of the forces rallied around the Democratic Revolutionary Front (FDR) and the Farabundo Martí National Liberation Front (FMLN).[5] This communiqué offered an alternative to the Reagan policy; comments to this effect in the U.N. General Assembly in 1981 indicated the degree to which various nations were willing to use the communiqué as a basis for resolving the conflict in El Salvador.

The Franco-Mexican communiqué brought to a climax Mex-

---

primeras dificultades"; and José Miguel Insulza, "La crisis en Centroamérica y el Caribe y la seguridad de los Estados Unidos." Both articles were published in *Centroamérica: Crisis y política internacional* (Mexico, 1982).

[5] The communiqué, released August 28, 1981, recognizes the FDR and the FMLN as "representative political forces," and calls upon the international community to "facilitate an understanding among the representatives of the opposing political forces in El Salvador with the aim of reestablishing peace in the nation and avoiding all outside interference in Salvadoran affairs."

ican efforts to promote a negotiated solution to the Salvadoran civil war; however, such a solution has proved elusive owing to internal and external circumstances. Although opposition forces declared their willingness to negotiate as of mid-1981, their declaration evoked no echo from the ranks of Duarte's government despite the confidence of some observers that pressure could be applied to the government by such groups as the church, students, intellectuals, and various members of the petit bourgeoisie.[6] Clearly, the crucial factor in bringing about negotiations would have been the easing of the U.S. government's insistence on pushing the formula, "Elections plus antiguerrilla warfare." This easing, however, appears unlikely as long as Central American affairs are viewed by the Reagan administration through a lens focused on the danger posed by Cuba and the Nicaraguan Revolution to the security and strategic interests of the United States.[7] Only the discovery of some way to minimize the deep suspicion with which the United States regards these two countries can lead to less hostile relations between the American government and the revolutionary movements in Central America.

Given these circumstances, the next step taken by the Mexican government took the form of a global initiative proposing a way to handle the whole Central American and Caribbean situation. President López Portillo formulated it in Managua on February 21, 1982, when he accepted the Order of Augusto César Sandino. He identified three "nuclei" of conflict in Central America: Nicaragua, El Salvador, and the relations between Cuba and the United States. In his opinion, the third nucleus was of greatest consequence, and the solutions of the first two depended on its resolution. With regard to El Salvador, López

[6] Cf. Román Mayorga's article, "Una solución política negociada para El Salvador," in *Foro Internacional*, no. 84 (April–June 1981).

[7] We must not lose sight of the fact that the Caribbean Basin is considered a "third border" of the United States. One-half of America's foreign trade, two-thirds of its petroleum imports, and a number of strategic minerals pass across this "border"; it is estimated that in the event of a war 50% of supplies for American troops in Europe would be transported across the same zone. This lends some credibility to the theory that Cuba and the Soviet Union might be interested in extending their influence among the countries in the area. Such an interest has yet to be demonstrated, but this has not prevented the Reagan administration from advancing the idea that United States security is endangered. True or not, it seems improbable that the U.S. government would allow any course of events in Central America that could lead to a military alliance with the Soviet Union.

Portillo reiterated the necessity of finding a negotiated solution to the internal crisis, and he emphasized that the elections of March 28, as then envisioned, would not put an end to the military confrontation. As for Cuban-American relations, he noted the value of an exchange of views on Central American affairs by both nations, and he announced Mexico's willingness to continue acting as intermediary between the two (it may be worth recalling that in November 1981 the Mexican government had arranged the meeting of Alexander Haig and the Cuban vice-president Carlos Rafael Rodríguez). With respect to Nicaragua, President López Portillo was even more explicit. He proposed talks between Nicaragua and the United States based on the following terms: (1) the United States would refrain from all threats and use of force against Nicaragua; (2) a program of mutual arms reduction would be set up and implemented; Nicaragua would stop arming on the assurance that Somocista bands operating on the Honduran border—and in the United States—would be disarmed; and (3) nonaggression pacts would be signed between Nicaragua and the United States, and also between Nicaragua and its neighbors. López Portillo asserted that Mexico was qualified to initiate dialogue between Nicaragua and the government of the United States.[8]

Mexico's proposal entailed the acceptance of new realities in the Central American–Caribbean region; at the same time, it recognized that the process of political change would be limited by the U.S. government's refusal to accept any military situation that might endanger American security. In fact, behind the proposal to open dialogue between Cuba and the United States and improve American relations with Nicaragua lay the implicit assumption that the United States would accept as irreversible the expansion from the Caribbean Basin of regimes that diverge from an orthodox capitalist model or display a diversity of international economic and political alliances. In compensation, the proposal advocated balanced arms reductions in Nicaragua, thus canceling the possibility of an arms buildup there that could lead to a situation similar to the Cuban Missile Crisis of 1962. Finally, in taking the initial step in setting up a new framework for international relations in the area and in offering

[8] Cf. the Mexican press on February 22–23, 1982.

its services as a mediator among the United States, Cuba, and Nicaragua, Mexico clearly established its status as a nation with regional influence.

THE REAGAN ADMINISTRATION AND THE CONSOLIDATION OF REGIONAL POWERS

The U.S. reaction to Mexico's peace initiative for Central America was not uniform. On the contrary, it reflected the dichotomy in approaches to Central American policy that exists between numerous sectors of public opinion on the one hand, and the Reagan administration on the other. Thus, while the news media and certain members of Congress responded favorably, the State Department displayed no interest in the proposal and set about discouraging the Mexican foreign minister from acting as a mediator in Central American affairs.

No action taken by Mexican diplomacy in the recent past has gotten such widespread coverage in the American press. It is worth noting that between March 5 and March 21, 1982, thirty-seven relevant news releases, and seventeen editorials and by-lined articles, appeared in the *New York Times*, the *Washington Post*, the *Christian Science Monitor*, and the *Wall Street Journal*. Their tone is reflected in the following excerpts:

"Mexico's effort," commented the *New York Times*,

can have an immediate and beneficial result. It can pull combatants apart before they strike irrevocable blows. And it can open space for diplomacy by other countries, notably Venezuela and Costa Rica, removing the odor of unilateralism from Washington's case. In fact, without Mexican involvement, there can be no Central American policy worthy of the name. . . . Why, then, has it taken so long for the Administration to warm up to Mexico's repeated calls for negotiation?[9]

Similarly, the *Washington Post* observed:

United States policy in Central America ought to be based on three elements. The first is support, meaning aid and the encouragement of reform, for friendly and reasonably worthy governments. The second is military nonintervention—the only position likely to bring an American president the requisite domestic leeway and international company, especially Latin company. The third is negotiation. The Reagan administration has not done all that it might on the first two points but

[9] *New York Times*, March 17, 1982, p. A22.

it has been especially deficient on the third. That is the significance of the latest meeting of the foreign secretaries of Mexico and the United States. It offered the brightest glimmer to date of American interest in the negotiating track.[10]

It is evident that opinions in favor of greater recognition of Mexico's point of view bore a direct relation to impatience with the Reagan administration's policies. However, the American government felt no need to make concessions to these outspoken critics. In the second half of March, Haig met with Secretary Castañeda in New York to discuss the Mexican proposal. The outcome of this meeting was negative. In Haig's opinion the proposal suffered from a serious deficiency in failing to note the central point of contention between the United States and Nicaragua: the shipment of arms to El Salvador. Furthermore, Haig recalled that the United States had—since August 1981—presented some proposals of its own for the normalization of relations with Nicaragua, but without success. The limited role Haig assigned to Mexico in the search for a solution to Central American problems is well expressed by the following statement:

Mexico can play an important role in facilitating contact. Secretary Castañeda already did that in November when I met with Cuban Vice President Rodríguez in Mexico City. I am hopeful that Mexico will continue and go on playing that kind of a role. It's most helpful. Of course any such meetings will have to be strictly bilateral, and the United States will present and receive proposals on its own behalf.[11]

As Haig made these remarks, the State Department telegraphed its major embassies to guard against the possibility that press reports might give the erroneous impression that Haig's meeting with Castañeda had modified to any extent the two current priorities of U.S. policy toward Central America: the holding of elections in El Salvador and the presentation of a development plan for the Caribbean. In short, the Republican administration does not share the editorial opinion that "without Mexican involvement, there can be no Central American policy worthy of the name."

The Reagan administration's disregard for Mexico's point of view may be explained in several ways. For one thing, as indi-

[10] *Washington Post*, March 16, 1982, p. A22.
[11] *New York Times*, March 16, 1982, p. A6.

cated above, the Mexican proposal entails a change in the hegemonic role assumed by the United States in Central American
affairs. It calls, moreover, for the recognition of a plurality of
regimes committed to diversifying their international alliances,
and also for the incorporation of regional powers in constructing a new international order for the area. A second explanation
is the adherence by various spokesmen of the Reagan administration to the "domino theory," according to which the ultimate target of Central American revolutionaries lies inside
Mexico's borders. Those who hold this view believe that the
Mexican government has been "misreading" events in Central
America, and that Mexico's understanding will correct itself
only when problems along its southern border force it to acknowledge that the defense of Mexican security coincides with
the American government's interpretation of events in Central
America.[12]

This is not to say that the Reagan administration has overlooked the advantages of seeming interested in Mexico's participation in Central American affairs. Nonetheless, the United
States has sought Mexico's participation primarily in the economic sphere, just as it has tried repeatedly to involve other nations on the continent in its economic policy toward Central
America. In mid-1981 the White House issued a report on Central America that emphasized economic concerns. To deal with
them, the report recommended a program of economic aid
so massive that it was described by commentators as a "mini-
Marshall Plan." However, from the beginning the American
government emphasized that it did not intend to pursue the enterprise single-handedly. Other nations with interests in the region were also expected to participate: Venezuela, Canada, and
Mexico. For this purpose, delegates of the U.S. government met
with the others in Nassau on July 10, 1981. This is not the place
to discuss the myriad factors that made the "Nassau Convention" unworkable, or the circumstances in which the Program
of Caribbean Development was finally unveiled to the American
public in February 1982 as a unilateral action on the part of the

[12] One might advance the hypothesis that certain American groups, particularly inside the CIA, have a specific interest in fomenting episodes in Southeastern Mexico that
would substantiate the danger posed to Mexican security by Central American revolutionaries. In this kind of enterprise Mexican-Guatemalan relations play a key role.

United States.[13] Suffice it to note the severe discrepancy between these invitations to assume responsibility for aid programs and the American decision not to take Mexico's voice into account in the handling of political issues.

The Mexican initiative could be rejected by the Reagan administration only in the wake of the elections in El Salvador. The very act of holding elections (a sign of the opposition's inability to paralyze activity in urban areas), and their manipulation so as to give the appearance of massive electoral participation, had the effect of neutralizing for a time the discontent within the United States. Nonetheless, once the publicity for the "triumph of democracy" had died down, the grave problems in El Salvador reasserted themselves. Moreover, the government established by the elections gave new strength to the more disreputable of El Salvador's ruling groups, whose repressive practices and opposition to economic reform are well known; the figure of Roberto D'Aubuisson is merely the most conspicuous example. The Reagan administration could no longer claim to be dealing with a reform government committed to the protection of human rights. Guerrilla warfare, in this context, seems more defensible; the elections have resulted in a greater polarization that in turn makes an end to Salvadoran violence even less likely. Not surprisingly, the critics of Reagan's Central American policy are once again raising their voices; hence, also, the growing fears of military intervention, which these critics hope to prevent through congressional action.

The conflict in the Malvinas Islands (Falklands) reduced Central American concerns to a secondary status, temporarily at least. Quite possibly, however, these concerns will resurface in the near future. What will happen then? Specifically, what hope

[13] The Reagan administration's economic initiative for the Caribbean is "a program which will create conditions in which creativity and private enterprise will flourish"; its chief elements include free trade in Caribbean Basin products exported to the United States for a period of twelve years. Despite the fact that 82 percent of these countries' exports already enter the American market tariff-free under the Generalized Preference System, it is somewhat disingenuously hoped that the economic plan will encourage fresh investments in the region. At the same time, to make the area more attractive to American investors, Reagan announced monetary incentives and an attempt to set up bilateral investment agreements with Caribbean nations. He also announced that Congress would be asked to approve a complementary allocation of $350 million for fiscal 1982, most of which would be channeled into El Salvador. For assorted commentary on this initiative, see *Foreign Policy*, no. 47 (Summer 1982).

is there for the Mexican attempt to activate mechanisms that can lessen the tensions in that part of the world?

Any speculation about the future political action of Mexico in Central America must be based on the assumption that the most probable scenario for the region, in the absence of a counteracting force, will be characterized by prolonged and extended guerrilla warfare in El Salvador and Guatemala and the consequent military involvement of the United States; increased difficulty for the Sandinist government in trying to pursue its program of economic reconstruction in the face of internal obstacles aggravated by the undercover actions of the United States; and the American effort, particularly at the level of rhetoric and propaganda, to implement a program of development in Honduras and Costa Rica on the model of the Program of Caribbean Development, including creation of a favorable climate for American investment, extension of tariff preferences in the United States for the products imported from those countries, and a modest program of economic aid.

In this context, also conditioned by the state of relations between the United States and the Soviet Union, there exists the danger of an escalated military conflict and the transformation of the area into a theater for East-West confrontation. The Mexican proposal's concern with minimizing tension in Central America and making room for a process of political change will thus continue to have relevance. This is not to suggest that the influence of the proposal, or even the continued presentation of similar proposals, is guaranteed; this will depend on a diversity of internal and external circumstances among which we may cite, in the first place, the rapport established by Mexican diplomacy with the revolutionary forces in Central America. In this regard it is worth pointing out that the Mexican initiative has been well received in Nicaragua, a fact confirmed by the Sandinists' call for the opening of talks with the United States—talks at which they requested the presence of representatives from Mexico. Meanwhile, the leaders of the FDR and the FMLN have set forth negotiation proposals that closely parallel the ideas in the Franco-Mexican communiqué. As for Cuba, it has openly shown an interest in opening dialogue with the United States, and Vice-President Carlos Rafael Rodríguez enthusiastically attended the meeting with Haig set up by Mexico in November 1981. In summary, Mexico is the only nation in Latin America that has gained the trust of revolutionary forces in Central America and the Caribbean. This fact should not go unnoticed, since it legitimates and renders indispensable Mexico's role as an international mediator.

The second major factor to take into account is the United States. We have cited the sympathy for the Mexican initiatives expressed in the American press. If the executive branch has ignored the call to listen to the Mexican proposal, this may be in part because it had other cards to play in Central America—the elections and the Program of Caribbean Development—and in part because it could count on the support of most Latin American countries for its policy in Central America, as confirmed by the vote taken in the OAS General Assembly in November 1981 concerning the elections in El Salvador. Both of these situations are in flux, however; neither the elections nor the outlined development plan were able to forestall either the conservative shift of the Salvadoran regime or the continuation of the guerrilla struggle. The chief weaknesses of Reagan's policy (and the reason it is continually under attack by public opinion) lie in its inability to deal with these two problems. More recently, the reaction of Latin American countries against the United States as a result of the aid given to Great Britain in its conflict with Argentina has provoked a serious rift in the alliances upon which part of the U.S. position in Central America rested. Argentina has recalled the military advisors it sent to El Salvador to support American actions; the Inter-American Treaty of Reciprocal Assistance cannot be invoked by the United States to justify intervention in Nicaragua; and it seems unlikely that there could be another OAS meeting at which Latin America votes solidly in favor of the United States' position. Thus, at least in the short run, Latin American support for the Reagan policy has diminished. Although this does not necessarily imply a shift toward the acceptance of Mexico's proposals, it does open the way for new alliances and approaches that could lend support to some of the points made in the proposals. Another thing to consider is the change in Venezuelan policy toward Central America and the Caribbean that could follow the election of an Acción Democrático candidate in 1983. As we know, a vulnerable point of the present Venezuelan government has been its identification with the United States in Central American and specifically Salvadoran affairs. Quite possibly, the internal discontent provoked by that policy could weaken the party in power and result in its replacement by a government that would almost certainly orient Venezuelan foreign policy in directions coinciding with those of Mexico.

Finally, it is necessary to round out this exploration of future scenarios with a look at Mexico's internal situation and its influence on the continuity (or lack thereof) of Mexico's political action in Central America. The intention of the Mexican political elite to follow the path traced by López Portillo's administration is by no means assured. Various indicators, among them the limited support afforded to the Franco-Mexican communiqué and reluctance to continue sending aid to Nicaragua in the face of Mexico's own grave economic problems, suggest that in recent years the official Central American policy has not fully taken hold of the Mexican political elite's imagination. Support for the policy has come mainly from the chief executive, the foreign minister, and certain sectors of the Partido Revolucionario Institucional (PRI). Their enthusiasm is not shared by the defense minister and other sectors of the government. Although rejection of Mexico's fundamental guiding principles in Central American policy (refusal to employ force, adherence to self-determination, and nonintervention) is unlikely, there might well be a policy reversal regarding negotiation with opposition forces, economic and political aid to the Sandinist government, and efforts to achieve, among other objectives, the opening of a dialogue between the United States and Cuba. Maintaining the Mexican policy as proposed would require the conviction that political change in Central America, within a framework of peaceful coexistence guaranteed by an understanding between Cuba and the United States, is related directly to Mexican interests in the economic sphere and also to its national security. This conviction is not widespread in Mexico, partly because of the traditional indifference of the society toward international problems that do not impinge directly upon its own interests, and partly because the geopolitical considerations linking Mexico's destiny to that of the Caribbean Basin have only recently been perceived and attended to by the Mexican political elite.

Despite the opinions so frequently expressed about Mexico's importance as a regional power, in fact the country has no such tradition. On the contrary, until recently Central America and the Caribbean occupied a minor place in the priorities of Mexican foreign policy. Interest in regional affairs is a new concern; not surprisingly, the Mexican government lacks well-articulated and persuasive arguments capable of weaving consensus among Mexican power groups to support its political action in Central America. It will take the next few years fully to assess the Mexican government's ability to popularize these arguments; also, some time must elapse before it is possible to assess the degree to which Mexico is committed to the role of limiting United States hegemony and making room for a political transformation of Central American nations in the direction of economic development and stability.

Mexican Policy Toward Central America in the Context of U.S.-Mexico Relations

Mario Ojeda

THERE ARE always two clear dangers in the analysis of conjunctural factors. The first is that, by the time the analysis is published, much of the content has been superseded by subsequent events. The second is that the author, who is necessarily immersed in the midst of the events themselves, can be excessively influenced by the mood of the moment and may confuse the essential with the merely accidental or peripheral, for lack of sufficient historical perspective. In other words, according to the old saying, he runs the risk of not seeing the forest for the trees.

At the risk of committing these errors, which are discussed more in order to warn the reader than to provide a precautionary justification for the author, this work attempts to analyze Mexican policy toward Central America in the context of United States–Mexico relations and in light of the situation that obtained in 1981–82. The principal problem is related to this latter point. In the author's judgment, the current situation suggests that important changes have occurred not only in the international-regional context within which relations between the two countries take place, but also internally within both countries. The magnitude and real effects of these changes on relations between the two countries cannot be accurately foreseen.

This paper begins with a brief review of United States–Mexico relations since President Reagan took office in Washington. It is followed by an analysis, split into several sections, of Mexico's policies in response to the so-called Central American crisis. Next, the transformation taking place in the international context which encompasses United States–Mexico relations is examined in light of four primary phenomena: the decline in international oil prices, the effects of this decline on the Mexican economy, the world economic recession, and alterations in the international subsystem of the region. Finally, some conclusions are drawn about the possible effects of these changes both on Mexico's foreign policy and on relations between Mexico and the United States.

MEXICO-U.S. RELATIONS, 1981—1982

The climate of relations between Mexico and the United States improved noticeably with Ronald Reagan's inauguration as president of the United States, despite his previous reputation as a hard-line ultraconservative. This improvement was due primarily to Reagan's own deliberate effort to better the state of relations. These relations had deteriorated during President Carter's administration as a result of a series of differences and misunderstandings, including the fiasco of the initial negotiations for the sale of Mexican natural gas to the United States. For his part, President López Portillo was aware of this deterioration and added his own effort to improve the climate of relations. Nevertheless, as Anthony P. Maingot properly points out, the personal sympathy that both leaders profess, despite their ideological differences, is not sufficient to resolve the problems between the two countries. These difficulties stem from structural differences in their respective national interests that are more powerful than the presidents.[1]

During 1981 the two great problems in bilateral relations that had monopolized attention in the recent past, namely hydrocarbons and illegal immigrants, lessened—the second, only temporarily. They gave way to a critical issue related to regional politics, the Central American and Caribbean crisis.

In reality, rather than receding, the hydrocarbons issue was stabilized after new natural gas negotiations yielded results satisfying to both parties and after verification of the hypothesis that Mexico's own internal needs would force an increase in the export of crude oil. The level of exports had been the United

[1] "Diplomacy and the Structural Realities of National Interest," *Miami Herald*, June 28, 1981, cited in *Latin American Studies Association Newsletter*, 12, no. 3 (September 1981), 16.

States' chief preoccupation in previous years, but after the second half of 1981, when excess supplies emerged in world oil markets, this concern became obsolete. The illegal immigration issue entered a kind of lull with the failure of President Carter's amnesty plan and with Ronald Reagan's arrival in Washington. At least at the beginning of his administration, Reagan showed signs of not being concerned about the problem. Given his economic philosophy of not interfering in the free play of market forces, some observers assumed that he therefore favored the status quo. It was not until the beginning of 1982, when the Simpson-Mazzoli bill on migration and refugees came before Congress, that the issue once again became prominent on the Mexico–United States agenda. In contrast to the status of these other two issues during 1981, the Central American and Caribbean problem rapidly acquired a high priority in Mexico–United States relations.

Reagan assumed office in January 1981. The change of government in Washington was very important not only because it signified the substitution of Republicans for Democrats, but more significantly because it brought the right wing of the Republican party to power. It was therefore felt that the new government must restore the United States' image as a great power, determined to defend and promote its interests in all parts of the world. This policy would restore the country's morale, dissuade the Soviet Union and its allies from embarking on new adventures, and reinforce United States' leadership in the Western world.

One of the primary places selected to show the world this new determination was the Central American and Caribbean subregion, where significant political changes had occurred and more were in gestation. As part of a reorientation in its foreign policy toward a more active stance internationally, Mexico had semi-adopted the Sandinist Revolution in Nicaragua and would therefore soon find itself inevitably confronting the new U.S. policy.

From a certain point of view, one might think that Mexico's and the United States' objectives in the region are not far different, since both countries are seeking stabilization of the area. However, the reasons for this objective and the tactics for achieving it employed are quite distinct and even mutually exclusive. Reagan's administration obviously wants the stabilization of the area, but it intends at the same time to maintain American hegemony. Therefore, it is unwilling to accept profound social changes. It is willing, however, to use coercive tactics, ranging from financial blockades to the covert use of military force, and it has already partially done so.

For its part, Mexico favors stabilization because of its own interest in deterring the creation of a nucleus of generalized unrest on its southern border. This position is congruent with its traditional policy of trying to prevent external issues from interrupting or obstructing the internal development process. For example, should present tensions in the area result in open warfare on a subregional scale, this policy would justify the arguments of those within Mexico who demand the modernization and expansion of the armed forces in order to provide greater protection for the southern oil fields. Meeting these demands would entail an increase in military spending at the expense of development projects, with the resulting distortion of priorities in resource allocation. Ultimately, it could jeopardize the present balance between civil and military power. Embarking on a militaristic course, however, would involve entering an arms race. Frequent escalations would be required in an endless effort to maintain the balance of military power, and continuous technological discoveries would fuel the process further.

Mexico favors tactics that foster negotiation between the parties to the conflict in order to avoid the initiation, extension, and internationalization of armed conflict and to allow for some basic social changes that can help make a negotiated solution more durable. The greatest difference between the Mexican and U.S. positions is on this last point. On the basis of its historical experience in the area, Mexico argues that it is politically necessary, as well as socially more just, to accept change. Otherwise, it would only postpone social explosion, which would be even larger in the future. Suffocating the revolution by force, as occurred in Guatemala in 1954, would only push the problems below the surface and condemn the region to permanent instability. Actually, over time Reagan's government has shown signs of moderating its initial belligerence toward the Salvadoran Revolution. This change has led certain observers to conclude that

Reagan has finally understood the problem; other observers think that Mexican diplomacy has had some effect on the moderation process.[2]

MEXICO AND THE NICARAGUAN REVOLUTION

Traditionally, Mexico followed an isolationist and basically passive foreign policy that rested on two fundamental principles: the right of self-determination and the principle of nonintervention in the internal affairs of other countries. These are often called the "twin principles" because one necessarily leads to the other. Even where this is not the case, these have been the prevalent criteria used in Mexican diplomatic practice. There have, however, been exceptions. In certain cases where it has been forced to choose between self-determination and nonintervention, Mexican diplomacy has favored the former. This explains why Mexico did not recognize Franco's government in Spain. Even though the Spanish government met the requirement of being a *de facto* government according to the Mexican interpretation, its victory depended upon support given by foreign powers. In other words, Franco's government was the product of foreign intervention and not of the self-determination of the Spanish people. Breaking with Pinochet's government in Chile is a similar case. From the Mexican viewpoint, Pinochet's government was illegitimate and violated the right to self-determination by defying the Chilean people's electoral decision and relying on the connivance of foreign powers, namely the United States, during the seizure of power.

An exception to Mexican foreign policy's traditional passivity was also made in the regional arena. Mexico has always maintained an active anti-interventionist stance in the Latin America region. The cases of Guatemala in 1954, Cuba from 1959 to the present, the Dominican Republic in 1965, and Chile in 1972–73 demonstrate this. Nevertheless, its opposition to interventionism never exceeded the limits of diplomatic forums. It was not until President Echeverría took office that Mexico decided to of-

---

[2] Other observers, however, think that the moderation of the Reagan government's stance was only a temporary tactic; that it was dictated as a result of strong internal and international criticism provoked by the counter-evidence totally discrediting the "White Paper on El Salvador," published by the U.S. government itself. See, for example, Richard R. Fagen, "The Real Clear and Present Danger," *Caribbean Review*, 11, no. 2 (Spring 1982), 19.

fer more than diplomatic support. Faced with the case of Salvador Allende's government in Chile, Mexico offered material
support of an economic nature to a government that it considered the product of a process of popular self-determination and
that was being threatened by intervention from the region's hegemonic power.

This once-passivist tradition was in the process of shifting
toward an even more active international posture in which
Mexico would declare the abandonment of its classic legalism,
emphasizing self-determination over anti-interventionism.[3] On
May 20, 1979, President López Portillo made the surprise an-
nouncement of his decision to break relations with Somoza's
government in Nicaragua. The major novelty was not simply
severing relations, even though the measure was directed against
a government that, in the final analysis, was already established
and had come to power through elections. The legitimacy of
these elections was clearly doubtful, but that was not sufficient
reason for the action, given the frequency of such an occurrence
in Latin America, even in Mexico itself. The major innovation
was the rationale upon which the decision was based. For the
first time in the recent history of Mexican diplomacy, Mexico
based its decision to break relations not on the origins of the
other government but on its political actions. The violation of
human rights, represented by blatant genocide, made it necessary to isolate Somoza diplomatically and to pressure for his
ouster.[4] It was also a departure for Mexico to go beyond unilateral action and embark on a campaign to recruit other countries
in the region to join the diplomatic blockade against Somoza.
Breaking relations with him seemed to indicate that Mexico was
sacrificing a juridical orientation for a political one. The U.S.
State Department took due note of this.

More important than determining whether this action constituted a significant juridical or historical change in Mexican foreign policy is identifying the political reasons that led the Mexi-

[3]It could be argued that this change actually began during Luis Echeverría's government. Nevertheless, its impact was less, perhaps because the problems he had to confront were not as serious or as close to Mexico and because he did not have the weapon
provided by oil.
[4]During Echeverría's government, Mexico requested Spain's expulsion from the
United Nations for reasons similar to those cited in the Somoza case. In the Spanish
case, however, the government had never been recognized by Mexico.

can government to abandon its traditional position. Of course, there is no official evidence available on the real reasons for this decision. Nevertheless, in light of certain occurrences it is possible to propose the hypothesis that Mexico saw itself pushed by circumstances to take sides in the Nicaraguan conflict. Furthermore, in this decision-making process, Mexico became aware of the strategic and political importance of stability in the Central American region. Once this decision was made, the Mexican government embarked on a determined political course, backed by the president's enthusiasm and supported by the recently acquired international status conferred by oil. In addition, the internal and external costs of supporting the Nicaraguan Revolution were not very great, given the movement's pluralist nature and nationwide support, as well as the fact that the Somocista government was the product of a quasi-hereditary dictatorship that elicited little sympathy in international circles.

Until Mexico's break with Somoza, the Nicaraguan Revolution had counted on the political and logistic support of Costa Rica, a country with great democratic prestige. In addition, Costa Rica had given refuge to a Sandinist government in exile. Panama was the other country that had offered the revolutionaries firm support. However, it was the Venezuelan government under Carlos Andrés Pérez that was able to provide economic aid, thanks to its oil revenues. In March 1979, however, Carlos Andrés Pérez's government left office and the new president, who is a member of the opposition party (Copei), came to power. The change of government and ruling party in Venezuela jeopardized the political and economic support for the Nicaraguan Revolution, and consequently the outcome of the revolutionary struggle as well. It was also feared that this situation would force the Nicaraguan revolutionary movement to solicit more extensive Cuban aid. The possibility of increased Cuban participation carried with it the danger of more direct and decisive United States involvement. Given this situation, there was no other alternative than to try to convince Mexico, the other country in the region with oil wealth and with a long tradition of civilian government, to fill the vacuum left by Venezuela. Otherwise, there was danger that the conflict would be internationalized and be converted into an East-West confrontation.

The president of Costa Rica, Rodrigo Carazo Odio, appears

to have been the one charged with convincing Mexico to step in. He scheduled a meeting with López Portillo for May 20, 1979, in Cancún, Mexico. However, it is possible that the Mexican government felt it necessary to consult with the Cuban government, or at least to inform it of its own decision beforehand, in order to avoid misinterpretations. As a result, a sudden invitation was issued, asking Castro to meet with López Portillo on the island of Cozumel, Mexico, three days before Carazo Odio's visit.

During Castro's visit to Mexico, there was no indication that the Mexican government would break with Somoza three days later. The only possible indication—and this can only be seen *a posteriori*—was Castro's allusion to Mexico as the "front line of Latin America" ("la trinchera de América Latina").[5] Carazo Odio arrived for his meeting with López Portillo on May 20, two days after Castro returned to Cuba. During the official banquet that day, López Portillo announced his decision to break with Somoza's government and outlined the reasons for his decision. Days later, however, he declared before the leaders of the Mexican Chambers of Deputies and Senators that "this has been a carefully considered decision that was simply announced during the dramatic denunciation [of Nicaragua] by the President of Costa Rica, a republic that is the pride of Latin America."[6]

Coincidentally with the breaking with Somoza, the Mexican and Costa Rican governments embarked on a campaign, which was not very successful, to recruit other countries in the region to join the diplomatic blockade of the Nicaraguan government. Shortly thereafter, rumors began to circulate in Washington that the Mexican government was providing arms to the revolutionaries. The accuracy of these rumors has never been confirmed. However, a year later an influential Mexican columnist wrote that López Portillo's government "provided much more concrete, wide-ranging, and effective aid to the Nicaraguan rebels than has been admitted so far."[7] At the same time, Mexico

[5] See Castro's speech during the official dinner on May 17, 1979. Some U.S. observers attribute the break with Somoza to the fact that López Portillo had substituted his previous, pro-U.S. Minister of Foreign Relations for a more nationalistic one barely a day before Castro's visit to Mexico. However, the reverse causation is more logical. Once the decision to support the Nicaraguan Revolution had been made, a new foreign minister more inclined to support this policy was named.

[6] See *Excélsior* (Mexico), May 25, 1979, p. 12-A.

[7] Manuel Buendía, *Excélsior*, Jan. 29, 1980, "Red Privada" column.

headed the group of countries that blocked a veiled United States initiative in the OAS in June 1979, aimed at forming an inter-American peace force to "reestablish order and assure democratic elections in Nicaragua."[8] Finally, on July 19, 1979, the Revolution triumphed in Nicaragua. From this point on, Mexico became the new government's international protector, which entailed being (1) its agent in Washington, trying to persuade the U.S. government not to intervene in Nicaragua and proposing a nonaggression pact with Nicaragua to that end on February 21, 1982; (2) its supplier, along with Venezuela, of the oil needed by the Nicaraguan economy; (3) guarantor of the external Nicaraguan debt before the international banking community; and (4) provider of a greatly disproportionate share of the economic and technical aid given by the donor nations. In exchange, Mexico did not demand anything openly and President López Portillo declared that "Mexico's aid will be unconditional." Nevertheless, it is obvious that Mexico expected, and continues to expect, that its presence would help to ensure the viability of the Nicaraguan economy, thus preventing the radicalization of the government and preserving its pluralistic character. It is also clear that Mexico expects that its participation will help to restrain the spread of conflict in Central America and gradually to reduce the presence in the region of "hegemonic powers of one or the other persuasion." This last objective demonstrates Mexico's intention of finding a "third way" for the region that is properly Latin American and is based on revolutionary nationalism, "which is a sufficiently broad term to be reinterpreted in accord with conditions in each country while ensuring independence from the great powers."[9]

Mexico's negative reaction, repeatedly stated indirectly in official declarations, to Managua's stated intention of buying sophisticated weapons from France demonstrates that these were the reasons for Mexico's presence in Nicaragua. For example, in his speech on February 21, 1982, when the Mexican president received the Augusto César Sandino medal of the "Batalla de San Jacinto" in Managua, he reminded "Sandino's people":

[8] Constantine Christopher Menges, *Current Mexican Foreign Policy, Revolution in Central America and the United States* (Arlington, Va., June 1980), p. 39.

[9] See the documents from the Conferencia Permanente de Partidos Políticos de América Latina (COPPPAL), held in Oaxaca, Mexico, in October 1979, organized by the Partido Revolucionario Institucional (PRI), the Mexican party in power.

"Two years ago I suggested that the Nicaraguan Revolution could become the point of contact—the historic link, I said then—of modern Latin American revolutionary history; today I reiterate my conviction. I am convinced of the Junta and the Sandinist Front's irrevocable determination to maintain the pluralistic, democratic and progressive stance outlined on July 19, 1979."[10]

During COPPPAL's reunion, held in Managua in February 1982, the official statement of the Mexican delegation from the Partido Revolucionario Institucional (PRI) expressed its agreement "with Comandante Daniel Ortega Saavedra when he pointed out yesterday that Nicaragua is stronger today than yesterday because it is making progress in carrying out its programs and meeting its goals, with its political pluralism, economic achievements, development of a mixed economic system, improvements in social welfare, and its exercise of freedom of expression."[11]

With the passage of time, Mexico's support for the Nicaraguan revolutionary government was complicated by two events that occurred after the Sandinist victory: the escalation of the revolution in El Salvador after 1980, and Ronald Reagan's assumption of office in Washington in January 1981.

MEXICO AND THE REVOLUTION IN EL SALVADOR

The escalation of the Salvadoran Revolution created one more unstable element in the already tumultuous Central American region, which alarmed Washington even more. The "domino theory"—which assumes that the countries of the region will fall under the control of Marxist revolutions one after the other—gained greater credibility. This created even more complications for Mexican policy in the area and revived the Mexico–United States differences over regional politics, especially since Mexico, according to the domino theory, is the last domino.

In the case of the Salvadoran Revolution, things became more complicated for Mexico for other reasons as well. In the first place, the national popular front to which the insurgents belong is not as clearly defined as Nicaragua's was. The political forces

[10] *El Día* (Mexico), Feb. 22, 1982.
[11] Speech by Bernardo Sepúlveda, PRI Secretary for International Affairs, cited in *Uno Más Uno* (Mexico), Feb. 24, 1982.

in El Salvador are more diversified, and popular support for each group is less obvious. Second, there is no solid front line of support made up of Latin American countries in the Salvadoran case such as there was in Nicaragua. Therefore, Mexico has lost important allies, including Venezuela and, most importantly, Costa Rica, which has undermined the legitimacy and force of the Mexican action. The legitimacy of its policy was undermined further when Mexico sought support for its policy in El Salvador from an extra-continental country, namely France.

In effect, the revolutionary movement in El Salvador does not present as united a front as Nicaragua's did. The Christian Democratic movement, which for years constituted the core of the political opposition in El Salvador, divided, and part of it collaborated with the military in a civil-military government; the rest joined the revolutionaries. This led Herrera Campins's Christian Democratic government in Venezuela to support the civil-military government in El Salvador and to oppose the insurgents. Costa Rica, which is profoundly anti-Somocista but also anti-communist, does not view the Salvadoran revolutionaries sympathetically, especially since the change in government in San José from Carazo Odio to Luis Alberto Monge.

Perhaps for all these reasons the Mexican government, contrary to what many observers expected at the time, did not break relations with Napoleón Duarte's government in El Salvador as it had with Somoza. However, on August 28, 1981, in the United Nations, it issued a joint communiqué with the French government, recognizing the Salvadoran revolutionary organizations as "representative political forces."

The Franco-Mexican communiqué provoked both positive and negative reactions. Those with critical reactions protested it as a flagrant act of intervention that encouraged the insurgents and granted them legitimacy. Furthermore, Mexico had invited an extra-continental power to interfere in regional affairs. Both the Mexican minister of foreign relations and President López Portillo denied that this was an act of intervention, arguing that it simply recognized a reality that needed to be taken into account if there was a true desire to reach a negotiated solution. In a clear reference to Reagan's government, President López Portillo declared that the real act of intervention in any case was the provision of military aid to one of the parties to the conflict. It is logical to expect that the Mexican government anticipated the strong criticisms that such a communiqué would provoke but considered it more important to take such a controversial position as an ultimate step in making "definitive action" against the revolutionaries by the United States and its allies more difficult.

On March 5, 1981, President Duarte of El Salvador created the Central Electoral Commission whose task was to draft an electoral law and establish procedures for an election of a Constituent Assembly in 1982. The assembly in turn would make the preparations for future presidential elections.[12] The first election was scheduled for March 28, and the Reagan administration pinned great hopes on this event, anticipating, on the one hand, that the mere participation of a large number of citizens would diminish the revolutionaries' legitimacy and, on the other hand, that the Christian Democrats would win. The guerrillas tried to disrupt the elections, with little success, by attacking diverse locations. In the end, there were high rates of participation. Spokesmen for the revolutionary movement argued, however, that the great majority of citizens voted because they were pressured by threats from the government or from rival political organizations. Before the elections, Mexico once again insisted to the United States, though ineffectually, that elections without prior political negotiation would not end the violence. Time will show that Mexico was correct.

The most important aspect of these elections, however, is that the winners were the ultra-rightist parties as a whole. Having decided to form a coalition, they ousted the Christian Democrats led by Napoleón Duarte and favored by Reagan. After the fact, Duarte denounced the antidemocratic tendencies of the new government, thus jeopardizing U.S. military aid to the Salvadoran government. All of these circumstances complicated the Salvadoran scenario even further. By the middle of 1982 it appeared to have become an unsolvable situation.

THE MEXICAN PLAN TO REDUCE TENSIONS IN CENTRAL AMERICA AND THE CARIBBEAN

The plan proposed by Mexico shortly before the Salvadoran elections for achieving a more relaxed climate that would lead

[12] United States, Department of State, *El Salvador: The Search for Peace* (Washington, D.C., September 1981).

toward peace, democracy, stability, and development in Central America and the Caribbean was more in line with Mexico's tradition and more acceptable politically, to judge by the support it received. President López Portillo made this proposal directly to the countries involved in the tensions on February 21, 1982, during his trip to Managua to receive the Augusto César Sandino medal.

On proposing this plan, the Mexican president said directly and frankly that there are three key factors determining the outcome of the conflict in the area: Nicaragua, El Salvador, "and, if one wants to see things realistically, relations between Cuba and the United States."[13] Therefore, he thought that if Cuba and the United States would continue the conversations already begun at Mexico's suggestion between the U.S. secretary of state and the Cuban vice-president, the dialogue might turn into negotiations.

The plan is directed first of all toward reducing tensions in order to create a propitious climate that could eventually lead to in-depth negotiations. According to President López Portillo, "It is not meant to be a global peace plan for the region, which would have great difficulty in succeeding. It is meant to set up mechanisms of negotiation, interchange, and formalization of concessions that could lead to a reduction of tensions. These mechanisms of negotiation would be established through separate channels which, however, would be parallel and might converge in the medium term."

The plan proposes three channels of action: first, the already mentioned continuation of the dialogue between Cuba and the United States; second, a negotiated solution for El Salvador in which Mexico, other friendly nations, and even United States' allies offer assurances to allay U.S. preoccupations about the consequences of a negotiated solution; and third, a series of non-aggression pacts between Nicaragua and the United States, on the one hand, and between Nicaragua and its neighbors, on the other. Mexico offers itself as an "intermediary" in this process: "We Mexicans want to be helpful, we want to be the intermediary, liaison, and means of communication between those who have stopped speaking or never have spoken to each other."

In his presentation of the plan, the Mexican president em-

---

[13] See *El Día* (Mexico), Feb. 22, 1982, for this and subsequent remarks of the president in this section.

phasized his repeated assertion that, in its policy toward the area, Mexico is not trying to fool anybody when it says that it does not defend one or the other ideology in the external arena but instead upholds principles such as people's right of self-determination and respect for the sovereignty of each country. He also reiterated the Mexican preoccupation with freeing the region from involvement in the East-West confrontation: "Central America and the Caribbean are struggling today to modify internal and external structures that in many respects resemble the colonial order that dominated those continents [Asia and Africa]. Just as most of these Asian and African struggles could not be forcefully inserted into the terrible East-West or capitalism-socialism dichotomies, the Central American revolutions today resist these Manichean dichotomies."

Reactions to the Mexican plan for reducing tensions were varied. Nicaragua and Cuba responded favorably, although the latter had some reservations.[14] Salvadoran President Duarte lamented what he considered meddling, but the revolutionaries declared their support for the plan. The United States' position, voiced by Secretary Haig, was a cold response, asserting that, in spite of the "convergence of perspectives" in the plan, it did not deal adequately with the issue of Nicaraguan aid to the Salvadoran insurgents. This stand-offish attitude obviously masked the United States' interest in waiting for the results of elections in El Salvador, scheduled for March 28.[15]

Despite all this, the Mexican plan is a realistic measure, and very suggestive as well. In the first place, it begins with the assumption that any solution for the area that does not take account of United States and Cuban involvement is unfeasible, and thus the current climate of tension will continue to prevail. In the second place, it does not pretend to be a general peace plan but only to reduce tensions in order to achieve a more propitious climate for eventual, in-depth negotiations. Nevertheless, it fails by not being wholly realistic about the possibility of distancing the regional conflict from the East-West confrontation, which is exactly contrary to President Reagan's strategy. According to his own guidelines, Reagan intends to use the con-

[14] See the letter from Fidel Castro to López Portillo in *ibid.*, February 24, 1982.
[15] *Guardian* (London), March 8, 1982, p. 6.

flict in the area as leverage in this global confrontation and thereby gain Soviet concessions on other fronts.

THE CHANGING CONTEXT OF MEXICO-U.S. RELATIONS

The context within which Mexico–United States relations takes place changed drastically with the set of conditions that emerged during the second half of 1981. The fundamental reason for the change was the decline in the price of oil; the economic recession in the industrialized countries and the change that occurred in the regional political structure also had a notable impact. Although these phenomena inevitably influenced both Mexican and U.S. foreign policy, as well as relations between the two countries, their impact was different, and even contrary, in each case. Therefore, it is important to analyze the specific weight attributable to each factor, in order to elucidate which one tends to prevail to a greater degree.

The Decline in International Oil Prices

The fall in oil prices has had a considerable effect on the structure of Mexico–United States relations. This is not to suggest that there is a mechanical relationship between petroleum and foreign policy. However, instead of being dominated by suppliers, the international oil market is now controlled by buyers as a result of the global excess supply of crude oil. This shift has obviously reduced the negotiating power of the exporting countries, both in the specific context of selling their own crude and in a broader and more general sense. This, in turn, necessarily affects the framework of Mexico–United States relations.

There is a further point. With the fall in oil prices, Mexico tried to offset the precipitous reduction of its oil export revenues by contracting new short-term international loans, despite the fact that its foreign debt was already the second highest in the world. In its negotiations, the Mexican government encountered a situation that was new for it: its economic solvency with the private international banks had been spectacularly reduced. With the decline in prices, oil was no longer a sufficient guarantee to assure the international banks of Mexico's capacity to service its external debt. The country was soon faced with a liquidity problem that threatened to force a reduction in public expenditure and a paralysis of development projects. With great difficulty, however, Mexico managed to contract large new loans at relatively unfavorable terms. Although these loans alleviated the immediate problem, they also eventually generated new pressures on the balance of payments by increasing the total debt and raising the proportion that consisted of short-term loans. As a consequence, by December 31, 1981, Mexico had the largest debt in the world.

The peso, on the other hand, which had been overvalued for a long time in order to stimulate oil exports, was subject to new pressures. Despite the fact that it had technically been floating since 1976, it had to be devalued 46 percent in February 1982. The discrepancy in inflation rates between Mexico and its principal commercial partner, the United States, which had been obvious since 1979, grew enormously in 1981. The 1981 inflation rate officially announced by the Mexican government was 28.7 percent, while the U.S. rate fell below 10 percent as a result of President Reagan's restrictive policies. Furthermore, Mexico began 1982 with an unprecedented inflation rate that escalated to 5 percent in January, while the U.S. rate fell even more. This phenomenon alerted the Mexican public, who increased pressure on the peso by buying dollars massively for speculative and defensive reasons. In February these pressures became so severe that on February 17, faced by what the president of the Republic himself would call a virtual "assault" on foreign reserves, the peso was devalued. The worst part of the situation was that, just as in 1976, the tendency to buy dollars continued, and the peso kept on sliding downward even after the devaluation.

The February 1982 devaluation also produced a new and appreciable increase in the size of the interest payments on the external debt, denominated in pesos. This eventually offset many of the benefits traditionally associated with devaluation, at the same time that it reduced Mexico's solvency with the international banks even further.[16]

Faced with this grave situation, President López Portillo was forced to issue an emergency decree on April 20, 1982, oriented

[16] On June 30, 1982, however, the Mexican government publicly announced the granting of a $2.5 billion credit by 75 banks from 12 different countries, "in a demonstration of solidarity and confidence in Mexico's future and in order to overcome problems that are not limited to Mexico, inasmuch as that the industrialized countries are also immersed in them" (*Excélsior*, July 1, 1982, p. 1).

toward "guaranteeing the continuity of development in the context of a more favorable external performance and of reduced internal inflationary pressures."[17] The decree consisted of a series of measures, contained in seventeen points, aimed at controlling the urgent situation. Overall, it is an economic stabilization program similar to those recommended by the International Monetary Fund, except that it will be self-imposed.

Among the measures adopted, the following stand out: (1) a drastic cut in public expenditures as well as a stricter control over their distribution; (2) the suspension of public works not directly related to the production process, and the postponement of new projects; (3) an increase in public revenues of 150 billion pesos, achieved by raising prices and tariffs on products and services under state control; (4) an upper limit of $11 billion on the net indebtedness of the public sector; (5) a limit on net credit allotted by the Central Bank to the federal government, to be determined by the amount of internal resources collected by the bank; (6) a control on the increment of total currency in circulation, which cannot exceed the increase in the Central Bank's net international reserves; (7) the reduction of $3 billion, as compared to 1981 levels, in the imports of both public and private sectors; (8) a policy on passive interest rates that is sensitive to the evolution of external rates and to movements in the exchange rate, establishing a prime rate favoring investments in pesos; (9) a policy with regard to active rates that gives preferential treatment to the most vulnerable socioeconomic sectors by setting maximum rates for certain categories of credit, at the same time avoiding disproportionate subsidies; and (10) a guarantee of better contracting and financing conditions for private enterprises in need of dollar financing.

The net result is that, instead of administering a surplus, which was expected to be generated after the 1976–77 crisis, we find ourselves in 1982 managing a crisis once again. In his second annual report, President López Portillo declared: "We have outlined successive goals that divide the national global development plan into three biennial stages: during the first two years, overcoming the crisis; during the next two, consolidating the economy; and during the last two, experiencing accelerated

---

[17] For this and the following paragraph, see Mexico, Presidency of the Republic, Decree of April 20, 1982.

growth."[18] In May 1982, however, the president admitted, in a visibly dramatic moment, that "the second period of consolidation overlapped with the accelerated growth that began before the economy was consolidated."[19]

It is true that the country was able to achieve unprecedented growth rates in recent years, with a 7.6 percent average for 1978–81,[20] and that employment, economic infrastructure, and productive plant in general also grew at an accelerated pace. But overheating the economy, and the resulting inflation, led the country to the present situation. No one foresaw the decline in the prices of oil; they were expected to rise indefinitely without interruption. This error in calculation reduced the government's prestige and the confidence accorded it in international circles.

On the internal political front the situation is also delicate. President López Portillo inherited a country in crisis from his predecessor and he, in turn, will bequeath to his successor a country in crisis. The difference lies in the fact that today there is no glimpse of a "lifesaver" such as oil provided in 1977. In addition, because it is a crisis that repeats itself in a similar form for the second time, there is a greater loss of credibility and public confidence in governmental institutions. Another difference is that on this occasion the crisis has been preceded by three years of economic bonanza. In any case, to stop providing work to those who have not had it is fundamentally different than to take it from those already employed. Finally, it should be taken into account that the crisis this year occurred just before federal elections. This fact is reflected in the vote, reducing the power and legitimacy of the party that has governed Mexico for the past fifty years.

Mexico from Bonanza to Crisis, 1981–1982

Between 1976 and 1981, the Mexican economy grew 7.4 percent per year on average, while the industrialized countries as a whole grew 2.7 percent and the Latin American nations 3.6 percent. The Mexican economy's extraordinary rate of growth gen-

---

[18] José López Portillo, *Segundo informe de gobierno* (Mexico, September 1978).

[19] José López Portillo, "Veinte mujeres y un hombre," interview, *Excélsior*, May 12, 1982, p. 1.

[20] In 1978, 7.3 percent; 8.0 percent in 1979, 7.4 percent in 1980, and 8.1 percent in 1981. See Banco de México, *Informe anual 1980* and *Informe anual 1981* (Mexico, 1981 and 1982, resp.).

erated an average 800,000 jobs annually during the same period and reduced open unemployment from 8 to 4.5 percent.[21] But overheating the economy led to the disparity between internal and external inflation rates, and international oil prices declined unanticipatedly. As a consequence, as we have seen, the economic bonanza began to fade during the second half of 1981. The year ended with a balance of payments' current account deficit significantly greater than that for 1980. In 1980 the deficit was $6.8 billion; it was $11.7 billion in 1981. According to the Banco de México's estimates, this enormous deficit was due to five sets of factors:

(1) The fall in prices in the international oil market. It is calculated that Mexico lost almost $5 billion in revenues as a result.

(2) The difference between the rapid economic growth internally and the slower growth of Mexico's traditional markets. This was a partial cause of both the continued contraction of nonpetroleum exports and the continued increase in imports. (The value of nonpetroleum exports equalled $5.4 billion in 1980 and $5.5 billion in 1981.)

(3) The widening of the internal and external inflation-rate differential, which led to a spectacular reduction in positive balances from tourism and border transactions. Net tourist revenues declined from $626 million in 1980 to $213 million in 1981. Meanwhile, the net yield from border transactions decreased over the same period from $593 million to only $94 million. It should be clarified here that U.S. sources reported a larger number of Mexican visitors to the United States (3,800,000) in 1981 than the total number of tourists leaving Mexico according to national sources (3,546,000). According to these same U.S. sources, the number of U.S. tourists (3,270,000) who visited Mexico that year was less than the already cited number of Mexicans (3,800,000) who visited the United States. This leads to the supposition that the tourist balance actually became negative between 1980 and 1981.[22]

(4) The persistence of high interest rates in international capi-

[21] José López Portillo, "Veinte mujeres y un hombre," as in n. 19 above.
[22] See Don Wynegar, *International Travel to and from the U.S.; 1982 Outlook* (Washington, D.C., December 10, 1981), table 5; cited by Rosario Molinero, *Mitos y realidades del turismo en México (1976–1981)* (Mexico, 1982), p. 60.

tal markets, which increased the capital outflow resulting from external debt servicing. Interest payments on the external public debt generated an outflow that grew from $4.0 billion in 1980 to $5.5 billion in 1981, for an increase of $1.5 billion. Payments on the private debt grew from $1.5 billion to $2.7 billion, for an increase of $1.2 billion.

(5) Loss of revenues from the sale of silver due to the depression in the world silver market.[23]

This large current account deficit was offset by net inflows of capital that reached the unprecedented level of $18.2 billion, which was $8.4 billion more than in 1980. Of these net financial resources 82 percent were obtained by external public sector borrowing ($14.9 billion). Private indebtedness also contributed significantly toward offsetting the current account deficit by generating a new inflow of reserves of $4.2 billion.[24]

These figures clearly demonstrate the pressures exerted on the peso that, added to the massive dollar purchases, necessitated a devaluation on February 17, 1982.

It was not easy for President López Portillo to make the political decision of converting the country into an oil exporter in 1976. In the first place, the historic precedent set when Mexico became a large exporter of crude in the 1920's had left bad memories because the oil sector did not generate many wider economic benefits and instead brought with it many international problems. Second, in 1976 a doctrine already existed, sanctioned by time, to the effect that nonrenewable natural resources should be reserved for internal development. Finally, the mere idea of converting the country once again into an exporter of hydrocarbons provoked a huge polemic in both governmental and nongovernmental circles that was contained only with difficulty. Therefore, it must have been highly frustrating for López Portillo to have to face a situation toward the end of his government similar to the one he had encountered when he came to power.

When comparing the crises that Presidents Echeverría and López Portillo had to face toward the end of their respective governments, the most notable aspect is not their differences

[23] Banco de México, *Informe anual 1981*, p. 74.
[24] *Ibid.*, pp. 76–77.

but their similarities, especially in terms of political management. It is well known that neither president was able to perceive clearly the great breach of confidence and credibility that had developed between the citizenry, or at least the attentive public, and the government. They were not able to see that, because of this breach, the public had reached the point of interpreting events in a manner totally contrary to official declarations. As a result, in cases such as the 1976 and 1982 devaluations, the public rejected the declarations intended to calm it and regain its confidence, and purchased massive amounts of dollars, thereby helping to make its own fears materialize as a "self-fulfilling prophecy." President López Portillo himself obviously contributed, inadvertently perhaps, to the rumors of an imminent devaluation with his declarations in the fifth annual report, which he continued to sustain for months afterward, that he would "defend the peso with the tenacity of a dog." After the February 1982 devaluation, he admitted that "at this moment a clerk who recommends to a woman that she should buy dollars has more credibility than the president of the Republic."[25]

The World Economic Recession

The world economic recession, and particularly the slowdown in the United States, tends to affect the context of Mexico–United States relations to the extent that it is an obstacle impeding Mexico's economic recuperation in the short term. The grave crisis that the external sector of the Mexican economy is experiencing has already been described. A massive transfusion of reserves is needed in order to attack Mexico's problem of international liquidity in the short term. On the one hand, however, the depressed international petroleum market is not likely to recuperate quickly unless there is some sudden change, such as the eruption of generalized armed conflict in the Middle East that would cut oil production and exports. On the other hand, despite the peso's devaluation, nonpetroleum exports do not face a hopeful future either. This is due to the effects of the world recession, particularly in the United States, Mexico's principal trading partner. It is estimated that the GDP of the twenty-four OECD members grew barely 0.25 percent in 1982, instead

[25] José López Portillo, "Veinte mujeres y un hombre," as in n. 19, above.

of at the 2 percent rate foreseen a year ago. Industrial production in the ten largest countries declined an average of 1.9 percent during the twelve months from mid-1981 to mid-1982,
and their average unemployment rate was 8 percent.[26] In addition, the recession has pushed the industrialized countries toward increasing protectionism and use of subsidies, which influence Mexico's nonpetroleum exports both in the importing
country itself and in third markets.

External indebtedness does not provide a short-term solution
either. We have seen that Mexico has the highest debt in the
world today and that the government itself has a self-imposed
limit on new loans in 1982. Even if this self-limitation did not
exist and if the international capital market reacted favorably to
Mexico's appeals for a larger volume of credit, the high interest
rates currently prevailing in the market would make this solution prohibitively costly.

A larger inflow of direct foreign investment remains as a possible short-term solution. It remains to be seen, though, whether
a depressed market like Mexico's is attractive to foreign investors at this time, except for those who might want to acquire
established firms at low prices. In addition, foreign investors
would be in a better position to impose conditions at the present. If this were the case, the government would weaken itself
politically even further, both internally and externally.

Changes in the Regional Political Structure

The political structure of the American continent has changed
and continues to do so. United States hegemony is no longer as
omnipotent as it was during the early Cold War. The Latin
American countries as a whole diversified their economic relations as the industrialized countries rebuilt their economies
after World War II. Today they are not as dependent on the
United States as they were in the immediate postwar period.

Cuba was the first country to shake off the United States' political tutelage, although it did so under Soviet protection. Other
countries have followed Cuba and, without necessarily becoming involved in armed confrontations, have distanced themselves from the orthodox U.S. line. A clear indication of this ten-

[26] Samuel I. del Villar, "Quiebra y tasas de interés," paper presented before the Commission on International Affairs of the PRI (Mexico, June 7, 1982).

dency has been the reduction in the Pentagon's influence over many Latin American armed forces and the substitution of arms from other suppliers for those of the United States.

On the other side of this issue, many observers claim that the United States allowed a power vacuum to develop in Latin America during Carter's government by not suppressing—as they had in 1965 in the Dominican Republic—the Sandinist Revolution in Nicaragua; by making concessions to Panama in the new Canal treaties; and by permitting the establishment of pro-socialist regimes in some of the Caribbean islands. However, it is clear that Reagan's government has not been able to stifle the revolution in El Salvador either, nor could it prevent the Falklands/Malvinas War between Argentina and Great Britain.

It would be naive, however, to derive hasty conclusions from these phenomena. The United States continues to have the ultimate capacity to suppress revolutions and control wars in Latin America. The difference is that today the cost and effort required would be greater as a result of the larger degree of effective pluralism in the world or, in other words, of the reduced unilateral dependence on the United States. There was a period in which simple diplomatic pressure or an indirect economic threat was sufficient to inhibit a potential violator of the status quo. This was before the Vietnam War and the oil embargo, when the "Pax Americana" reigned absolute in the farthest corners of the Western world. Since then, circumstances have changed, and Reagan's government has had trouble in adjusting to this new situation.

Whatever the reason, it is certain that today both the Monroe Doctrine and the Inter-American Treaty of Reciprocal Assistance (Río Pact) are showing spectacular fissures. In the Central American and Caribbean conflicts, not only has international communism become involved but also the Socialist International and International Christian Democracy—all this in open challenge to the Monroe Doctrine, since these organizations derive their origins and force from European countries.[27] Both the conservative and the newly developed left wing of the Catholic Church have also been important actors in local conflicts. Some

[27] Isidro Sepúlveda, "Apuntes y consideraciones sobre la seguridad nacional en México," paper presented at the Seminar on International Relations, El Colegio de México (Mexico, June 1982).

Protestant denominations—to judge by the military's orientation in Guatemala—have demanded a more active role in politics as well. Even the Palestinian Liberation Organization and
Libya have involved themselves in the conflict.

The war over the Malvinas has made both the Río Pact and
the Monroe Doctrine more vulnerable. The former has been affected because the United States, far from avoiding the war, supported Britain materially and politically against Argentina. At
the least, this signifies that NATO has prevailed over the Río
Pact. The Monroe Doctrine was weakened because the United
States allowed an extra-continental power like Great Britain to
settle accounts directly with a Latin American country. The war
in the Malvinas has precipitated a realignment of the countries
of the region with old allies confronting each other, e.g. Argentina and the United States, and former rivals helping each other,
e.g. Cuba, Nicaragua, Panama, Peru, and Venezuela giving aid
to Argentina.

Given this situation, it should not be surprising that emerging
regional powers like Venezuela and Mexico, or other countries
in the region, like Costa Rica and Panama, claim their right to
participate in the process of restructuring the Central American
and Caribbean regional political subsystems. In other words,
because these nations are adjacent to the countries in conflict,
they feel that they have a greater right than other extra-regional
forces to influence the area's political future.

These changes in the regional political structure affect Mexico–United States relations to the extent that Mexico is part of
these changes. Relations are affected to the degree that Mexico
is an emerging regional power, disposed toward influencing
events in the area, and to the degree that the United States is
willing or unwilling to accommodate itself to this new situation.
Relations are also influenced to the extent that the two countries resent the changes and, perceiving them differently, adopt
divergent positions.

CONCLUSIONS

Mexico, forced by circumstances to participate in Central
American regional politics more actively and, more concretely,
to take sides in the internal Nicaraguan conflict, has become

newly aware of the Central American subregion's political and strategic importance. This new Mexican activism, then, appears to represent one more step toward abandoning its traditional foreign policy, characterized by passivity and legalism. This change could take place in large part because of the new international status that Mexico acquired as a result of its oil.

Furthermore, for the current economic crisis in Mexico—the result of the fall in oil prices in 1981 and the high inflation rates in effect during the past few years—no solution is foreseen for the short term because, on the one hand, sources of international credit are exhausted, and, on the other, the recession in the United States, Mexico's major trading partner, discourages nonpetroleum exports from Mexico and reduces income from tourism.

Given this grave situation, it is logical to assume that (1) once again, as in 1977–78, the country is entering a period of introversion; (2) the new government, understanding the country's malaise, will moderate Mexico's new international political activism and return to "discrete diplomacy" in order to avoid accusations of "lighting the street while keeping the house dark"; (3) given its weak financial situation, Mexico will probably reduce its actual presence in the Central American countries; but, above all, (4) given the reduction of the leverage provided by oil, the country's capacity for international negotiation with the world and especially with the United States will decrease as well.

Nevertheless, we should consider other factors that may tend to have the contrary influence, in particular the changes occurring in the region's international subsystem. Mexico cannot abandon its participation in the new political plan that is gestating, unless it is willing also to abandon the future of the region to external forces and to sacrifice its own political and strategic objectives. The latter would be served by the political stabilization of the area and by its isolation from the East-West conflict. Furthermore, there is a long-standing tradition in Mexico that foreign policy belongs more to the state than to any specific government. As a result, the changes in administration every six years tend to have only a small effect on the continuity of these policies. Finally, while it is true that Mexico's lack of international liquidity places a real constraint on its economic aid programs, supplying oil is still a form of economic cooperation "in kind" that can be used to bolster its foreign policy.

Faced with the conjuncture of these factors, the new government that will come to power in Mexico on December 1, 1982, may choose an intermediate solution. This decision would entail maintenance of essentially the same foreign policy, but in effect with a reduced presence in the Central American region, at least during the first two years of its term.

Mexico and the Guatemalan Crisis

Adolfo Aguilar Zinser

FOR Mexico's foreign policy, Central America begins in El Salvador. Guatemala constitutes a different reality and thus a special challenge. Historically, relations between Mexico and Guatemala have been characterized by mutual tension and suspicion. Except for the period 1944–54, during which Juan José Arévalo and Jacobo Arbenz carried out significant reforms, incidents between Mexico and Guatemala have followed one after another. Mexico has, however, put little emphasis on its relations with Guatemala, in view of its continuing concern with the northern border, the source of the most obvious threats and aggression toward its sovereignty and integrity. Only in specific historical circumstances have we turned to the south to confront outbursts of Guatemalan nationalism.

Mexican economic, political, and cultural policy toward Guatemala has generally been minimal, perhaps from the fear that an aggressive plan of commerce and economic expansion might arouse Guatemalan nationalist feeling. Nevertheless, there are more or less important economic exchanges between the two countries. For example, some Mexican business sectors have an interest in the Guatemala market and investments in Guatemala. And in Guatemala, as in the rest of Latin America, Mexican cultural products (books, music, cinema, etc.) enjoy a remunerative market.

For Guatemala, on the other hand, we are nothing less than the "Colossus of the North." Guatemalan nationalism has always fed on animosity toward Mexico; in many ways we are to Guatemala what the United States is to us. In the first place we are the aggressor who swallowed up an important portion of

Guatemala's territory: the state of Chiapas. Our culture, firmly rooted among the Guatemalan people, is frequently decried as an example of "cultural penetration." Mexican investments in Guatemala are seen as dictated by international conspiracies. Recently, the increase in migration between Guatemala and Mexico has led the Guatemalan military, which is committed to denying this migration's true causes, to denounce Mexico's maltreatment of the immigrants in much the same terms as Mexicans use to characterize the migration of undocumented workers to the United States.

Yet such parallels can be carried too far. The interests of the United States in Mexico are of overwhelming importance: its cultural and political influence are decisive for our country. By contrast, Mexico is neither economically nor politically central to the conduct of Guatemalan affairs, nor has Guatemala truly been an object of Mexican expansion. Still, for reasons of their own the dominant classes in Guatemala want to view us as a threat. Faced with their lack of secular legitimacy and their isolation from the most numerous sectors of society, they have frequently attempted to gain legitimacy and support by citing supposed Mexican aggressions. In the current crisis this anti-Mexicanism has taken on particular importance.

MEXICO'S POLICY TOWARD CENTRAL AMERICA

Guatemala has not in effect figured as a Central American country in Mexico's policy toward the region as a whole. Three central aspects of that policy are absent with respect to Guatemala.

First, Mexico has viewed the political, social, and economic upheavals that have racked Central America since 1978 as signs of a necessary break with a sociopolitical order based on traditional dominance under the hegemonic influence of the United States. Mexico has gradually, although cautiously, dissociated itself from the repressive, transnational, and oligarchic state in Latin America, and has recognized the legitimacy of new and contending forces, not so much for ideological reasons as from the simple argument that new social sectors within each country should decide the destiny of their countries. At the same time, it has taken care not to violate the dearly held principle of nonintervention. Mexican foreign policy thus attempts to reconcile traditional diplomatic positions with the difficult and as yet unpredictable process of change.

Second, and as a consequence of the foregoing, Mexico has publicly repudiated repression, authoritarian methods, human rights violations, and violence as a solution to the crisis. In particular it has argued that human rights violations have consequences not only for Central America but also for the entire international community.

Third, Mexico has vigorously opposed the interventionist policies of the United States, which deny the historical reality of Central America and only impede the search for true solutions based on self-determination. For Mexico, the essence of U.S. national security is not threatened by what is happening in Central America. If the traditional structures that sustain U.S. hegemony are being questioned, this does not necessarily entail a threat against the genuine national interest of the United States. Nor does Mexico see any threat to its own security from the political crisis in Central America. The region should simply be allowed to develop in its own way.

These three elements are present in the statements, actions, and initiatives of Mexico with respect to Nicaragua and El Salvador. By contrast, Mexican government spokesmen avoid explicit reference to the Guatemalan crisis and abstain from making judgments that might associate events in Guatemala with events in other countries in the region. Since to dissociate these phenomena is practically impossible, Mexican statements about Central American conflicts tend to include Guatemala in a general way, but specific mentions of Guatemala are typically ambiguous. In particular, Mexican authorities treat the Guatemalan military regime, unquestionably the most repressive in Central America, very delicately.

Events in Guatemala have not, however, gone unnoticed in Mexico; indeed, they have been discussed at length both within and outside the government. Some sectors have apparently begun to define the Mexican national interest vis-à-vis Guatemala in the same terms as those employed by U.S. officials—that is, the fear that subversion might extend to our country and have repercussions for its political stability. It would be too much to say that Mexico has already renounced its traditional distaste for the U.S. thesis of national security. Nonetheless, its actions with respect to Guatemala reveal, at the very least, confusions and contradictions that suggest a certain parallel between its policies and those of the United States.

ANTI-MEXICANISM IN GUATEMALA

Simple geographic contiguity is central to understanding Mexican policies toward Guatemala. Not surprisingly, Mexico is uneasy about the breakdown of social and political order on its very borders.

Historically, the independence of Mexico came about at the same time as the independence of Central America, which had been integrated into the colonial system under the Captaincy General of Guatemala. On September 15, 1821, in Guatemala City, the five countries of the Captaincy General (Guatemala, El Salvador, Honduras, Nicaragua, and Costa Rica) declared their independence from Spain. Soon afterward, Mexico attempted to annex Central America to its territory. Only El Salvador opposed this annexation, but the existing Mexican government was itself unstable and fell in 1823. The so-called United Provinces of Central America then declared their independence from Mexico and created a federation that lasted from 1824 to 1838. Mexico recognized the independence of these states in 1824.[1]

The state of Chiapas had declared its independence from Spain in August 1821, even earlier than the five countries of the Captaincy General of Guatemala. Soon afterward, along with all of the five except El Salvador, it recognized the Mexican Empire as the sole authority and government in the region. With the fall of the empire, Guatemala attempted to persuade Chiapan authorities to join the United Provinces of Central America. Faced with this threat, the Mexican government sent General Vicente Filisola to dissolve the Junta of Representatives created to support Chiapas's separation from Mexico. After a brief rebellion, a plebiscite held in 1824 resulted in the peaceful annexation of Chiapas to the Mexican nation.[2] The region of Soco-

[1] C. Vázquez Andres, *Bosquejo histórico de la agregación a México de Chiapas y Soconusco* (Mexico, 1923).
[2] *Diccionario porrúa de historia, biografía y geografía de México*, 3d ed. (Mexico, 1970), I.1: 595–97; and *Enciclopedia de México* (Mexico, 1977), III.3: 590–644.

nusco, which since 1569 had been part of Chiapas (but as a separate entity), also opted to integrate itself into Mexico in 1824.

The local Guatemalan government did not accept this decision and sent military forces from the city of Tapachula to take charge of Soconusco. The despotic nature of Guatemala's action, under the mandate of Colonel José Pierson, justified the intervention of Mexico, which sent a large military contingent to Soconusco under the command of General Juan Pablo Anaya. Guatemala retreated without resistance, but the preference of Soconusco's inhabitants remained unclear. For fifteen years the region remained in an undefined autonomous state, governed by its own municipal authorities. Only in 1841 was it finally incorporated into Mexican territory as part of the state of Chiapas.

To Guatemala this outcome was also unacceptable, and the dispute with Mexico over Soconusco and Chiapas smoldered for nearly fifty years. In 1882, after arduous negotiations, Mexico and Guatemala signed a bilateral border treaty that took effect in April 1895.[3] But even this was not enough for Guatemala's dominant classes, who have argued ever since that they were deprived of an important part of their land. This claim, along with their claim to Belize, has been the basis of and fuel for their precarious nationalism.[4]

Juridically this claim has lacked substance, and politically it has never been an issue in negotiations between the two countries. Nevertheless, it remains a source of tension and animosity. It was not of great interest to the powerful landholding oligarchy that monopolized Guatemalan economic resources for most of this century. To them Guatemala was a business, not a country, and Guatemalan nationalism was comparatively unimportant. But it has become important again in the rhetoric of Guatemala's military rulers.

The Revolution of 1944 marked the start of a period of reforms that appeared to be leading Guatemala toward a truly participatory political life. Similarities between Jacobo Arbenz's

---

[3] *Diccionario porrúa*, II.2: 2002.

[4] Belize, which in the colonial era was part of Guatemala, was in fact ceded to England in exchange for lumber exploitation privileges. Since the middle of this century, when Beliceños began to demand their independence, Guatemala has called for its annexation.

reform policies and those of the Mexican Revolution created a new framework for relations between the two countries, and the reformists brushed aside the conservative animosity against Mexico and gave their approval to modest programs of cooperation between the two countries. However, in 1954 this process was abruptly terminated by United States intervention. With help from Washington, the dominant classes regrouped to re-establish their power. During the final months of Arbenz's mandate, the United States attempted to isolate Guatemala internationally. In response, Mexico echoed Arbenz's denunciations of U.S. policy.

In March 1954, under the auspices of Washington, the Tenth Conference of Foreign Affairs Ministers of the Interamerican System was held in Caracas. Its purpose was to accuse Arbenz of allowing extra-continental communist intervention in Latin America. The reality was that the United States felt damaged by the reforms implemented by the regime, notably the agrarian reform, which sought to deprive the United Fruit Company of its properties in the country. Mexico proposed substantial modifications to the resolution resulting from the conference, but the U.S. position prevailed, causing the Mexican and Argentine representatives to abstain from voting. In May the United States claimed that the Arbenz government had received a shipment of communist arms from Czechoslovakia. On June 19 Colonel Carlos Castillo Armas, financed by the CIA, invaded Guatemala from Honduras and toppled the Arbenz government.[5] From this point on, the Mexican government and the Guatemalan military regime began a tense and distant relationship. Guatemalan anti-Mexicanism was reinforced, and anti-Mexican incidents resumed.

The restoration of oligarchic power was achieved at the cost of cruel repression. The military decided to divert political attention from internal problems by vigorously reviving anti-Mexicanism. On the morning of December 31, 1958, five Mexican fishing boats in Mexican waters near Guatemala were attacked by the Guatemalan Air Force. Three Mexican citizens were killed and sixteen wounded, and two boats were destroyed. On January 23 Mexican President Adolfo López Mateos an-

[5] Gordon Connell-Smith, *El sistema interamericano* (Mexico, 1971), p. 197.

nounced the severance of diplomatic relations.[6] In subsequent negotiations conducted with the help of Chile and Brazil, Guatemala argued that, although the boats were effectively outside Guatemala's borders, as the Mexicans alleged, they were nevertheless inside Guatemala's historical borders, i.e., off the coast of Chiapas. The incident ended with Guatemalan apologies, the payment of damages, and the resumption of diplomatic relations in September 1959.

During the 1960's and the early 1970's, the Guatemalan Army, with U.S. technical assistance, dealt efficiently with outbursts of armed opposition. Mexico, unthreatened, turned its attention elsewhere, give or take the occasional border incident. The Guatemalan Army's antiguerrilla campaign of the 1960's did not create major displacements of civilians toward the Mexican border, since the insurgents were isolated from the population and were confined mainly to the northeast.

Over time, however, the deepening of political contradictions, the intensification of repression, and the incapacity of the Guatemalan regime to design consensual solutions brought increasing numbers of the indigenous population over to the revolutionary side. The army was no longer only an instrument of the dominant classes. Through corruption and monopoly over privileges, it became a nucleus of economic power rivaling that of the oligarchy and the bourgeoisie.

In due course, counterinsurgency against a popular revolutionary movement became the regime's only possible strategy for retaining power. In 1981 the army put into effect the policy of *tierra arrasada* ("razed" or "ravaged" land), which consisted of annihilating and dispersing populations susceptible to revolutionary influence. Towns and villages were systematically attacked, and thousands of refugees fled the scene, many of them to the Mexican side of the border.

It is now clear that, like it or not, the Guatemalan political crisis has important consequences for Mexico. The areas of Guatemala adjacent to Mexico—Huehuetenango and San Marcos, the mountainous zones of Las Verapaces and El Quiché, the jungles of Petén—are the scene of significant counterinsurgent

---

[6] *México a través de los informes presidenciales, la política exterior* (Mexico, 1976), pp. 459–60.

activity. This is not coincidental. Not only do these areas have large indigenous populations that have been persistently repressed and exploited, but their difficult terrain is ideal for guerrilla warfare. The sharp increase in counterinsurgent activity along the Mexican border has two fundamental implications for our country. First, thousands of Guatemalan refugees have entered Mexico. Second, the presence of these refugees has added a new element to the anti-Mexicanism of the Guatemalan military.

For the Guatemalan Army the Mexican border presents serious dangers. Not only is there the possibility that refugees in Mexico will transport arms and other supplies through Mexican territory to Guatemala, but there is also the possibility of Mexican political support for the revolutionary movement. Moreover, the possibility of fleeing across the Mexican border makes the regime's terrorist policies less effective, and the presence of refugee camps in Mexico shows up those policies for what they are. Finally, the army fears that the refugees might tighten their links with the revolutionary movement and become a permanent threat to the regime.

WASHINGTON AND GUATEMALA: ALLIED FOR INTIMIDATION

In its attempts to intimidate Mexico, Guatemala's biggest ally is the United States. In late February 1982 Secretary of State Alexander Haig told the *Washington Post* that "the arms destined for the Guatemalan guerrillas come from a variety of sources, and part of the traffic passes through the southern zone of Mexico."[7] On March 4, in an interview with the *Los Angeles Times*, Haig reiterated his opinion that Guatemala was on the verge of a crisis similar to that of El Salvador, a crisis that he deemed "a very large threat to Mexico." He went on to describe the Mexican authorities as unable "to take what a foreign observer would consider to be logical actions," i.e., one presumes, to block the flow of arms to Guatemala through Mexican territory and to prohibit all activity carried on by Guatemalan revolutionary organizations within Mexico. The Guatemalan military clearly agrees with these ideas and would love to see Mexico take this line.

Encouraged by Haig's statements, the Guatemalan govern-

[7] *Washington Post*, Feb. 28, 1982.

ment stepped up its accusations against Mexico, denouncing the alleged use of Mexican territory for activities supporting the Guatemalan guerrilla movement. Five days after the fraudulent elections of March 7, Benedicto Lucas García, then army chief of staff and brother of the president, asked the Mexican government to collaborate in the guarantee of the security of the border. "Perhaps the Mexican civil authorities, as is the case here [in Guatemala]," said Lucas, "are not sufficiently strong to stop subversive activities on the border, which is why I consider a greater militarization of the Mexican side of the border to be advisable." He went on to say that the ministers of defense of the two countries had met for a preliminary discussion of the issue.[8]

The agreement between the vision of the Guatemalan military and the strategic conceptions of the United States with respect to Mexico and Guatemala is obvious. If the Guatemalan military were not so primitive, one might even suspect that Guatemala and Washington were acting in concert with respect to Mexico. Washington urges Mexico to protect its territory from subversive activities; Guatemala urges Mexico to police the refugees to diminish tension along the border. Not much difference there. The panorama is completed by Mexico itself, which officially denies the existence of training camps for Guatemalan guerrillas[9] while simultaneously stepping up migratory surveillance by military and police forces on the border and throughout the country.

MEXICAN-GUATEMALAN FRICTIONS

These actions, however interpreted, are harmless enough in themselves. What is not easily forgiven is the harshness of Mexican policy toward the Guatemalan refugees and the large-scale police abuse of Guatemalan and other Central American exiles in Mexico. These developments, together with the increased presence of the Mexican Army on the border, have not been sufficiently explained and justified by our government. On the contrary, they suggest that some powerful sectors in Mexico, or even sectors of the government itself, believe, as in Washington and Guatemala, that insurgency in Central America threatens

[8] *Excélsior*, Mar. 12, 1982.
[9] *Ibid.*, Mar. 13, 1982.

their own stability. Or perhaps these activities are intended to demonstrate to U.S. strategists that the Mexican state is capable of caring for its own interests, while at the same time making it visible to the Guatemalans that, as part of its politics of neutrality, the Mexican state will not permit the use of its territory for the realization of direct or indirect activities against itself.

Several big questions are raised by current Mexican policy toward Guatemala. At what audience is Mexican policy aimed? At the Guatemalan military? At the government of the United States? Or perhaps at certain possessors of economic and political power, both inside and outside of the Mexican government, who perceive a threat to their interests in the South and identify more each day with the United States? Since the answers to these questions are not yet clear, I shall restrict myself in what follows to the dilemmas confronting Mexican-Guatemalan bilateral relations and to the possible contradictions they entail.

Despite the grave crisis in Guatemala, its effects in Mexico, and the worldwide loss of prestige suffered by the Guatemalan regime, Mexico maintains fully normal diplomatic and political relations with its southern neighbor. Such restraint has not characterized Mexico's relations with other countries in the region. In 1979 the Mexican government severed diplomatic relations with the Somoza dictatorship in Nicaragua, and in 1981 it recognized the insurgent Frente Democrático Revolucionario-Frente Farabundo Martí para la Liberación Nacional (FDR-FMLN) in El Salvador. Indeed, Mexican Foreign Minister Jorge Castañeda publicly described the Salvadoran government as responsible for innumerable deaths—irrefutable proofs of which were in the hands of the Mexican government. Yet, in the case of Guatemala, the Mexican government has limited itself to voting in favor of reports issued by human rights commissions of the U.N. and the OAS, charging Guatemala, along with Chile, Argentina, and El Salvador, with grave violations. Mexico's tone here is very different from that of most other countries. We need only remember that Guatemala was not invited to participate in the Central American Democratic Community by governments such as that of El Salvador. Even the U.S. government, in the end the most interested in keeping the Guatemalan military in power, has found it necessary, owing to pressure from public opinion and Congress, to denounce Guatemala for human rights violations, and even, under Carter, to formally suspend its program of military and economic assistance.

In 1979 Mexico's effort to maintain a climate of normality in its relations with Guatemala took the time-honored form of a presidential visit. In September of that year, when the Guatemalan government of Romeo Lucas García was already considered one of the most repressive in the world, President José López Portillo had a cordial meeting with his Guatemalan colleague in Tapachula, Chiapas. In the company of United States officials, the two presidents visited laboratories in which Mediterranean fruit flies were being raised and sterilized. They talked about other problems of mutual interest, and discussed the construction of a hydroelectric dam on the Usumacinta River that would benefit both countries.[10]

As tensions rose after 1979, subsequent presidential meetings became more problematic. A return visit by López Portillo to Guatemala was originally scheduled for early 1980. On January 31 of that year, a group of Guatemalan peasants occupied the Spanish embassy in Guatemala. The government responded by burning the embassy with all of its occupants, including Guatemalans who were inside to negotiate with the peasants. Only the Spanish ambassador and one peasant survived, and police subsequently removed the peasant from the hospital where he was being treated and killed him. These events caused an angry international protest in which Mexico joined, and López Portillo's visit to Guatemala was postponed.

In August 1981, the Mexican government announced that López Portillo would travel to Guatemala on September 5, returning Lucas García's 1979 visit. But owing to increased anti-Mexican activity by the Lucas regime and anti-Lucas statements from the Mexican left, the visit had to be postponed again.

International developments also had worsened relations between the two regimes. Only days before the scheduled visit, Mexico and France released a communiqué recognizing the Salvadoran FDR and FMLN. This communiqué drew angry reactions in Guatemala, where, among other things, three previously unknown organizations, the Liga de Protección al Guatemalteco, the Liga Guatemalteca Antimexicana, and the Comando

[10] *Uno Más Uno*, Sept. 19, 1979.

Guatemalteca Pro Recuperación de Belice, published a statement in the local Guatemalan press threatening President López
Portillo with death if he visited Guatemala. Belize was at this
time preparing itself for independence from Great Britain contrary to Guatemalan wishes, and Mexico had announced its intention to recognize the new country and back its immediate en-
try into the United Nations. The frictions between Mexico and
Guatemala could hardly have been more evident. Yet whereas
accentuating these frictions was an integral part of the Guatemalan government's domestic policy, the Mexican government
persisted in its policy of minimizing these frictions at almost any
cost.

In September 1981, soon after the frustrated state visit of
López Portillo, a Mexican official in Guatemala, Jesús Silva
Mendo, and two other Mexican citizens living in that country,
Carlos Guadalupe Méndez Pérez and José Luis Méndez Pérez,
were declared missing. Silva Mendo—the Mexican consul in
Malacatán, San Marcos—and Carlos Méndez disappeared while
trying to locate José Luis Méndez, who had been missing since
August 18. The Mexican embassy in Guatemala City officially
notified the Guatemalan government of its concern and solicited
its cooperation; and Mexico's foreign minister sent José Caba-
llero Bazán, director of the consular service, to speak with Guatemalan authorities.[11]

Subsequent developments in the case have not been made
public, save for a response made in June 1982 to renewed Mexican inquiries by Efraín Ríos Montt, head of the military junta
that overthrew Romeo Lucas García in March. In a statement to
the daily *Uno Más Uno* Ríos Montt made the following remarks: "From the diplomatic point of view, let Foreign Relations issue a statement and consider the affair closed. From the
military point of view, my God! What am I supposed to do
about it?"[12]

The original discretion of the Mexican government was understandable and even appropriate in this situation. Its continued
silence seems less justified. It did, to be sure, close its consulate
in Malacatán in May 1982, allegedly as a measure of "economic

[11] *Prensa Libre* (Guatemala), Sept. 23, 1981.
[12] *Uno Más Uno*, June 4, 1982.

austerity."[13] But why no more than this? The government's response to another incident of the same period is equally disturbing. In May 1982 thirteen Guatemalan peasants occupied the Brazilian embassy in Guatemala City in an effort to publicize the killings that were taking place under the new Ríos Montt regime. These peasants were exiled to Mexico, where, though they were granted exile status, they remained under the strict surveillance of the Ministry of the Interior, which denied them access to the media.

MEXICO'S GUATEMALAN POLICY: A POLICY OF MANY VOICES

The caution that characterizes Mexico's foreign policy toward Guatemala has several apparent causes. One is a failure to think hard about how best to combat the hostility of Guatemala's governing military. Another is the fear that taking a definitive position toward Guatemala's political crisis will lead to greater friction with the Generals and stronger pressure from the United States. A third is the lack of a true consensus in the government concerning how to think about the Guatemalan issue.

Still a fourth is a structural difficulty. Mexican policy toward Guatemala is not solely the province of the foreign ministry. Matters concerning Guatemala must also be dealt with by the ministers of the Interior, Labor, and Defense, to name only a few of the most important ones, who must in turn be attentive to different views within their ministries. The governments of border states (Tabasco, Chiapas, and Quintana Roo) must also have their say, not to mention political parties, the Catholic Church, business interests, and the press. Nevertheless, and with all allowances for the complexity of the situation, a certain disconcerting consensus of policy emerges: not to attack the Generals. This posture is expressed at the highest levels of the federal government in the declaration of absolute neutrality with respect to what is happening in Guatemala.

Why? The facts are clear, if only from the presence of thousands of Guatemalan refugees in Mexico. There is ample evidence to support a denunciation, implicit or explicit, of the Guatemalan government. Yet the official attitude of neutrality

[13] *Excélsior*, May 16, 1982.

and the actions that accompany it have become, in practice, an implicit support of and collaboration with the Guatemalan regime. Among these actions are incidents of repression against Guatemalan citizens in Mexico, which, be it added, are then denounced with incredible gall by Guatemalan officials. Whatever can be said for such a policy, it clearly serves to discredit Mexico's foreign policy and its international image.

High-Level Policy Toward Guatemala

In November 1981 President José López Portillo, when asked by an NBC interviewer about Mexico's view of developments in El Salvador and Guatemala, acknowledged the existence of lawless violence in both countries but distinguished between El Salvador, where "we want the solution to this situation to be a political one so that the violence can end," and Guatemala, where "we are totally detached from this problem and we simply lament that they have it." Of Guatemala, he added, "As we say in bullfighting language, leave them alone in the ring."[14]

In the case of El Salvador, the factual situation, which entails violence, repression, and conflict between different forces, is recognized; and, owing to the international character that this conflict has taken on, Mexico feels obliged to recognize the actors involved and to opt for a political solution. In contrast, though there is admittedly a problem in Guatemala, it remains undefined. Earlier, in an interview with a Tunisian journalist on the same subjects, López Portillo remarked, "We have to clear up the situation. We have to order the world so as to give life to viable solutions for countries like El Salvador and Guatemala." But he immediately added, "The latter is not in the condition of the former."[15] Always, when there is a specific reference to Guatemala, an exception is made.

In one way Guatemala did not in fact resemble El Salvador at the time of these remarks by López Portillo: there did not yet exist a clearly constituted political and military front for all Guatemalan insurgents. This could be taken to mean that Mexico did not yet perceive an alternative organization with respect to which new policy options toward Guatemala could be formu-

[14]Dirección General de Información y Relaciones Públicas, Presidencia de la República, *El Gobierno de México*, no. 60 (Nov. 1981), p. 55.
[15]*Ibid.*, no. 56 (July 1981), pp. 76–77.

lated. Since then, however, the revolutionary military organizations fighting the Guatemalan government have unified into the Unidad Revolucionaria Guatemalteca (URG); and another organization, the Comité de Unidad Patriótica de Guatemala, headed by Luis Cardoza y Aragón and including important political and intellectual figures from Guatemala, was formed in Mexico in February 1982. Plainly, then, the lack of an alternative to the regime of the Generals is not responsible for Mexico's continued neutral posture toward Guatemala.

Nor does the Mexican government seem to worry about the possibility of a socialist regime being established in Guatemala. There is no reason to doubt the sincerity of President López Portillo's response in February 1982 to a CBS interviewer's question about the possible consequences of an insurgent victory in Guatemala: "Well, a system would be established, the result of Guatemalan self-determination, and nothing more. In Cuba there is a communist regime, and we have magnificent relations with Cuba. We have magnificent relations with China and the Soviet Union." But how, more precisely, would Mexico view a Marxist regime in Guatemala? The president responded, "Nothing would happen. Normal commercial and tourist relations, etc. Nothing would happen." [16]

Where, then, lies the problem? Even Mexico's foreign minister, Jorge Castañeda, who has probably had more than anyone else to do with Mexico's independent foreign policy in Central America, has revealed himself to be particularly cautious with respect to Guatemala. On the one hand, he has rejected the possibility that the Guatemalan revolutionary movement could extend to Mexico: "Nothing like the struggle of the Guatemalan peasantry would make sense in Mexico, since we experienced this stage sixty years ago. We know how costly it was. I am convinced that the problem affecting Guatemala will not cross the border." Despite this unusually straightforward reference to the nature of the social upheaval in Guatemala, Castañeda argues that conditions are not conducive to a Mexican initiative of any sort: "The situation has not become internationalized and thus does not merit or permit actions like those taken by Mexico in other cases (Nicaragua and El Salvador). The situations are dif-

[16] *El Día*, Mar. 23, 1982, cited in Jacobo Vargas Foronda, *¡Hasta cuando!* (Mexico, 1982), mimeographed version, p. 78.

ferent."[17] Castañeda was obviously referring to a peace initiative or the search for a political solution. He did not go on to contrast Mexico's vigorous opposition to U.S. interventionist policies in El Salvador and Nicaragua with its silence on this matter in respect to Guatemala; or Mexico's unhesitating denunciation of the repressive character of the Salvadoran regime and the Somoza dictatorship with the absence of any such denunciation of the Guatemalan military. The time is not ripe, he says. Why not? "The situations are different." How?

Meanwhile, little has changed in Guatemala. The regime presided over by General Efraín Ríos Montt has to a certain extent modified its rhetoric with respect to Mexico, and Ríos Montt himself has even proposed a presidential visit.[18] But it is clear that his concern is with enlisting Mexican support against Guatemalan guerrilla activities on the Mexican side of the border. Despite the pleasantries of Ríos Montt, the fundamental attitude toward Mexico has not changed, nor have the climate of repression and the killings of peasants in the zones closest to the border.

In effect, no change is likely so long as Guatemala's rulers can bolster their claim to legitimacy by appealing to the widespread anti-Mexicanism of Guatemala's people. It is in the logic of the situation for the Guatemalan military to denounce alleged guerrilla activities in Mexico, to limit the flow of refugees into what it perceives as enemy territory, and to obtain help from wherever possible, including the Mexican Army, in expelling refugees and sealing off the border.

Military Activity

If we take into account only the public statements of Mexican officials, the independence of Belize would appear to be the only point of contention between Mexico and Guatemala. We do not hear about the increasing presence of the Mexican Army along the Guatemalan border, or about the mounting problem of dealing with Guatemalan refugees. Yet these phenomena exist, and ignoring them merely compounds the problems involved.

What is the reason for recent increases in Mexican military strength along the border? Are they designed to prevent Guate-

[17] *Excélsior*, June 24, 1982.
[18] *Uno Más Uno*, June 4, 1982.

malan insurgent activity within Mexico? To protect the southern border against threats from the Guatemalan military? Whatever the reason, one result is the increased surveillance of Guatemalans who, for political reasons, reside in different parts of our country. The motive for this surveillance seems to be fear lest Guatemalan insurgency infect Mexico and threaten its political stability.

Actual border incidents, however—at least those reported in the national press—have been wholly the work of the Guatemalan Army. According to charges made by Mexican peasants in March 1982, "every fifteen days, three or four Guatemalan patrol boats enter Mexican territory in the jungle zones of Chiapas" in the border region.[19] Other peasants reported that "at least twice between June 1981 and March 1982 soldiers have entered Mexico in search of refugees from Guatemala," and that these soldiers "swear to kill Guatemalans, even on the Mexican side."[20] According to still other accusations, the Guatemalan Army robs and beats up Mexicans who cross the Usumacinta River to sell their goods in Guatemalan towns. Even the Mexican minister of defense took note of this last matter, claiming that it had been taken care of by his Guatemalan counterpart. He denies, however, that Guatemalan troops have entered Mexican territory.[21] By contrast, the director of the Mexican Interministerial Commission on Aid to Refugees, Luis Ortiz Monasterio, has admitted to "sporadic incursions" by Guatemalan troops, but does not consider them serious since they are clearly "aimed at provoking the Mexican government into closing its border to peasants fleeing from the violence in Guatemala."[22]

All in all, Mexican military authorities seem to be more worried about Guatemalan insurgent activity than about incursions of the Guatemalan Army. As Mexico's minister of defense has stated, the Mexican Army's main concern along the border is Guatemalan guerrillas. If guerrillas enter the country, Mexican forces are to "apprehend them, arrest them, and deliver them to the appropriate authorities."[23]

What does the Mexican Army fear? Does it fear that these

[19] *Ibid.*, Mar. 31, 1982.
[21] *Proceso*, no. 282 (Mar. 29, 1982).
[23] *Proceso*, no. 282 (Mar. 29, 1982).

[20] *Ibid.*, Mar. 8, 1982.
[22] *Uno Más Uno*, Mar. 25, 1982.

subversive groups will also become committed to stirring up political instability in Mexico? Is it simply trying to ensure that Mexican territory is not used for activities that threaten the Guatemalan regime? The answers are not clear. Yet in the actions of the Mexican Army one detects a certain sympathy with the cause of its Guatemalan counterpart, a more than neutral eagerness to collaborate.

In December 1981 Mexico's armed forces staged a military exercise in the Southeast. The operation consisted of repelling the invasion of an extra-continental enemy that first captured several Caribbean islands, then "invaded a neighboring country, surprising its armed forces, and continued its operations into our territory with the goal of occupying the oil region of the Gulf of Mexico."[24] The operation based on this scenario involved mobilizing some 40,000 men. Guatemalan military personnel were invited to observe the exercise, and also, according to Defense Minister Félix Galván, "to tour the regions with me where it has been claimed that guerrilla training camps were located. Some fourteen or fifteen officials landed their helicopters at points they themselves selected, to get better proof that no such camps existed."[25]

GUATEMALAN MIGRATION

Migration between Mexico and Guatemala has a long tradition. During the annual harvest periods, especially the coffee harvest, sixty to seventy thousand Guatemalans cross into Mexico without legal papers. Most perform agricultural tasks, but many others seek work in services and other activities, including oil drilling in Campeche and Tabasco. Some Guatemalans and Central Americans do not stay in Mexico but pass through en route to the United States. Most illegal immigrants remain in Mexico only a few months before returning to Guatemala: proportions aside, the pattern is similar to that of seasonal migration from Mexico to the United States. This migration pattern is attributable to Guatemalan economic problems preceding, and not directly related to, the repressive activities of the military in the peasant communities. Its similarity to the illegal migration of Mexican workers to the United States is striking: illegal Gua-

[24] Otto Granados, "Regreso a las armas?," *Nexus*, no. 50 (Feb. 1982).
[25] *Proceso*, no. 282 (Mar. 29, 1982).

temalan workers, for example, are subjected to various forms of humiliation and extortion by the Mexican immigration service.

Alternatively, Guatemalan workers are imported by agreement between landholding Mexican *empresarios* and their Guatemalan counterparts. Also, many Guatemalans, including several military leaders, own rich coffee plantations on the Mexican side of the border. This phenomenon was publicized before the Guatemalan elections of March 7, 1982, when Amnesty International and the Comité de Ayuda a Refugiados Guatemaltecos denounced the Guatemalan regime for coercing Guatemalan workers on Guatemalan-owned Mexican farms to return to Guatemala to vote. From March 5 to March 8, Mexican farms in the border areas suspended work to enable peasants to return to vote in the Guatemalan elections.[26]

In recent years a very different type of migration has taken place. Thousands of Guatemalan peasants and Indians, direct victims of the Guatemalan military's policy of *tierra arrasada*, have sought refuge in our country. The first public denunciations of this phenomenon were made by the Catholic Church in April 1981, when the archbishop of Oaxaca, Bartolomé Carrasco Briseño, charged that hundreds of Guatemalans, mostly women, children, and old people, had fled to Mexico rather than fall into the hands of the military. This same denunciation noted the repression and maltreatment of these people in Mexican territory.[27]

In July 1981 the refugee problem took on large-scale proportions. Mexican authorities began to expel Guatemalan refugees in considerably increased numbers and with less regard to niceties. On July 3, two Guatemalan peasants arrived in Mexico City, representing eight hundred immigrant families, to ask that refugee status be granted these families. They claimed, among other things, that Mexican authorities had allowed them to cross the river "because they know us and are well aware of what is happening in Guatemala."[28]

Nevertheless, from July 14 on, the Mexican Army and migration officials began massive deportation operations. Soon, some 1,900 Guatemalans had been forcibly returned to their country, typically after acceding to Mexican demands for money to pay

[26] *Uno Más Uno*, Mar. 6, 1982.   [27] *Excelsior*, Apr. 18, 1981.
[28] *Uno Más Uno*, July 3, 1981.

the costs of returning them. Beyond doubt, some (perhaps many) of the repatriated refugees were killed by the Guatemalan Army.[29]

The angry public reaction to these events took Mexican authorities by surprise; they could only note that all governmental actions on the border had been in strict compliance with immigration laws. In any case, these events amply revealed the lack of a refugee policy, the absence of coordination between military and immigration officials, and the ineffectuality of the newly created Interministerial Commission on Aid to Refugees. Gabino Fraga, head of the commission prior to Ortiz Monasterio, could only resign in protest over the arbitrary actions of the Mexican government.

The Guatemalan military regime, not surprisingly, took a different view of the refugee question. In September 1981, Guatemalan ambassador to Mexico Jorge Palmieri complained, among other things, that Guatemalan refugees in Mexico were systematically mistreated by their employers, and "when the time comes to be paid, they are reported to the migratory officials and deported without even getting the pay they are owed."[30] An ex-president of Guatemala, Carlos Arana Osorio, added that Guatemalan peasants emigrated to Mexico not to escape repression, but (one supposes) to create trouble back home. "When a hundred Guatemalan families left for Mexico, they made a big scandal. They said that the Army had thrown them out, which is absurd since they live in better conditions here than in Mexico."[31]

In short, the refugees are either emigrants in search of work, guerrillas bent on establishing bases in Chiapas and Tabasco, or possibly, according to Benedicto Lucas García, peasants forced not by the Guatemalan Army but by guerrilla organizations to emigrate against their will.[32] In June 1982, Ríos Montt took the first of these lines, that Guatemalan migration to Mexico responds to the same impulse as the migration of Mexicans to the United States, namely "the need to work." He added fervently, "Blessed be God that we have Mexico there and ready."[33]

Three months after Arana's statement, in December 1981, eight hundred Guatemala families that had settled on the lands

[29] Miguel Concha, "Refugiados guatemaltecos," in *Uno Más Uno*, Aug. 7, 1981.
[30] *Uno Más Uno*, Aug. 28, 1981.
[31] *Prensa Libre* (Guatemala), Sept. 4, 1981.
[32] *Excélsior*, Mar. 12, 1982.
[33] *Uno Más Uno*, June 4, 1982.

of the Buenos Aires Farm in Chiapas were deported by Mexican immigration officials. On their arrival in Guatemala, they were fired on by troops and armored helicopters of the Guatemalan military. Many survivors fled to the mountains, and others were able to return to Mexico, but the reports spoke of hundreds of casualties. In the following weeks, other events of this sort were reported.[34]

Faced with the charges made by *Uno Más Uno* and carried also in the international press, the Mexican government again reacted in a confusing and contradictory manner. Luis Ortiz Monasterio, new head of the Interministerial Commission on Aid to Refugees, stated that the massive deportations violated the Treaties of San José on refugees, to which Mexico is a signatory, and would end immediately. The Office of Migratory Services of the Ministry of the Interior disagreed. The disagreement has not been publicly resolved, and government policy in the matter is accordingly unclear.

By this time the refugee problem was attracting international attention. The U.N. High Commissioner for Refugees, who until then had handled matters relating to Mexico from San José, Costa Rica, announced on January 22, 1982, that a branch would be opened in Mexico. In February 1982 a commission of bishops from the dioceses of Chiapas, Oaxaca, and Morelos visited the border zone to familiarize themselves with the plight of the refugees.[35] On March 30, amid growing public concern about the migration of Guatemalans across the Mexican border, the Foreign Relations Committee of the Chamber of Deputies summoned Ortiz Monasterio to inform Congress about the situation of the refugees. He reported that his organization and the Ministry of the Interior had already worked out a way of protecting the refugees: they had been assigned the immigration classification FM-8, which permitted them to reside in Mexico and to go back and forth between the two countries. This classification was necessary, he said, because the refugees were not workers in search of permanent residence in Mexico, but Indians and peasants fleeing the repression and hoping to return to their communities when conditions improved. Ortiz Monasterio explained that the new classification, good for a period of

[34] *Ibid.*, Jan. 19, 1982.
[35] *Ibid.*, Feb. 28, 1982.

three months to three years, was an attempt to deal with a problem for which no provision was made in existing laws.

TWO REFUGEE POLICIES

It is nevertheless clear that Mexico has had two policies toward the refugees. On the one hand, although in ambiguous fashion, the highest Mexican authorities have acknowledged that most immigrants from Guatemala are truly refugees. President López Portillo himself has used this term. Moreover, three of his cabinet ministers form part of the Interministerial Commission on Aid to Refugees, which in cooperation with the U.N. High Commission offers the refugees all types of services, including medical care, and whose member ministers keep the issue prominent in the deliberations of the federal government. On the other hand, the Mexican government frequently presents a view of the refugees that is incompatible with the work carried out by the commission.

In the border zones of the country, the two official policies coexist. At the same time as the refugee commission locates Guatemalans scattered throughout the jungles and mountains of Chiapas and Tabasco, setting up camps for them and providing aid, immigration officials hunt down other Guatemalans and deport them. Typically, the local peasant population supports and protects the refugees, at times against Mexican immigration officials, who pursue them for a variety of motives, including extortion. In March 1982, *Uno Más Uno* reported that "six new immigration checkpoints have been set up in Tenosique (Tabasco), Frontera Echeverría, Ixcán, El Pedernal, Vicente Guerrero, and Llano Grande, making a total of eighteen on what could be called the border of Chiapas." According to this report, "On almost all roads leading to the Guatemalan border, there are groups of soldiers who check each vehicle, one by one, to ensure that it is not carrying arms into Guatemala, and to see that nobody gets into Mexico without having his immigration papers in order." [36]

Mexican policy toward refugees is thus a contradiction: one arm of the government views the refugees as subversive agents and disruptive factors, while another views them as victims of

[36] *Ibid.*, Mar. 8, 1982.

the brutality of the Guatemalan military. In espousing the former position, the Mexican government's purpose is not clear: whether to please the Guatemalan Generals, or to show Washington that Mexico is capable of controlling its border, containing subversion, and prohibiting actions against its allies in Guatemala. At any rate, in the eyes of the Office of Migratory Services, nominally the authority responsible for dictating official policy in this area, there are no refugees.

A revealing statement on this point was made in May 1982 by Diana Torres, Director General of Migratory Services of the Ministry of the Interior, in a discussion of immigration from Central and South America generally.[37] Torres described this immigration as "creating serious pressures in the labor market, for social, educational, housing, and urban services, as well as in the fight against delinquency," and as causing "a serious distortion in the tertiary sector of the economy." She acknowledged that in the previous three years "political and military conflicts . . . in Guatemala and El Salvador" had caused many people from those countries to emigrate to Mexico, but denied that Guatemalan migration to Mexico involved significant numbers of people directly affected by counterinsurgency. On the one hand, she argued that "the number of political exiles is relatively low, since a true combatant remains at the place of struggle." On the other hand, she suggested that "the great majority are part of a migratory current seeking work and resettlement."

Her concern was with the effect on Mexican society. Not only might immigrants create unemployment among Mexicans, leading to resentment and strife between the two groups, but many of the immigrants were delinquents and gangsters, and most would put a strain on public health services and the urban infrastructure generally. In Torres's view, Mexicans would not respond well to "the presence of foreigners in their places of work and study," and to "their antisocial behavior." In sum, she considered immigration to Mexico the cause of "an increase in social disintegration, a rise in population, unemployment, poverty, promiscuity, ignorance, delinquency, violence, anarchism,

[37] Diana Torres, *Intervención en la mesa redonda sobre corriente migratoria hacia México*, organized by the Tribuna de la Juventud, Tuxtla Gutiérrez, Chiapas (May 21, 1982). The remaining citations attributed here to Diana Torres were taken from the text of this conference.

etc." To the Ministry of the Interior, then, this is not only a migration of the economically destitute in search of work, but also a migration of persons bent on subverting the public order and political peace of Mexico.

Despite the legal arguments used by the Ministry of Interior to justify its restrictions on the migration of refugees, it is clear that the true motive is not juridical but political, a reflection of the policy of strict neutrality followed vis-à-vis Guatemala. Torres has stated: "Mexico has geographical and political borders with countries that have very different political systems, very different levels of development, and very diverse internal problems. It must ensure that the movement of people from its neighbors, the United States of America, Guatemala, Belize, Cuba, and other Caribbean countries, does not lead to frictions or international problems." This means that, according to the Ministry of the Interior, migration policy is an integral part of foreign policy and as such must be careful not to draw Mexico into conflict with its neighbors.

With respect to policy toward Guatemala and particularly toward the refugees, different positions within the government have blocked any consensus. At issue are a debate over national security and a struggle between contending political and economic interests. In March 1982 the industrialist José Luis Coindreau, leader of the Confederación Patronal de la República Mexicana (COPARMEX), decried both "guerrilla infiltrations on the southern border" and "undue flirtations with foreign ideologies."[38] He later urged that the border "be sealed to infiltrations and ideological contaminations," and complained that "the communists take advantage of everything, especially now that we have political, economic, and social problems to fan the flames."[39]

In the same vein, Pablo Emilio Madero, the conservative Partido de Acción Nacional (PAN) candidate for the presidency of the Republic, publicly asked that the Mexican Army be strengthened on the southern border. According to Madero, "The real danger to Mexico is the greed awakened by communism in the southeast of the country, where the oil is. Additionally, the

[38] *Proceso*, no. 281 (Mar. 22, 1982).
[39] *El Día*, Mar. 18, 1982.

training of guerrillas, which goes undetected in our country, is not to the liking of the Guatemalan dictatorship since they are outside of its borders and can't be apprehended."[40]

These statements express a view that is widespread among business groups and in some sectors of the Mexican middle class. They see the Central American revolution, and especially the Guatemalan revolution, as a development that, if unchecked, could someday threaten their economic interests in Mexico. They share with the U.S. State Department the notion that south of Mexico's borders the flames of a communist conspiracy are being fanned.

CONCLUSION

In this essay we have examined the evolution of Mexican policy toward Guatemala within the context of the government's diplomatic relations with the Reagan administration and the Guatemalan military. This evolution has in fact been ambiguous and confusing. In a word, Mexico's highest representatives have elected to take shelter behind a supposed neutrality so as not to denounce the regime of terror that the Guatemalan military has imposed on its country.

Within this general orientation, different agencies of the Mexican government have responded differently. The foreign ministry has been extremely cautious in all matters involving Guatemala, including the disappearance of a Mexican consul and two other Mexican citizens in September 1981. The Ministry of Defense, whose chief worry seems to be that Guatemalan revolutionary groups will transfer their activities to Mexican soil, has concentrated its efforts on seeing to it that this does not happen, to the point of permitting the Mexican Army to assist immigration authorities in deporting refugees.

The Ministry of the Interior, together with other government offices, has put into practice two policies regarding the migration of Guatemalans. On the one hand, the migrants are officially denied refugee status, are denounced as disruptive factors and causes of social instability, and are subjected to restrictive practices in Mexico. On the other hand, the Interministerial Commission on Aid for Refugees, a fundamental part of the Ministry

[40] *Excélsior*, Mar. 6, 1982.

of the Interior, makes a significant effort to assist the refugees in meeting their most urgent needs.

A debate has accordingly developed, in which various information media, ecclesiastical groups, and organizations representing the intellectual and political left denounce Guatemala's repressive regime and urge the state to repudiate it, while business organizations and rightist political groups express distaste for the Guatemalan revolutionary movement and characterize Guatemalan refugees as a threat to the social peace of Mexico. At this writing, the ambiguous stance of the Mexican government has served only to confuse public opinion and strengthen the position of the right.

Guatemala: Crisis and Response

Piero Gleijeses

IN JUNE 1954 the government of the United States scored a
signal victory by achieving, at little cost, the overthrow of
Guatemala's president, Jacobo Arbenz. Over a quarter-century
later, the Guatemalan people are still paying a heavy price for
Washington's victory. But the "Pax Americana" now faces a
challenge far more formidable than the one represented by Arbenz, and the efforts of the Reagan administration to prevent a
victory of the revolutionary left appear increasingly futile.*

THE LEGACY OF THE U.S. VICTORY OVER ARBENZ

In 1953–54, while clamoring for a U.S.-sponsored overthrow
of Arbenz, many American liberals urged that the "Red President" be replaced by a moderate leader—a Guatemalan Figueres. Men like Adolf Berle and, in Costa Rica, José Figueres himself argued that a "third force" (the magic "center" that liberals
would later seek again in Guatemala and in other countries of
the Western Hemisphere) would be more satisfactory morally
than a highly repressive regime and, above all, would best guarantee the indispensable pro-American stability in the long term.[1]

As on later occasions, however, the liberals' argument, if sincere, betrayed a deep misunderstanding of Guatemalan reality.
There was no political center in that country to serve Washington's interests. The weak middle class largely supported Arbenz.

---

*This essay is based not only on written sources, but, in addition, on a series of inter-
views with U.S. officials, Guatemalans of different political persuasions, and other observers. For their protection, their names will not be listed. The author's most recent trip
to Guatemala was in September 1982.

[1] Adolf Berle, *Navigating the Rapids* (New York, 1973), pp. 616–19; personal interview with José Figueres.

The only forces that could replace the Arbenz government—
and had been desperately seeking its overthrow—were those
powerful landed groups who bitterly opposed any change that
might affect, however slightly, their entrenched privileges. There
was no realistic choice between a "liberal" and a "reactionary"
coup: the only choice, of marginal significance, was between intransigent conservatives like Colonel Carlos Castillo Armas and
General Miguel Ydígoras Fuentes.[2]

For their part the liberals, despite their lamentations, preferred the overthrow of Arbenz, whatever the nature of the
coup, to a continuation of his government. In the same vein,
nine years later, John F. Kennedy preferred a military coup to
the "threat" of Arévalo's return to the presidency; and, in 1980,
the Carter administration, despite its criticism of the Lucas government, preferred it to the only existing alternative: an eventual victory of the guerrilla forces and their civilian allies.

The same logic that dictated the character of the coup against
Arbenz has marked the nature of the Guatemalan political system in subsequent decades. Over the years the most important
change within the system was not the diversification of the
bourgeoisie into agro-exporting, industrial, commercial, and financial sectors, but rather the shift in the relative importance of
the military vis-à-vis the bourgeoisie. In the wake of Arbenz's
overthrow, the army was the junior partner of the triumphant
landowning class. Discredited and divided into a series of cli-
ques, it was stained, in the eyes of Castillo Armas's *Liberacio-
nistas* and of its U.S. mentor as well, by its earlier tolerance of
Arbenz—a stain that its last moment betrayal could not erase.

The military became progressively the senior partner in the
alliance with the bourgeoisie, largely in response to the guerrilla
challenge of the 1960's (which enhanced its role as the guardian
of the status quo) and to the remarkable degree of unity that the
institution had developed over the years. As a result, the military acquired, particularly in the 1970's, its own independent

[2] Much to General Ydígoras's indignation, the CIA finally selected Colonel Castillo
Armas to head the plot to overthrow Arbenz; for Ydígoras's self-serving explanation of
why the CIA passed him over, see his highly entertaining if misleading account in *My
War with Communism* (Englewood Cliffs, N.J., 1963), pp. 49–51. Ydígoras's turn finally came in 1958, when he became president of Guatemala following Castillo Armas's
assassination.

economic base, and became the country's strongest political "party," ruled by a "central committee" of a few senior officers.[3] From 1970 on, this party selected Guatemala's presidents—always a general—resorting in 1974, 1978, and again in 1982, to flagrant electoral fraud. As a result, even the civilian leaders of the bourgeoisie were reduced to a secondary role, and the presidential elections, already meaningless for a large majority of Guatemalans, became increasingly irrelevant for the civilian parties of the right as well.[4]

Despite minor quarrels over the division of the spoils, the alliance between the armed forces and the bourgeoisie continued to function quite satisfactorily until the latter years of the Lucas government. Both partners reaped immense benefits in the process, profiting from the sustained growth rate of the economy[5] and the benefits of a laissez-faire capitalism that encouraged state intervention only to advance forcibly the interests of a selected

[3] The senior officers can be considered a part of the bourgeoisie. Although the younger officers belong to the middle class, their primary loyalty remains with the military.

[4] The 1965 *Ley electoral y de partidos políticos* stipulates that political parties must be authorized by an electoral council, permitting many procedural techniques to deny or delay legal recognition. As a result, there have been parties not officially recognized, but with greater popular following than those receiving the council's imprimatur (as in the case of the left-of-center Frente Unido de la Revolución [FUR] until its recognition in 1979).

Until 1978 there were only four recognized political parties: Partido Revolucionario (PR), Movimiento de Liberación Nacional (MLN), Partido Institucional Democrático (PID), and Democracia Cristiana Guatemalteca (DC). Since that time, the Lucas government authorized four more: the Central Auténtica Nacionalista (CAN), the Partido Nacional Renovador (PNR), the Frente de Unidad Nacional (FUN), and the FUR. This apparent democratization was only cosmetic, since the party system was more restricted than ever. A ninth party, the Partido Social Democrático (PSD), has not been granted recognition. Of the nine parties, only three (FUR, PSD, and DC) belong, broadly speaking, to a political center encompassing moderate left to moderate right.

In the 1970's, parties served to express the political will of the armed forces. In the 1974, 1978, and 1982 elections the political parties represented different factions within the military, which explains why in 1974 and 1978 more than one presidential candidate has been a military officer. The armed forces have successfully played one party against another, but the political parties have been unable to play factions of the military against one another. A political party refusing to perform its assigned role was subjected to different forms of pressure, such as bribes, covert threats, physical elimination of its leaders and other members, among others.

[5] The overall rate of economic growth accelerated significantly from the 1950's, when it averaged less than 4% per year. Participation in the Central American Common Market, beginning in 1960, helped raise the annual growth rate to an average of 5.5% in that decade. Since the mid-1960's Guatemala's growth has generally been the Latin American average (for the period 1965–73, for example, the median growth in GDP in Latin America was 4.7%, compared to Guatemala's 6.1%).

minority at the expense of the populace. This economic growth was not accompanied, however, by even modest social reforms, and while the economy prospered, the conditions of the lower strata of the population worsened. The expansion of export crops, soil erosion, and population increases exacerbated the pressure on small landholders, further disrupting the traditional world of the Indians in the Altiplano, while the fledgling industrial sector and commercial agriculture, both capital intensive, could not absorb the growing numbers of unemployed and underemployed.[6]

Under such conditions, only violence could maintain the social status quo. Waves of extreme violence (as in 1966–68, 1970–73, and since 1978) alternated with periods of selective repression (as in 1974–77), depending on the degree of pressure from below on the bourgeoisie and the military.[7] Repression was not limited to left-wing groups and "subversive" peasants. The fury of the regime fell on the political center whenever the latter threatened to take meaningful positions, and the increasingly large middle class, though allowed a modest share of economic benefits, was permitted no independent political role.

[6] The lack of social reforms limited the growth potential of the economy. The chronic low productivity of the *minifundia* restricted the growth of agricultural production of the export sector and created the need for unnecessary and expensive imports of basic foodstuffs. The extremely low educational level (even by Latin American standards) affected the productivity of the work force, creating a serious shortage of skilled and semi-skilled labor, particularly evident in manufacturing. Moreover, the subsistence level of the mass of the population has limited domestic demand and dangerously increased industry's dependence on exports. As a recent study of the World Bank noted, "With a major portion of the population living outside or at the margin of the monetized economy, and with the recent inflation eroding the purchasing power of the wage earners, the inadequate domestic demand for consumer products has been a significant constraint on expansion of domestic production. Economic growth could be accelerated substantially if the effective purchasing power of the bulk of the population, particularly in the rural areas, were increased." (*Guatemala: Economic and Social Position and Prospects* [Washington, D.C., 1978], p. iii.)

[7] The best analysis of this process is provided by Gabriel Aguilera Peralta, Jorge Romero Imery, et al., *Dialécticas del terror en Guatemala* (San José, Costa Rica, 1982). Numerous articles on the subject include Aguilera Peralta, "El proceso del terror en Guatemala," *Estudios Sociales*, 4 (Aug. 1971), 35–66, and "Terror and Violence as Weapons of Counterinsurgency in Guatemala," *Latin American Perspectives*, 7, no. 2–3 (Spring–Summer 1980), 91–113; Kenneth Johnson, "On the Guatemalan Political Violence," *Politics and Society*, 4, no. 1 (Fall 1973), 55–82; and John Booth, "A Guatemalan Nightmare: Levels of Political Violence, 1966–1972," *Journal of Interamerican Studies and World Affairs*, 22, no. 2 (May 1980), 195–223. Particularly valuable are the reports by Amnesty International, and the classic *La violencia en Guatemala* (Mexico, 1969), by the Comité de Defensa de los Derechos Humanos.

This reality was strikingly manifest during the administration of President Julio César Méndez Montenegro (1966–70), a well-respected moderate who won the elections as the candidate of the centrist Partido Revolucionario (PR). Méndez Montenegro was allowed to assume the presidency only after his written guarantee that the armed forces would effectively rule the country during his tenure[8]—a bargain he kept scrupulously. For four long years he provided a veneer of international legitimacy while the social reforms promised by the PR remained a dead letter and the armed forces, in a U.S.-supported campaign of indiscriminate terror, massacred thousands of peasants and a handful of guerrillas. The military also kept their side of the bargain. To the surprise of many, and the applause of others, the nimble Méndez Montenegro was allowed to remain in the presidential palace until the end of his constitutional term, while the discredited and demoralized PR abandoned all but the most flimsy pretenses of reformism.[9]

THE 1974–1977 "MODERNIZING PERIOD"

The extreme repression that characterized the period of Méndez Montenegro continued unabated throughout most of the presidency of General Carlos Arana (1970–74). The victims of the terror included the last remaining guerrilla nuclei and those moderate political leaders who opposed armed struggle but sought some social reform, as well as thousands of hapless individuals who could have been branded as subversives only in a system gripped by paranoia. In the first three years of the presidency of General Kjell Laugerud (1974–78), however, the Guatemalan government took the unusual step of implementing some modest social reforms—notably, it provided financial assistance for cooperatives in the Altiplano and allowed them to receive aid from foreign development sources. Moreover, even in the last months of the Arana period, the repression had ac-

---

[8]The text of the secret pact of May 4, 1966, was eventually published in the Guatemalan daily *La Hora* of Nov. 26 and 27, 1973, by Clemente Marroquín Rojas, who had also signed the document as Méndez Montenegro's elected vice-president of the Republic.

[9]The PR was soundly defeated in the 1970 elections—and not through fraud. Thereafter the party's moderate elements were expelled or left; others were bought off; and what remained of the PR—the strongest centrist party of the 1960's—limped along throughout the decade (and to this date) as a loyal tool of the regime, meekly supporting the president of the moment.

quired a more selective character, and on repeated occasions
Laugerud refrained from "settling" strikes by force.

The combination of these developments—so modest in another setting, yet uncharacteristic of post-1954 Guatemala—
afforded hope to elements of the political center and moderate
left of an incipient opening in the ruling system that might eventually lead, by the 1982 elections, to a degree of democratization without the need for a hard and bloody fight.

By 1978, however, it was evident that this had been a naive
hope. The government's "modernizing" effort had assumed that
a limited amount of circumscribed reforms, accompanied by a
decrease in repression, would succeed in coopting strategic sectors within the popular strata. But the reforms were too modest
to allow any significant degree of cooptation. On the other
hand, the slackening of the repression, the number of successful
strikes, the hopes awakened by the government's timid steps—
and the frustration that resulted from their shallow character—
all contributed to radicalize large sectors of the population. In
the countryside, instead of a meek and government-controlled
cooperative movement, the militant and politically conscious
Comité de Unidad Campesina (CUC) rapidly gained strength. In
the cities, the trade unions, while still small, had by early 1978
reached their highest peak in numbers and militancy since 1954.
Guerrilla activities had once again begun, if on a small scale, in
several areas in the countryside.

Thus, viewed in rational terms, the Guatemalan ruling class
faced stark alternatives. It could, in order to pursue a more realistic attempt at cooptation, embark on more significant, and
painful, social reforms, or it could unleash a wave of terror.
Given the nature of the regime, the latter was the only logical
choice. The last months of Laugerud's administration saw the
beginning of yet another period of fierce repression, a further
demonstration that the alternating cycles of extreme and moderate violence were influenced little by the personal attitudes of
the men in power.[10]

[10] It is interesting to note that a number of observers, focusing on formal symbols
hardly relevant in the Guatemalan context, characterized the Lucas administration at
the outset as center-right. They were misled by the fact that Lucas was also supported by
the formerly centrist Partido Revolucionario, and that he chose as his running mate
Francisco Villagrán Kramer, a man with a respected reformist past. In fact, until his
resignation in September 1980, Villagrán Kramer stolidly performed his role as a conve-

THE LUCAS GOVERNMENT

Laugerud's ineffectual modernizing effort was replaced by violence that soon reached levels unprecedented even by Guatemalan standards. The fledgling political center, which had once more begun to develop under Laugerud, was again ruthlessly persecuted. The assassination in early 1979 of Alberto Fuentes Mohr and Manuel Colom Argueta, the charismatic leaders of the Partido Social Democrático and the Frente Unido de la Revolución respectively, was only the ominous beginning; soon their parties felt the regime's wrath. Particularly striking is the fate that befell the Democracia Cristiana (DC), the tamest of the country's centrist parties. It was the only party—outside the extreme right—to participate in the April 1980 municipal elections, thus lending some credibility to a meaningless exercise in which only 12.5 percent of the electorate bothered to vote. It scored relatively well in the ballots. In the following two years, scores of DC mayors were murdered and the death squads of the regime decimated the rank-and-file of the party—a most effective object lesson for those who held to the delusion of peaceful change.[11]

Within the logic of the Guatemalan state, this systematic assault on the center was quite rational, for the regime had consistently opposed any moderate alternatives. By all other standards, the policy was self-destructive and impractical, since it increased the regime's isolation, at home and abroad, at a time when the threat from below was rising to levels never reached before. This threat was represented by the growing strength of the guerrillas, which in numbers, capability, and popular support are far different from their predecessors of the 1960's.

The guerrilla groups of the 1960's—young middle-class *Ladinos* who refused to be coopted by the regime—had fallen victim to the delusions of the *foco* theory.[12] They offered their lives

---

nient if increasingly ineffectual cover for the atrocities of the regime, just as Méndez Montenegro had done twelve years earlier.

[11] And yet the DC chose once again to "play the game" by accepting to participate in the March 1982 elections. In fact, beginning in the late 1970's the party leaders had moved into a position on the moderate right. Opposing a victory of the guerrillas even more vehemently than a continuation of the status quo, they felt they had little alternative but to persist in the hope that the regime would reform. (Instead, the FUR and the PSD refused to join the electoral farce.)

[12] For some incisive studies of the 1960's guerrilla struggle in Guatemala, see Regis Debray, *Les Epreuves du feu*, vol. II of *La Critique des armes* (Paris, 1974), pp.

for the liberation of an oppressed peasantry, but neglected all but the most perfunctory efforts to gain the peasants' support. They felt deeply the immense injustice to which the Indians had been subjected for centuries, but lacked the knowledge to penetrate their secret world. They were a vanguard with little or no contact with those they sought to free. They fought alone, but did not die alone: the government's blind terror also inflicted countless casualties on the helpless civilian populace.

However, the guerrilla groups that have emerged in the mid- and late 1970's, after a few years of deceptive tranquility, have learned from the errors of the past. Rejecting a purely military approach, they began by concentrating systematically on the development of a peasant base. Indeed, the Ejército Guerrillero de los Pobres, the first of the new guerrilla groups, initiated military action only after three years of secret work among the Indians of the Altiplano.[13]

A confident regime responded to the emerging guerrilla struggle with the use of terror—terror had always proved effective. For the first time, however, it proved counterproductive—and this, rather than the levels of terror and corruption, is the most significant feature of the Lucas period. While the patient work of the guerrillas among the peasantry was a critical factor, other elements, too, contributed in shaping the popular response. The deterioration of the already abysmal living standards of the populace that marked the Lucas period added intolerable pressures;[14] the "overindulgence" of the Laugerud administration had unwittingly allowed the emergence of combative popular organizations in the cities and in the countryside; the army proved unable to crush the guerrillas, and the guerrillas proved

281–380; Richard Gott, *Guerrilla Movements in Latin America* (Garden City, N.Y., 1971), pp. 39–118; Adolfo Gilly, "The Guerrilla Movement in Guatemala," *Monthly Review*, May 1965, pp. 9–40, June 1965, pp. 7–41; Robert Lamberg, *Die Guerrilla in Lateinamerika* (Munich, 1972), pp. 65–92; Eduardo Galeano, *Guatemala: clave de Latinoamérica* (Montevideo, 1967); and, for the testimony by a participant who is now a major guerrilla leader, see Ricardo Ramírez, *Lettres du front guatémaltèque* (Paris, 1970).

[13] For a fascinating account of a participant of the origins of the EGP in Guatemala, see Mario Payeras, *Los días de la selva* (Mexico, 1980).

[14] The crisis is due in part to purely economic factors: imported inflation, which further compressed real wages; deterioration of the terms of trade; and, in 1981–82, the high interest rates abroad that negatively affected capital movements. The major reasons for it, however, are of a political nature, related to the instability throughout Central America and at home.

increasingly able to afford a degree of protection to supportive peasants and to castigate government informers in the countryside. The attitude of the clergy was of particular importance. While many, following Cardinal Casariego, remained pillars of the regime, a larger number became increasingly critical, and some even joined the revolutionary forces.

It was a process whose seeds had been sown well before 1978, and it developed over time during the Lucas years, largely overshadowed by the more dramatic events that were taking place first in Nicaragua in 1978–79, and immediately thereafter in El Salvador. For careful outside observers, however—if not yet for the Guatemalan regime—this process began acquiring ominous characteristics by late 1980, as it became apparent that in growing numbers Indians were reaching out to support or join the guerrillas and left-wing mass organizations (such as the CUC). For the first time in the history of Guatemala, caste division began to give way to the realization of a common class interest. Such an evolution, if it persisted, would inflict a devastating blow on a ruling class that has traditionally profited from the contradictions between caste prejudice and class interest.

The agony of the regime had in fact begun. The increasing challenge from below was met by mounting yet ineffectual terror. The lucrative tourist industry and domestic investment were increasingly diminished by the war, as were both foreign private investment and credits from foreign banks and international organizations.[15] Guatemala's status as an international pariah affected potential assistance from friendly governments (notably the United States) and reinforced the reluctance of organizations such as the World Bank to lend. The government's growing inability to cope with the political, economic, and military crisis also accelerated the capital outflow provoked by the shock of Somoza's fall, and by the worsening Salvadoran situation. The net outflow of capital was in turn a major cause for the deterioration in Guatemala's balance of payments. The high level of international reserves that Guatemala had traditionally main-

[15] Private investment, which had demonstrated vigorous growth until 1978, decreased in 1979 by 12%, and in 1980 by 21% (Consejo Monetario Centroamericano, Secretaría Ejecutiva, *Estudio sobre la situación económica y financiera de los paises centroamericanos en 1980 y sus perspectivas para 1982*, Memorandum CPM/167/81, pp. 67–108). It is estimated that in 1981 it remained at the depressed levels of the previous year.

tained withered away to the point that by the end of 1981 they were down to $171.8 million (less than the equivalent of two months of 1981 merchandise imports), compared with a peak of $763.2 million at the end of 1978. At the same time, Guatemala found it increasingly costly to borrow abroad. Under such conditions, an efficient administration of public finances would have been all the more necessary, but the corruption and incompetence of the Lucas government, though not unusual by the standards of the post-1954 regime, were particularly glaring in the face of an unprecedented crisis.

Predictably, the terror also claimed the lives of many members of the middle class, while the severe economic strains hurt the pockets of many more. This time, however, the regime no longer appeared all-powerful. The growing manifestations of its weakness and incompetence, its intransigent refusal to allow space to the centrist parties, Guatemala's status as an international pariah, and the mounting opposition of the clergy, all created a sense of deepening frustration. Had they made a more sustained effort, the groups of the revolutionary left could have better exploited the feeling of despair among many members of the middle class.

This, then, was the new reality of Guatemala as the country entered the 1980's: for the first time since 1954 a variety of forces had joined against the regime and were reinforcing one another, while the Lucas government, increasingly besieged, appeared blindly obstinate.

THE CARTER ADMINISTRATION—IN SEARCH OF A CENTER

Broadly defined, Carter's policy toward Central America had two major phases, separated by the period between the summer of 1978 and the summer of 1979, when Somoza was overthrown. In the first phase the administration felt little threat from the left in Central America. Hence, it appeared possible to advance a human rights policy without endangering U.S. interests. After the shock of the Sandinist victory, the administration saw the pro-American stability in the area suddenly threatened by revolution. It reacted to this unexpected nightmare with an effort to coopt the Sandinists in Nicaragua. In somewhat contradictory fashion, it sought to strengthen the military in Hon-

duras while simultaneously encouraging an opening of the political system. In El Salvador it pushed forward a "third force"
experiment with mounting disregard for reality.[16]

In Guatemala, after the fall of Somoza, the U.S. administration continued, as before, to press for "democratization," arguing that a centrist solution, however difficult to achieve, would
in the long run prove the most effective way of preventing a
popular explosion and a victory of the radical left. In the mean-
time, any slackening of repression and implementation of even
modest reforms were seen as positive steps to help defuse tensions. The Carter policy toward Guatemala failed miserably.
The Guatemalan ruling class—never known for its political
sophistication—became increasingly convinced that the State
Department was dominated by Marxists (including men like
William Bowdler and James Cheek, who, they believed, had
cunningly persecuted and finally removed from his post the
staunchly anticommunist ambassador Frank Ortiz). Continuing
pressure and public chastening from Washington led only to a
break in communication between the two governments, while
within Guatemala repression wrought havoc among those centrist groups that enjoyed Washington's support.

By 1980 a debate began in earnest within the administration.
The Defense Department, the National Security Council, and
"hard-liners" in the State Department argued that the policy of
the "stick" toward the Lucas government had failed. They therefore advocated an improvement in relations and the resumption
of military assistance. By proffering the "carrot" the Carter administration, they claimed, would regain the confidence of the
Guatemalan regime, and could eventually persuade it to adopt
some reforms. While this proposed policy shift was rejected, it is
important to understand the rationale of those State Department "liberals" who opposed it. They, too, strongly preferred a
Lucas government (however unredeemed) to a Sandinist-type
victory in Guatemala. They would have advocated military assistance had they believed that it was necessary for the survival
of the regime. In their eyes, however, Lucas was not yet seri-

---

[16] For a more detailed assessment, see Gleijeses, "The Search for the Center in Central
America," *Working Papers* (Nov./Dec. 1981), pp. 30–37, and "The United States and
Turmoil in Central America," in *The 1980s: Decade of Confrontation?* (Washington,
D.C., 1981), pp. 129–42.

ously threatened; hence the United States could afford to wait (while military assistance was provided by Argentina, Israel, and other countries). In this fashion, the Carter administration would avoid dirtying its hands and would preserve the facade of its human rights policy as long as possible. Meanwhile, the frustrating effort to moderate the Guatemalan government continued in an atmosphere of increasing tension.

THE REAGAN ADMINISTRATION AND GUATEMALA

The Reagan administration came to power saying that it would return America to its former grandeur; it promised to redress Carter's policy of "blunders" based on humiliating concessions to Communist and radical states, and vowed to end the betrayal of loyal allies like Anastasio Somoza and the Shah of Iran.

Geography and history made it inevitable that Central America would occupy a critical place within a vision that stressed the need to reassert America's will. In order to project the image of an effective, resurgent America, an immediate foreign policy victory would be most advantageous. Neither Afghanistan nor the Persian Gulf were appropriate places for a swift and easy success—but Central America's proximity to the United States, the smallness of the nations threatened by "Communist aggression," and the ease with which the United States had traditionally imposed its will on the region, all seemed to hold out this promise. The Reaganites' intense desire to make Castro pay for his past actions was an added incentive to reassert U.S. will in the area. Hence Central America was thrust in the forefront of Reagan's foreign policy.

Within this imperial logic, the "test case" selected to demonstrate the United States' new-found will was El Salvador—in fact, since January 1981 U.S. policy toward Nicaragua has been largely a function of developments in El Salvador. As had been the case under Carter, Guatemala was seen as a less urgent problem by the incoming Reagan administration, for the guerrilla challenge, while growing, did not yet appear an imminent threat.[17]

Within the administration, a majority of high-ranking officials (in particular new Reagan appointees) saw the Lucas govern-

[17] For a more detailed assessment of Reagan's policy in Central America, see Gleijeses, *Tilting at Windmills: Reagan in Central America* (Washington, D.C., Apr. 1982).

ment as a "moderate repressive" regime whose excesses should be understood within the violent context of Guatemala's history and the "aggression from Communist terrorists abetted by Cuba and the Soviet Union." The United States must provide assistance to a beleaguered and loyal ally, rather than indulge in intemperate and naive criticism of a deeply-rooted social reality. Reforms were welcome, but only at the pace and within the scope accepted by the Guatemalan ruling class.

Another group—which included perhaps a majority of career officials working on the region, especially within the lower- and middle-ranking echelons—acknowledged that Guatemala desperately needed social reforms. For them, the Guatemalan regime was repressive to a degree that could not be justified either by the country's history or by aggression from the left; in the end it might well prove self-defeating. They argued, however, that Carter's intolerance had failed to persuade the Lucas government to temper its own policies. By resuming the "dialogue," Washington might eventually succeed in convincing the Guatemalan ruling class that, in its own best interest, it should accept some reforms. In any case, they concluded, the United States had no other alternative.

Thus, both approaches stressed the need to provide military assistance and maintain a close relationship with the Guatemalan government. The "hard-liners" overlooked the need for reforms; those with a more pragmatic bent acknowledged their importance, but emphasized that the Guatemalan government must be pressured, and had in any event to be supported. Their case rested on the hope that the Guatemalan ruling class would at last reveal instincts for self-preservation. Both approaches also agreed on the administration's need to make support for the Guatemalan regime more palatable to Congress by improving the sordid image of the Lucas government.

REAGAN AND LUCAS: FOURTEEN MONTHS OF FRUSTRATION

U.S. efforts to improve the image of the Guatemalan regime proved an abject failure. Assuredly, the administration was unlucky: its campaign had just begun to unfold when Amnesty International released the most incriminating report it had ever published on Guatemala. By documenting conclusively, for the first time, that "tortures and murders are part of a deliberate and longstanding program of the Guatemalan government," Amnesty struck an untimely blow to Washington's emerging argument that right wing terror was independent of government responsibility.[18] Moreover, Reagan's stated intention to reverse his predecessor's policy on Guatemala helped to draw attention to the country, attention already focused by the continuing escalation of the guerrilla war.

The administration's largest stumbling block to a rapprochement with Guatemala was that country's own government. The Reaganites hastened to show their goodwill toward Lucas in their rhetoric, as well as in concrete gestures that were to serve as a prelude to more important steps (the sale, for example, of $3.2 million of military trucks and jeeps in June 1981 in violation of the spirit, if not the letter, of U.S. law).[19] All they asked, in return, was that Lucas help them to help him, by making minor concessions that would mollify Congress. For Lucas, however, any concession was unreasonable.

Not only did the scope of the atrocities continue to increase, but in August 1981 the Guatemalan government gave further proof of its insensitivity to Washington's needs by announcing that the defense minister, General Aníbal Guevara, would be the official candidate for the forthcoming presidential elections in March 1982. Guevara's selection was a cruel blow to the Reagan administration, which had pleaded that a civilian with less bloodied credentials be allowed to succeed Lucas in the Presidential Palace. In practical terms, a moderate civilian president would hardly affect the course of events in Guatemala, but would be a prisoner of the military, as Julio César Méndez Montenegro had been. Nevertheless such a civilian would have better served the image-building efforts of the State Department, which was stressing the importance of the March 1982 elections in the democratization underway in Guatemala. Indeed, before Guevara's selection, some hard-pressed U.S. officials argued privately that although Lucas might be beyond redemption, his successor would be a man of different stamp,

[18] Amnesty International, *Guatemala: A Government Program of Political Murder* (London, 1981), p. 3. A major source of the report was Lucas's own former vice-president, Villagrán Kramer.

[19] The administration sidestepped the law banning sales to governments such as Guatemala's by removing these items from the proscribed list.

thanks to the new policy of dialogue established by the Reagan administration[20]—a naive hope that the Lucas government hastened to contradict. In fact, the government's insistence on Guevara was all the more frustrating for Washington, since his three competitors were all men of a solid conservative stamp.

Thus, a most unhappy relationship developed between Washington and Guatemala, based on mutual lack of comprehension and disappointment. The Guatemalan regime grew increasingly skeptical of the resolve of the Reagan administration and saw symptoms of creeping Carterism without Carter,[21] while in Washington disappointment grew even among a majority of hard-core Reaganites. Senior officials like Vernon Walters, who had initially argued and perhaps even believed that the Guatemalan government was only moderately repressive, were soon forced to acknowledge that the repression was not only indiscriminate but counterproductive, and that the rampant corruption and blind intransigence only strengthened the forces of revolution.

It was not moral revulsion, however, that prevented the Reagan administration from coming to the assistance of its Guatemalan protégés. Rather, more practical considerations stayed Washington's hand. By mid-1981 the administration had at last realized that the guerrillas in El Salvador did indeed represent a formidable foe—an awareness that would deepen in the following months. Simultaneously, both Congress and public opinion in the United States were becoming increasingly skeptical of the administration's Salvadoran policy, and Reagan's own popularity was beginning to feel the shocks of the deepening economic recession at home.

However, the battered reputation of the Salvadoran junta appeared untainted and even virtuous when compared with Lucas's disastrous record, which provoked deep abhorrence among an overwhelming majority in Congress. Indeed, as a dispirited lobbyist lamented, "nobody wants to put himself on the line on the Hill by asking for weapons for Guatemala—even conservative

---

[20] The administration's favorite candidate was Gustavo Anzueto Vielman of General Arana's Central Auténtica Nacionalista.

[21] One of the few U.S. officials whose goodwill was not in question was Roger Fontaine, Latin American expert at the National Security Council and a key figure in Reagan's transition team for Latin America. However, Fontaine's good intentions appeared frustrated by an obvious lack of influence.

Congressmen don't want to get involved." By asking Congress
for assistance to Guatemala, the administration would have met
certain defeat and courted the risk of a backlash that could have
affected support for its Salvadoran policy. Beginning in the summer of 1981, contrary to its original intentions, it wisely refrained from any effort to seek assistance for Guatemala. This
caution was accompanied by the feeling that the Lucas government, though weakened, was still not in immediate danger.[22]

By the end of 1981, however, a sense of urgency began to
emerge within the Reagan administration, following a year of
growing guerrilla military strength and popular support while
the economy sharply deteriorated.[23] Some U.S. officials even began to wonder whether Guatemala would replace El Salvador as
the next "domino" in Central America. The administration's
alarm was given concrete expression by its decision, in early
February 1982, to test Congress by requesting $251,000 in mili-
tary assistance for Guatemala, breaking the four-year ban (it
claimed, to soften congressional resistance, that it did not intend to appropriate the money unless human rights conditions
in the country improved).[24]

Thus, the administration approached the coming presidential
elections (March 1982) in Guatemala with mounting anxiety.
While proffering hollow declarations that the elections would

---

[22]This was called a "wait and see" policy by many State Department officials; others
frankly acknowledged: "we have no policy" (personal interviews).

[23]Haig called Guatemala "clearly the next target of Communist insurgency in Central America," and said it "soon will be a parallel case to El Salvador" (Michael Gettler,
"Reagan to Ask More Foreign Military Aid," Washington Post, Feb. 28, 1982).

[24]The $251,000, which was included in the administration's FY 83 Security Assis-
tance Act, would finance U.S. military training for Guatemalans—for the first time since
1977, when all U.S. military assistance had ended. Commenting on the administration's
move, the New York Times remarked: "Quietly, in a tricky little maneuver revealed in
the fine print of the security program, the Administration now names Guatemala . . . as
deserving renewed help. The symbolism is important, and Guatemalans know it. Just a
few American dollars buy a lot of respectability for a cruel regime. . . . Whatever the
argument . . . there is no case for sanitizing Guatemala." ("Sanitizing Guatemala,"
March 7, 1982.) Already in late December 1981, Jack Anderson noted "evidence that
the administration is planning to send a modest amount of military aid to Lucas García,
about $2 million worth of helicopter spare parts. . . . Congressional sources report that
State Department officials have secretly visited key legislators in the House and Senate to
test their reactions to the proposed military aid. . . . According to Capitol Hill sources,
the State Department emissaries have met almost universal negative responses in their
visits to Congress. But at least some of the legislators got the impression that the administration was not deterred by their objections." ("Regime Blamed for Violence in Guatemala," Washington Post, Dec. 22, 1981.)

represent a positive step in the development of Guatemala's democracy, the administration hoped against hope that Lucas, in a moment of rationality, might indeed allow free competition among the four competing candidates rather than impose Guevara. On March 8, 1982, the official candidate was soundly defeated at the polls, only to be proclaimed the victor once the official results were announced. In all likelihood, the electoral fraud had been no more flagrant than in 1974 or 1978, but never before had the international media focused with such intensity on Guatemalan elections. For the first time since Arbenz's overthrow, the Guatemalan regime seemed mortally threatened, which led many foes of the guerrillas to argue that "these elections are our last chance and everybody knows it"[25]—a graphic expression that was widely used by journalists and other observers.

In 1974 and 1978, defeated opposition candidates had complained as bitterly as in 1982 of the official fraud, and their complaints had met the same harsh response—but never before had the divisions among different sectors of the ruling class been as glaring as in the March 1982 elections. They were now fed not only by personal ambition and greed, but by fear that the Lucas administration was threatening the very survival of the ruling class by imposing Guevara. At the same time, the outcome of the elections deepened disaffection amid the middle class, heightening the danger that in despair it would turn in significant numbers toward the revolutionary left. It seemed, indeed, as if the Guatemalan regime was bent on accelerating its own demise. Guevara's "election" was as costly as a series of resounding guerrilla victories, promising to intensify the regime's isolation to a degree hauntingly reminiscent of Somoza's plight in the last months of his rule.

The Reagan administration, which had suffered a string of humiliations in Guatemala and whose pleadings Lucas had consistently scorned, nevertheless hastened to the defense of the battered regime. With profound disregard for contrary evidence, the State Department indicated that the elections had been fair, and declared that it would press for military assistance for Guatemala, while President Reagan sent Guevara a "warm congrat-

[25] Raymond Bonner, "Guatemalans Vote for New Leader," *New York Times*, Mar. 8, 1982.

ulatory note."[26] The administration's cynicism was not gratui-
tous—Washington was a prisoner of its own logic and of the
intransigence of the Guatemalan government. If the alternative
of a left-wing victory was unacceptable, then assistance had to
be provided to the Guatemalan regime regardless of its excesses.
Indeed Lucas's own blunders, including the handling of the
March elections, made such assistance even more imperative.
Under such conditions the Reagan administration had to forget
its *amour propre* and seek congressional acquiescence for assistance to Guatemala, however difficult and politically costly this
might prove.

Thus, the administration had come full circle since January
1981, for there was little point in attempting to "hold the line"
in El Salvador if Guatemala were to be lost.[27] While it prepared
to embark on a desperate gamble, however, some pragmatic
U.S. officials privately conceded that even if Congress were to
grant aid to a Guevara government, the administration's policy
offered no long-term solution. Acknowledging that Guevara
represented no improvement over Lucas, they concluded that,
short of military intervention, U.S. aid would fail to prevent a
guerrilla victory, increasingly likely over the next couple of years.
Nor would military intervention reestablish pro-American stability over the long term. A U.S. occupation would fail to reform
the Guatemala ruling class, but would more probably increase
its intransigence by indicating that the United States could be
relied upon to prevent a revolutionary victory. Following the inevitable departure of the American troops, the guerrilla tide
would gather strength again, and the United States would, in a
few years' time, be faced again with the need to intervene. And
yet, these analysts concluded, no other policy was possible, for
Washington could not accept a guerrilla victory.

However shortsighted, the administration's policy acquired a
perverse logic when contrasted with the stance of most of its
congressional critics. If a majority in Congress opposed assis-

---

[26] Beth Nissen, "Guatemala: God Has Changed Things," *Newsweek*, Apr. 5, 1982,
pp. 49–50.
[27] In the words of a State Department official, "It wouldn't do us much good, for example, if our investment in El Salvador was to pay off only to find that we're facing a
worse threat in a larger and more important country like Guatemala" (John Goshko,
"U.S. is Still Fumbling for Solution in Central American Situation," *Washington Post*,
Jan. 31, 1982).

tance to Guatemala, it was as firmly opposed to what the administration correctly presented as the only realistic alternative: a victory of the revolutionary left. This fundamental and unresolved contradiction afforded the administration its only hope. Congressional opposition to aid to Guatemala might weaken before the growing specter of a guerrilla victory, amid pious expressions of concern for human rights, assurances that Guevara would introduce some reforms, and a barrage of accusations of "outside communist aggression." It was, indeed, a desperate gamble, where an unlikely but not impossible success in the short term would only lead to a more humiliating defeat over time.

THE RIOS MONTT JUNTA

The March 23, 1982, coup that overthrew Lucas apparently took the Reagan administration by surprise. After some initial hesitation, however, Washington was ready to welcome the three-man military junta led by retired general Efraín Ríos Montt; in the words of Assistant Secretary Enders, "Since last month's coup led by junior officers, violence not directly connected to the insurgency has been brought virtually to an end. . . . Concrete measures have been taken against corruption. . . . All political forces have been called to join in national reconciliation."[28]

Many U.S. officials may indeed have hoped that the new junta would result in a regime of the modernizing right—that is, a regime willing and able to coopt strategic sectors of the popular classes by means of significant (but not radical) social reforms and by the use of selective rather than indiscriminate repression.

This hope was fortified by signs that were seen as encouraging in some quarters. General Ríos Montt had been the 1974 presidential candidate of the centrist Democracia Cristiana and, like Duarte two years earlier in El Salvador, had been deprived of his victory at the polls by brazen fraud. After four years of diplomatic exile in Spain, he had returned to Guatemala, where he underwent a profound religious experience and remained aloof from political activities until March 1982.

Moreover, the young *golpista* officers claimed that their coup was motivated by the high levels of corruption, brutality, and

---

[28] Robert Kaiser, "Reagan May Lift Ban on Military Sales to Guatemala," *Washington Post*, Apr. 22, 1982.

incompetence of the Lucas administration, as well as by the recent electoral fraud. Their actions seemed to fit the model of "young modernizing officers" rather than that of a clique of ultra-conservative senior officers. This initial impression was reinforced when the junta appointed some respected technocrats to high-level bureaucratic positions. In the days immediately following the coup, the junta's assurances that the guerrillas would be dealt with firmly, but without indiscriminate violence, seemed vindicated by several moves: the infamous Cuerpo de Detectives was disbanded; a few leading police officers were dismissed; the repression in the cities decreased; and no reports of government terror in the countryside reached the press. But even if it appeared that "the government has come out of the darkness into the light,"[29] as U.S. Ambassador Frederick Chapin claimed, in words attuned to Ríos Montt's religious phraseology, appearances can be deceiving.

Even at first sight ominous signs are in evidence. The Cuerpo de Detectives has been reestablished under a different name. The Guatemalan armed forces have remained almost intact; indeed only seven out of twenty-seven or twenty-eight generals, and a mere handful of colonels, have been retired. Therefore, the current equilibrium between senior and younger officers is at best unstable; this precarious balance may persist, paralyzing the "modernizing" aspirations of the younger officers, or it may provoke further and more disruptive coups, threatening the unity of the military institution. Moreover, not only are Ríos Montt's reformist credentials controversial at best, but—more importantly—his mental equilibrium is questioned by many.[30]

The uncertain balance between younger and senior officers and Ríos Montt's mental stability may not, however, be the critical issue. The evidence indicates that there is no significant modernizing group among the young Guatemalan officers. Neither Ríos Montt, nor the young officers, nor even the technocrats

---

[29] "Guatemala Hallelujah!," *Economist*, May 1–7, 1982, p. 71.

[30] Ríos Montt was Army Chief of Staff from 1970 to 1973—one of the worst periods of repression in Guatemala. There are credible allegations that his gracious acceptance of the 1974 electoral fraud was rewarded not only by a post in Madrid but also through a generous sum of money. In any case, he left the military a rich man, well beyond what his salary could suggest. His psychological condition is a source of concern to several sympathetic but increasingly apprehensive U.S. officials. A reading of his own public statements since March 23 makes U.S. uneasiness understandable.

brought into the government, have proposed or intend to introduce the social reforms that any formula of the modernizing right desperately requires. Indeed, the young officers' political contacts before the coup were not with centrist parties, but rather with the Movimiento de Liberación Nacional (MLN) of Mario Sandoval Alarcón—and the MLN has consistently demonstrated over two and a half decades that its answer to insurgency is not reform but more political terror.

While the young officers, and Ríos Montt, have indeed criticized the widespread repression of previous years, their actions belie their words. After the silence of the first days, graphic reports of massacres in the countryside have reached the outside world. In fact, the level of government violence in rural areas has already surpassed that of Lucas, as evidence from Amnesty International, church groups, U.S. and foreign journalists, and other observers amply illustrates, and as even conservative Guatemalans acknowledge in private.

Sheer self-interest would have dictated that the Guatemalan regime adopt a modernizing formula long ago. This clashes, however, with the "logic" permeating the rationale of an entire generation that emerged from the nightmare of Arbenz's "Red Government"—the premise that salvation would depend on repression and that reforms are a threat. The dogma was reinforced by the experience of the following years, when terror proved a most effective means for governing. On the other hand, the failure of the modernizing effort of the Laugerud period also seemed to demonstrate that concessions led to radicalization rather than cooptation, contrary to claims of "naive" foreigners. Finally, the increasing guerrilla strength in neighboring El Salvador since October 1979 also suggested that overzealous reforms may bring chaos rather than stability.

This point of view is reflected in the new, post-1954 generation—not only in the children of the bourgeoisie, but also in generations of officers who have learned, in the military academy and in the barracks, a primitive anti-communism that identifies reforms with subversion.

This mentality is reinforced by other, more practical factors. Even if it were not too late, it would require immense determination and large economic resources to pursue at this late stage a program of the modernizing right. It would also require a high degree of sophistication to use selective rather than indiscriminate repression—particularly in the countryside where, as the officers have been taught (and at times have learned through bitter experience), it is impossible to distinguish between "peaceful" peasants and guerrilla sympathizers, and where women and children often play supportive roles for the guerrilla. This problem, also confronting the Salvadoran military, is complicated in Guatemala by the fact that the army officers are *ladinos*, while the peasants in the guerrilla areas are mostly *indígenas*—and the *indígenas* are by definition inscrutable, hiding bitter hostility and thirst for revenge for centuries of oppression behind their passive demeanor.

Large economic resources, which the Guatemalan state no longer possesses, would be required to implement significant social reforms. An agrarian reform within a capitalist framework would demand not only considerable amounts of money to pay a "just price" for the expropriated land, but also outlays for credits and technical assistance. The establishment of cooperatives in the Altiplano to increase the productivity of the peasant *minifundia* would be less costly—but in order to develop an effective cooperative movement it would be necessary to allow an independent peasant leadership to develop. In the eyes of the Guatemalan armed forces (generals and younger officers alike) as well as the bourgeoisie, the emergence of such a leadership would be an intolerable threat—and their fears are, at this date, not wholly unjustified.

These considerations do not, however, deter the Reagan administration. Focusing on the slackening of repression in the major cities, and exploiting congressional fears of a guerrilla victory, it is attempting to persuade Congress that the Guatemalan regime is reforming and deserves assistance. If these efforts are successful, a familiar cycle will then unfold. The administration will exploit Congress's initial support to seek additional assistance—and it will be argued, as in the case of Vietnam and now El Salvador, that U.S. credibility is at stake.

The war, however, will not abate. The government's scorched-earth tactics and massacres only provide fresh recruits to the rebels. The army is beginning to show signs of passivity in its fight against the guerrillas, while showing savage zeal against unarmed peasants. Following the March coup, weakening discipline and growing factionalism are evident in the officer corps, as was demonstrated in August by the misfortune of Colonel Morales Díaz, a strict disciplinarian appointed by Ríos Montt as the commander of the important military zone of Quetzaltenango. Morales Díaz was ousted *manu militari* by his subordinates, and Ríos Montt had to acquiesce.

Moreover, as a top official of the Central Bank told the author in September, the economy is "in a dead-end street": nothing has changed since March, and foreign banks, leery of the country's political plight, still refuse assistance, despite the pleas of those respected technocrats who have been brought into the Ríos Montt government largely to attract foreign loans. As the war rages on, the economy will continue to deteriorate, and the middle class—which had welcomed the coup, but is increasingly disillusioned by the government's dismal performance—will once again lose heart; many will drift toward the opposition, since the guerrillas' program now offers them a role in a future Guatemala. Finally, amidst intensifying violence and mounting fear of defeat, even cosmetic changes may be jettisoned, and the bloody image of Lucas will again be bared.

FACING REALITY

Washington has only two alternatives: to provide military and economic assistance to the Ríos Montt government (granting the one without the other would weaken the purpose), or to remain aloof and accept the increased likelihood of a guerrilla victory. To dream of a centrist alternative is as realistic as to imagine that Fidel Castro will turn into a pliant U.S. ally. If the United States chooses to assist Ríos Montt, it must do so with open eyes. The aid will be granted not because the regime is reforming, but because its inability to reform makes U.S. support imperative. Indeed, aid must be conceded in full awareness that it will only reinforce the regime's obstinacy, and in the hope that increased terror might become, once again, an effective means of social control.

How many weapons, how many millions will be necessary to turn the tide? Will it also prove necessary to send, in ever increasing numbers, U.S. military advisors to a country that is far more suited than El Salvador to a guerrilla war? It will be an uncertain adventure, divisive at home and damaging to U.S. prestige abroad. And it would not be realistic to rule out the possibility that an initial involvement might eventually lead to the need for direct military intervention—for U.S. prestige will appear tied to the fortunes of an increasingly beleaguered regime. On the other hand, to provide assistance with the intention of not going beyond a certain point means to risk a humiliating withdrawal (which would expose U.S. weakness, rather than its flexibility) after having fixed the hatred of the Guatemalan guerrillas.

No one seriously expects the United States to support the guerrillas actively, but Washington can refuse assistance to a regime that is threatened by the revolt of a people it has too long oppressed. If the regime falls, it will not be because of a nonexistent or minimal Cuban involvement, but because of its own, unredeemable weakness.

What are the risks of passivity? To be sure, if Washington chooses to pursue an aggressive policy there will be no possibility of a *modus vivendi* between the United States and a revolutionary government in Guatemala. This is the lesson of U.S.-Nicaraguan relations under Reagan. The key question, however, is whether the Guatemalan guerrillas, once in power, would be inclined to seek a cooperative relationship with Washington. Much depends, of course, on how the United States would define such a relationship. Demanding a pro-American stability would defeat the purpose. Nor is it likely that a guerrilla-led government would adhere to all the strictures of Western democracy—something that very few countries in the Third World have achieved. Surely, this should not be of undue concern to the United States, which has shown great capacity to work with regimes that hold both political and social democracy in contempt. It is crucial, from a U.S. perspective, that a revolutionary government be willing to adopt a flexible foreign policy that, while not necessarily pro-American, would not endorse the Soviet Union. In this regard, the Guatemalan guerrilla movement does indeed offer excellent prospects for a *modus vivendi*.

There are obviously hotheads and doctrinaires within the guerrilla movement—particularly among the small Fuerzas Ar-

madas Rebeldes and the Núcleo de Dirección del Partido Guatemalteco del Trabajo. But the EGP and the Organización Revolucionaria del Pueblo en Armas (ORPA), which together make up
between 80 and 85 percent of the guerrilla strength, are of a different mold. It is true that the leaders of EGP and ORPA see the
Reagan administration as a dangerous enemy, and not without good reason. Still, both their publications and their private
statements indicate not only that they are very much aware of
the need for a *modus vivendi* with Washington, but also that
they are free of a doctrinaire spirit and a naive confidence in the
virtues of the Soviet Union as an ally or as a model. Indeed, their
sympathy for Fidel Castro is tempered by their realization that
the Cuban mode has little to offer to their own country.

Those skeptics who argue that guerrillas show their true col-
ors only when they are in power, should also consider a unique
aspect of the Guatemalan guerrilla movement: the strength of
its *indígena* component.

Indígenas constitute not only a majority of the rank and file,
but also an important and ever-growing number of the com-
manders of guerrilla columns of the EGP and ORPA—indeed,
a frequent accusation against both organizations is that they
are too *indigenistas*. The *indígenas*, however, have in fact little
taste for Marxism; rather, they are firm champions of private
property. They want their own land, an end to cultural dis-
crimination, and a large degree of autonomy. This deeply entrenched outlook, when combined with their high level of participation in the war, will profoundly affect the course of a future
Guatemala.

Rather than generating a "Second Cuba," a guerrilla victory
will in all likelihood bring to power a left-wing government
ready to follow a flexible course in both foreign and domestic
matters. It is hardly relevant that from a U.S. perspective the
ideal solution would have been a centrist pro-American regime;
no such solution exists. The issue, then, is one of opportunity
costs. For the United States to accept a guerrilla victory is likely
to prove far less costly than the efforts to sustain the present
bankrupt regime. Sober realism is not, however, an attribute of
the Reagan administration in the Caribbean Basin. Congress
alone can restrain the administration from embarking upon a

self-defeating policy, by refusing economic and military assistance to Ríos Montt. A timely recognition of Guatemalan realities would undoubtedly enhance U.S. prestige among many of
its allies—including the West Europeans, the Mexicans, and the
Japanese—who see Washington's primary weakness not as lack
of will, but as inability to adapt to new circumstances.

The Discussions at Guanajuato:
An Afterword

Clint E. Smith

THE discussions at Guanajuato were dominated by criticism of U.S. policy toward Central America. These criticisms, however, did not go unanswered. Everett E. Briggs, Deputy Assistant Secretary of State for Inter-American Affairs, who was present, responded forcefully to the dominant point of view on several occasions. The main elements of the critique and Briggs's response can be summarized as follows:

(1) President Reagan came to power certain that he could and should impose his will on Central America in order to demonstrate to the world that under his administration the United States was determined to recapture its traditional hegemony in the hemisphere and—by implication—in the rest of the world. Reagan was, however, less certain about how to proceed. The early efforts by Secretary of State Alexander Haig to "take charge" of the situation in Central America were doomed to failure, in part because of his lack of understanding of the basic social and economic realities of the region. More specifically, an attempt to portray El Salvador as an East-West issue resulted in an early administration fiasco: the publication of the now-discredited White Paper *Communist Interference in El Salvador*.[1]

Thus, the critique continued, the first eighteen months of the administration's policy in Central America have been dominated by a view that focused on the struggle between the United States and the Soviet Union. For example, events in Nicaragua, El Salvador, and even in Guatemala were seen as resulting from covert Soviet or Cuban activities, with little or no recognition

[1] *Communist Interference in El Salvador*, Special Report no. 80, February 23, 1981 (Washington, D.C., Department of State, 1981).

given to the economic and social problems that are the true roots of conflict in the region.

Briggs acknowledged that some uncertainty marked the early days of the administration, and that members of the "transition team" sometimes gave strong signals that the battle with Cuba and the Soviet Union was the key factor in Central America. However, although certainly concerned with East-West issues, the administration subsequently has been far more sensitive to Central American realities than early statements might have suggested. Thus, Briggs continued, criticism of this sort—though it may have been valid for the first few months of the administration—does not apply to current policy.

Briggs further emphasized that the U.S. government is well aware of the social and economic inequities in Central America: in fiscal 1982 the administration requested $783 million in economic assistance for Latin America and the Caribbean. Of this amount, Briggs said, about 85 percent is for economic as opposed to security assistance. Thus, he continued, the oft-repeated charge that the Reagan administration views the situation in Central America as a simple East-West struggle is not supported by the facts.

Elaborating on this theme, Briggs said that the administration recognizes that Cuban (and Nicaraguan) intervention is not the primary source of instability in the region. The origins of unrest lie in historic social and economic inequities that have long generated frustrations among Central Americans struggling to improve their lot. It should not be forgotten, he noted, that these crises have subjected institutional structures to stresses that have made them more vulnerable to the appeals of violent radical groups backed by the Soviet Union and Cuba. The readiness of the Soviet Union and Cuba to exploit such situations imposes serious obstacles to economic progress, democratic development, and self-determination in Central America. Hence the opposition of the United States to Cuban and Soviet actions.

(2) With respect to Nicaragua, most participants agreed that the true long-term national interests of the United States have been harmed by the outright hostility the Reagan administration has shown toward the revolutionary government in Managua. Covert actions by the United States (revealed in detail in

the fall of 1982) have been directed toward the destabilization of the Sandinist regime.[2] Such actions, however, will almost surely result in the radicalization of the regime.

In addition, there was agreement among most participants that stability will not come to Central America until the United States has learned to accept the reality of revolutionary change— not only today in Nicaragua, but possibly tomorrow in El Salvador and Guatemala. In any event, the current test case is Nicaragua, and unless the United States is willing to pay an exorbitant price and risk direct military intervention, it must learn to live with the Sandinist regime. United States influence in Nicaragua can be gained only by good faith negotiations with the revolutionary government. Applying overt and covert pressures of the kind now being used will only drive Nicaragua more to the left.

Briggs strongly disagreed with much of this criticism. Far from showing unwarranted hostility, he said, the Reagan administration has made repeated efforts to open a meaningful dialogue with the Sandinists. Assistant Secretary of State for Inter-American Affairs Thomas O. Enders visited Managua in August 1981, to meet with Nicaraguan leaders. Against the background of increasing restrictions on domestic dissent, the discussions there focused on the regional security problem caused by Nicaragua's military buildup and provision of arms to Salvadoran guerrillas. In exchange for Nicaraguan action on these U.S. concerns, Briggs said, Enders offered resumption of economic aid and cultural/technical exchanges, in addition to assurances that the United States would not aid groups seeking to overthrow the Nicaraguan government. Despite the lack of a Nicaraguan response to these proposals, further efforts at negotiation were made by Secretary of State Haig and by the U.S. ambassador to Nicaragua.

Is the United States really, Briggs asked, pushing the Sandinists "into Castro's arms"? By mid-1982 the United States had contributed almost $125 million in aid to Nicaragua. Noting that in the period immediately following Somoza's overthrow, the United States was ready to label the new revolutionary gov-

[2]See, for example, "A Secret War for Nicaragua," *Newsweek*, Nov. 8, 1982.

ernment "truly democratic," Briggs added that one should look
carefully at what has happened since that time. Opposition
voices have been silenced; minority groups such as the Miskito
Indians have been subjected to inhumane and unjust treatment;
there are 4,500 political prisoners in Nicaraguan jails; the army
has grown to more than twice the size it was under Somoza;
Nicaraguan pilots are being trained in communist countries;
and some 2,000 Cuban military advisors are working with the
Nicaraguan armed forces. Furthermore, Briggs claimed, the
Sandinists have embarked on a program to reduce the influence
of the church. As for free elections, Briggs continued, Comandante Daniel Ortega of the government junta has referred to
them as "bourgeois raffles."

Briggs expressed his disagreement with the notion that the
concern of the United States with these matters represents "unwarranted intervention." The actions of the Sandinists, he noted,
represent a legitimate concern to other powers in the hemisphere, including the United States and—one might hope—to
Mexico as well. The United States is still trying to talk with the
Nicaraguans; and the administration does not believe that Nicaragua is "lost to communism," as long as there are some alternative voices remaining in the country: the church, businessmen,
labor, opposition political parties, nongovernmental media.
The United States also hopes that other governments and groups,
for example the Social Democrats in Europe, will continue to
use their influence to help maintain political pluralism and individual rights in Nicaragua.

Finally, Briggs pointed out, this concern for the internal situation in Nicaragua is coupled to international concerns. Specifically, the United States is worried that a Nicaragua increasingly
allied with Cuba and the Soviet Union will continue to be used
as a base for terrorist operations aimed at democratic governments in Honduras and Costa Rica. It is unfortunately true, he
claimed, that evidence of such activity has surfaced. The United
States feels strongly that attempts to destabilize these small de-
mocracies are pernicious and should be opposed.

(3) In the discussion of the situation in Guatemala, where the
Ríos Montt regime had taken power only three months earlier
(March 23, 1982), there was general consensus that the pros-
pects for an improvement in the human rights situation were

not increased by the coup. It was also generally felt that the Reagan administration had been too quick in announcing its support for the Ríos Montt regime, trying to pretend that it is a "modernizing right" (Gleijeses's term) government.

Only when the U.S. government is ready to accept the taking-of-power by a left-dominated movement in Guatemala—the critics continued—will U.S. policies be in consonance with the realities of the region. The United States must recognize that the "democratic middle," to the extent that it ever existed in Guatemala, has been destroyed by officially sanctioned violence. With the middle destroyed and the right unable to resolve the social and economic problems of the country, a left alternative looms as ever more necessary.

In response to this critique, Briggs stated that the United States had not yet (June 1982) reached any final conclusions about the three-month-old Ríos Montt regime. It would appear, he noted, that the indiscriminate violence that marked the previous (Lucas García) regime had been dramatically curtailed. The new government, he continued, appears to be reaching out more to rural areas in an effort to give them the resources to develop their communities. In any case, the United States does not support human rights violations in any country. To the contrary, the Reagan administration strongly condemns them, whether in Guatemala, El Salvador, Nicaragua, Cuba, or elsewhere.

Briggs concluded by noting that great admiration for revolutionary ideas had been expressed at the conference. In reality, he said, the ideas that the United States advocates are the truly revolutionary ones. People should be allowed freely to choose their own leaders. People should be allowed to change things as they see fit through elected representatives within a system that recognizes a pluralistic society and the rights of minorities.

In the Introduction to this volume and in the papers by Ojeda, Pellicer, and Aguilar, Mexican policy toward the region is analyzed from a number of complementary perspectives. The discussions at Guanajuato were not in general nearly as critical of Mexican policy as they were of U.S. policy. Nevertheless, some important comparative and more general points were made.

Professor Clark Reynolds noted that, while economic growth

and social development are indeed at the heart of any long-range solution to the crisis in Central America, order and stability are also vital ingredients of any regional settlement. In thinking about social and economic alternatives in Central America, the United States stresses the need for order and stability as a precondition for development. Mexico, on the other hand, insists on profound social and political changes as a precondition for both stability and development. Given these differing perspectives, a clash between Mexican and U.S. policies toward the region is almost inevitable, even though both governments may share similar visions of a preferred, long-range future for the area.

Referring more specifically to Mexican policy, Professor Joseph Nye observed that, although it is clear that Mexicans in general are critical of U.S. policy toward Central America, it is less clear that they have made their concerns known in a useful and positive way. All too often, he noted, potential Mexican influence on the United States is diminished because of the form that criticism takes. Mexico has something important to tell the United States, and it is in the U.S. interest to listen. But this will happen only if Mexicans appreciate more fully the vital U.S. concern with balancing and containing Soviet power.

Paraphrasing the historian John L. Gaddis to the effect that the United States over the last three decades has alternated between "comprehensive" and "limited" approaches to containment, Nye noted that the comprehensive approach had led to the debacle of Vietnam. Ironically, George Kennan's original vision of containment emphasized a more limited approach relying on indigenous nationalist forces to contain Soviet power. Thus, at the height of the Cold War, the United States supported Communist Yugoslavia. There is a lesson for Central American policy here. Mexico cannot reverse our concern about Soviet power, but it can try to get us to follow a limited approach to containment that accepts domestic social change while relying more on nationalist forces.

Thus, according to Nye, in order to be effective Mexico must help to guide such nationalistic forces in Central America in directions viewed as more acceptable in the United States: political pluralism, respect for human rights, genuine nonalignment.

In fact, Mexico has its own national interest reasons for opposing extra-hemispheric hegemony over its smaller southern neighbors, even though the play of domestic politics in Mexico sometimes impedes taking those actions that would make its policy preferences clear.

In conclusion, it seems useful to consider what has happened that might change the overwhelmingly critical evaluation of the Reagan administration's policy as expressed at Guanajuato by almost all participants not officially representing the U.S. government.

Certainly, the departure of Secretary of State Haig shortly after the Guanajuato conference, and his replacement by George Shultz, was followed by a notable lessening of confrontational rhetoric. Indicative of the new tone was the speech given in San Francisco on August 20, 1982, by Assistant Secretary of State Enders.[3] In that speech, Enders stressed the following points: (1) Central America is an area that suffers from severe economic troubles and social tensions; (2) the solution to problems in Central America lies in the hands of those "who believe that democracy and the rule of law—not violence—are the only feasible paths to progress"; (3) the United States has kept to its basic course of economic and social assistance under two quite different administrations; (4) there should be reciprocal, verified pullouts of foreign military advisors from Central America, until none remain; and (5) U.S. troops will not provide the solution. What can make a difference is a sustained U.S. commitment to help restore and develop economies and democratic institutions.

Unfortunately, however, changes in the style and, to some extent, in the content of public statements during the second half of 1982 appear not to be reflected in the administration's overall policy and operational approaches toward Central America. The secret war against Nicaragua continues, as do the basic policies toward El Salvador, Guatemala, and Honduras. Voices within Washington's career foreign policy community counseling moderation and shifts in direction apparently fell on deaf ears in the White House and elsewhere. As 1982 comes to an

[3] "Building the Peace in Central America," in Department of State, *Bulletin*, 82, no. 2067 (Oct. 1982)

end, a growing feeling within this community is that the administration may well be embarked on a Central American adventure that *inter alia* could have serious effects not only on the region, but also on United States relations with Mexico and other traditional friends in the hemisphere and around the world.

Index